Illicit Drug Policies, Trafficking, and Use the World Over

Illicit Drug Policies, Trafficking, and Use the World Over

Caterina Gouvis Roman, Heather Ahn-Redding,
and Rita J. Simon

LEXINGTON BOOKS

A division of
ROWMAN & LITTLEFIELD PUBLISHERS, INC.
Lanham • Boulder • New York • Toronto • Plymouth, UK

LEXINGTON BOOKS

A division of Rowman & Littlefield Publishers, Inc.
A wholly owned subsidary of The Rowman & Littlefield Publishing Group, Inc.
4501 Forbes Boulevard, Suite 200
Lanham, MD 20706

Estover Road
Plymouth PL6 7PY
United Kingdom

British Library Cataloguing in Publication Information Available

The hardback edition of this book was previously catalogued by the Library of Congress
as follows:

Roman, Caterina Gouvis, 1966–
    Illicit drug policies, trafficking, and use the world over / Caterina Gouvis Roman,
    Heather M. Ahn-Redding, and Rita J. Simon.
        p. cm.—(Global perspectives on social issues)
    Includes bibliographical references and index.
    1. Drug abuse—Cross-cultural studies. 2. Drug traffic—Cross-cultural studies. 3.
    Narcotics, Control of—Cross-cultural studies. I. Ahn-Redding, Heather. II. Simon,
    Rita James. III. Title. IV. Series.

HV5801.R618 2005
362.29—dc22   2004029298
ISBN-13: 978-0-7391-0998-4 (cloth : alk. paper)
ISBN-10: 0-7391-0998-7 (cloth : alk. paper)
ISBN-13: 978-0-7391-2088-0 (pbk. : alk. paper)
ISBN-10: 0-7391-2088-3 (pbk. : alk. paper)

Printed in the United States of America

⊖™ The paper used in this publication meets the minimum requirements of American
National Standard for Information Sciences—Permanence of Paper for Printed Library
Materials, ANSI/NISO Z39.48–1992.

Contents

Tables

Preface

ILLICIT DRUG POLICIES, TRAFFICKING, AND USE THE WORLD OVER is the ninth in a series of volumes that examines a major social issue using an explicitly comparative approach.

In this volume we provide a brief history and analysis of the current laws and policies vis-à-vis illicit drugs in twenty-four countries all over the world. The countries vary by geography, political and social institutions, economic status, religion, and ethnic and racial characteristics. We examine the extent of the use of different types of drugs, natural and manmade, historically and currently, and focus particularly on cannabis, cocaine, and heroin. We also report on and discuss the international laws or conventions enacted from 1912 (the Hague Convention) to the present.

In 2003, the United Nations Office on Drugs and Crime estimated that there are 200 million consumers of illegal drugs around the world. Further discussion of this issue is reported in chapter 2. The remaining chapters provide country-by-country data and analysis.

The organizing focus of this series of World Over Volumes is the analysis of important social issues about which many societies in the world have enacted laws and statutes, and about which most of its members have opinions that they voice in the public arena. They are issues that receive extensive media coverage as well as judicial attention. Thus far volumes have included the following issues: abortion, euthanasia, capital punishment, marriage and divorce, pornography, immigration, education, and juvenile justice institutions. Each volume is intended to serve as a handbook containing empirical data and comprehensive references on the social issue, problem, or practice in question.

—Rita J. Simon

Acknowledgments

WE ARE INDEBTED TO DAN FALLON, Joyce Coninx Wright, and Kate McNamee for research assistance in the preparation of this book. We began this book at a time when government reports were not readily or routinely available on the Internet, which made the data collection process very challenging and sometimes overwhelming. Special thanks goes to John Roman for his continued support over the many years it took to complete the manuscript. In addition, we want to thank Graham Farrell for his monthly urgings to finally publish the manuscript.

PART I

1

Introduction

THE DEMAND FOR DRUGS throughout the world is great. The gross volume of business in illegal drugs makes it one of the most important industries in the world. Entire nations depend on drug production for their economic survival (e.g., Turkey, Colombia, and Bolivia). Other countries are so embroiled in the production and distribution that they would be severely affected economically if the demand dropped significantly (Chambliss 1992). With regard to drug use, the United Nations Office on Drugs and Crime estimates that the annual global prevalence rate of illicit drug consumption is in the range of 3.3 to 4.1 percent of the world population—about 140 million people worldwide (United Nations Office on Drugs and Crime 2003).

Research available on common indicators reveals that consumption is increasing throughout the world. Nations are reporting increased drug-related hospital admissions and mortality and arrests of drug-law violators. Illicit consumption of cannabis is widespread, and the less prevalent, but more harmful, abuse of heroin has become a major health threat to many nations. Undoubtedly, drug use and abuse have played a large role in worsening already serious problems: the spread of AIDS, property and violent crimes and prostitution, babies born addicted to drugs, and the waste of otherwise productive lives. Medical costs associated with drug abuse have climbed into the billions of dollars. Countries in Eastern Europe and those liberated from the Soviet Union, who had little past experience with drug problems, are now facing the need to develop policies and formulate strategies.

The meager information available on the extent of local drug abuse in many nations around the world limits the ability to curtail drug abuse and its related issues. Although a growing number of countries have undertaken studies in recent years on the incidence and prevalence of drug abuse, only a few countries have data that can be compared cross nationally.

This book examines the laws and policies vis-à-vis the sale and consumption of drugs, the prevalence of consumption and trafficking[1] of illegal drugs, as well as the punishments handed out for trafficking and use in different societies. At times, we include discussion regarding drug production and drug seizures, as indirect indicators of consumption. To set the stage for the research, our discussion of each country includes a brief outline of each country's government structure and legislative system. We have chosen a sample of countries from different regions in the world, with different levels of industrial development and types of governments, where solid, reliable information is available. This text does not aim to provide an analytical comparison of cross-national drug policy by comparing and contrasting laws, policies, and related drug statistics. Nations differ in a myriad of ways making it difficult to draw direct comparisons or generalizations. Furthermore, generalizing about how the scope or nature of the drug problem changes over time *within* nations can be problematic as societies evolve rapidly. The intent of this book is to provide a backdrop from which readers can begin or continue their own examination of cross-national drug issues. The book provides information that can assist readers in examining critical issues that are part of the international debate: Have the nations of the world begun to converge with respect to drug policy? Has international cooperation and continued public discourse on the ills of drugs created more uniform policies and practices to reduce the world's drug problems? Which countries have remained apart from the international dialogue and have not been party to the anti-drug treaties and conventions? Are there countries that have taken steps to forge new or more liberal policies stressing education, treatment, and alternative community-based intervention?

After reading through dozens of texts related to international drug policy and cross-national drug issues, we concluded that a text cataloguing the historical information and data across countries would be useful to continued dialog about drug policy. With the exception of a few reports from the United Nations Office on Drug and Crime, research providing an in depth synthesis of drug issues for more than a few countries at once is scarce. Many research reports or texts are limited to regional analysis or are edited volumes with no particular consistency in themes across chapters. We hope this volume fills a void in the research literature. Overall, data quality is not high, but it is improving. Definitions of key terms and methods for collecting data differ across countries. When aware of these differences, we document them.

The countries included in this book, by region, are:

1. North America: United States, Canada, and Mexico
2. South and Central America: Colombia, Brazil, and Costa Rica
3. Western Europe: Great Britain, France, Italy, Spain, and the Netherlands
4. Eastern Europe: Russia, Poland, Bulgaria, and the Slovak Republic
5. Middle East: Iran and Israel
6. Asia: China, Japan, India, and Thailand
7. Africa: South Africa and Nigeria
8. The South Pacific: Australia

Notes

1. This manuscript focuses primarily on intra-country trafficking, such as low-level sales between individuals, as opposed to international drug trafficking related to illicit criminal organizations.

2. For basic backround information on the criminal justice systems of each of the countries discussed in this book we relied primarily on two sources: (1) The World Factbook of Criminal Justice Systems, which is a U.S. Department of Justice, Bureau of Justice Statistics Website that provides descriptions of forty-five countries (www.ojp.usdoj.gov/bjs/abstract/wfcj.htm) and (2) the World Factbook by the Central Intelligence Agency (CIA) (www.cia.gov/cia/publications/factbook/index.htm). The CIA factbook is updated periodically throughout the year.

References

Chambliss, William J. 1992. "The Consequences of Prohibition: Crime, Corruption, and International Narcotic Control." In *Drugs, Law and the State,* eds. Harold H. Traver and Mark S. Gaylord. New Brunswick, N.J.: Transaction Publishers.

United Nations Office on Drugs and Crime. 2003. Global Illicit Drug Trends 2003. www.unodc.org/unodc/en/global_illicit_drug_trends.html (accessed October 24, 2003).

2

The Definition of Drug Use

IT IS IMPORTANT TO DISTINGUISH DRUG USE from drug abuse—drug abuse is based on the relationship an individual has with drugs. Any drug can be abused, no matter how accepted it is in any given culture. The effects of drugs depend on the person, place, and time. The set and setting play a large role. The set is the person's expectations; the setting is the physical, cultural, and social environment. Drug use is universal, although some countries do not consider drug use or abuse a major policy concern. Almost every culture throughout history has used one or more psychoactive drugs (Weil and Rosen 1993).

In their book *From Chocolate to Morphine*, Weil and Rosen (1993) provide a variety of reasons as to why people use drugs. They include:

- To aid religious practices;
- To explore the self;
- To alter moods;
- To treat disease;
- To escape boredom and despair;
- To promote and enhance social interaction;
- To enhance sensory experience and pleasure;
- To stimulate artistic creativity and performance;
- To improve physical performance;
- To rebel/to establish identity; and
- To go along with peer pressure.

Types of Drugs

Drugs can be natural or manmade. In addition, our bodies produce some drugs, though not discussed here—drugs such as endorphins. In many cases, the synthetic or partially synthetic are meant to mimic these drugs. The majority of psychoactive drugs come from plants. In the *crude form* of the plant, the drug usually is very weak, has an unpleasant taste, or brings unwanted side effects. This natural form (the plant itself) is generally the safest type of drug, with lower potential for abuse. Opium is a well-known drug often used in its natural state.

The *refined forms* of drugs are synthesized in laboratories. Some refined drugs, such as mescaline, are not altered that much from the original form. Others have much more complex molecular structures. The refined powders are much more toxic and have a higher abuse potential.

Semisynthetic drugs are drugs that have had their chemical structure changed from the more refined natural components. Chemical groups are added to molecules to make them stronger. By adding two acetic acid groups to morphine, it becomes heroin, a semisynthetic drug more potent than morphine. There are also wholly *synthetic* drugs like LSD, where the end drug is very different from the natural drug with which the chemist began. Wholly synthetic drugs have no natural properties.

We have limited the scope of this book to the natural, refined, and semisynthetic drugs that have given societies trouble since the mid-nineteenth and early twentieth centuries. The drugs covered in this book are cannabis (marijuana), cocaine, heroin, and heroin's derivative drug, opium. We have excluded tobacco and alcohol because of their general acceptance and legal status worldwide.

A History of Drug Use

Cannabis

Also called hemp, *Cannabis sativa* is the Latin name given to the plant whose dried tops of flowers are what is commonly known as marijuana. Hashish is the resin from the plant. The active ingredient in all forms of the drug is tetrahydrocannabinol (THC). Cannabis is considered a sedative having psychoactive properties.

The history of cannabis goes back to early Chinese dynasties hundreds of years before the birth of Jesus (Escohotado 1999). In the twenty-eighth century B.C., Emperor Shen-Nung began to prescribe marijuana for constipation, gout, malaria, rheumatism, and absent-mindedness. A few centuries later, marijuana was used to treat eyesores in Egypt. The ancient Greeks were known to trade cannabis and used it to treat earaches, edema, and inflammation. Passages from the *Arabian Nights* show that cannabis was used throughout Asia and the Near East for its fiber as well as its psychoactive properties. There are reports that the Celts exported hemp ropes and fiber to the Mediterranean in the seventh century. During the Roman Empire in the first century it was common to smoke the female hemp flowers (marijuana) in gatherings. Knowledge of how to smoke hemp was gained from black slaves in Brazil who used the plant in Africa. In addition, central and southern Europe used hemp for cloth in the thirteenth century and in later generations. Historians say Napoleon Bonaparte and his troops introduced the drug to Europe after they returned from the invasion of Egypt. Eventually, the practice of smoking marijuana spread to Mexico and into the United States at the turn of the twentieth century by Mexican migrant workers. Although there are reports of the drug being smoked after World War I, cannabis did not really catch on until the 1960s, when it became associated with youth movements on college campuses.

Cocaine

Cocaine use dates back centuries with the growth of the coca plant in South and Central America. Coca leaves were discovered on the northern coast of Peru during the Huaca Preita settlement between 2500 and 1800 B.C. The Incas used cocaine mainly in the highlands of Peru and Bolivia. Cocaine was chewed and used to make tea. It was also used as a medicine and for religious ceremonies (Grinspoon and Bakalar 1976). When the explorer Pizarro came upon the Inca Empire in 1530, the nobility was using the coca plant liberally. During the Spanish Conquest, Spaniards sanctioned the use of coca by all people, and the use of coca for consumption spread rapidly. For the next 200 years, Spanish authorities traded and taxed coca throughout South America (Escohotado 1999). The trade of coca brought in as much as 8 percent of a country's revenue by the mid-1800s.

The first citing of coca leaves in Europe appears to be in the middle of the nineteenth century, and in 1844 cocaine was chemically isolated from coca leaves. When Sigmund Freud became interested in the drug two decades later, a wave of research was initiated, resulting in findings that advocated cocaine as a type of wonder drug that not only produced euphoria, but increased muscle strength and reaction times. German soldiers were known to use cocaine to fight fatigue. Freud also supported use of cocaine for withdrawal from morphine addiction, a large problem at that time.

But it was one of Freud's colleagues, Carl Koller, who established cocaine's place in modern medicine as an effective local anesthetic. Around the same time, the coca leaf was used in a tonic known as the Vin Mariani, which was a combination of wine and coca-leaf extract. This drink won various prizes and received backing from Thomas Edison and Pope Leo XIII (Alexander 1990). Similarly, in 1886, a Georgia pharmacist produced coca cola. It was marketed as an "intellectual beverage." By 1903, cocaine was removed from the formula as the public began to recognize the addictive powers and ensuing problems related to cocaine use. The reform movement in the United States and Canada in the early 1900s took up a crusade against cocaine. By 1930, the Depression pushed cocaine out of the center of public attention. But by the 1960s, cocaine's popularity returned, connected with the liberal attitudes of the hippie movement. The federal government soon attempted to quell renewed usage of the drug as epitomized by New York's "Rockefeller laws," drafted in 1973. These state laws provided mandatory minimum life sentences for possession of more than two ounces of cocaine (Grinspoon and Bakalar 1976).

Opium and Heroin

Worldwide, opium is the most well-known narcotic. The word narcotic comes from the Greek work meaning "stupor." Narcotics produce stupors by depressing brain functions in a different way than sedatives and general anesthetics. Gummy-like, opium is made from the poppy, a flower that originated in Asia Minor (the western extreme of mainland Asia) and the countries bordering the Mediterranean Sea. Botanically classified as *Papaver somniferum,* the genus is named from the Greek noun for poppy and the species from the Latin word meaning "sleep inducing" (Booth 1996). Of 250 species of poppy, only two—*Papaver somniferum* and *Papaver bracteatum*—produce opium in a significant amount and the latter is not used as a commercial drug source. When the poppy flower dies, the green pod swells as it ripens. During the time when the pod is not ripe, it contains a juice, that, when dried, is crude opium. Opium is only produced during a ten-to-twelve day period as the pod is ripening.

There are many drugs derived from opium compounds, including heroin. All opiates produce similar effects, acting on the central nervous system, although they differ greatly in potency, duration of high, and how active they are when taken by mouth. Heroin is a semisynthetic form of opium.

According to history books, opium has been used for over ten centuries for its therapeutic agents. Smoked, eaten, or consumed in liquid form, it was used as a painkiller and tranquilizer, and also to increase sexual potency and enhance strength. The first written evidence of opium appeared in the third millennium B.C. in Sumerian tablets. It is believed that the Sumerians—the world's first civilization—cultivated the opium poppy along the Tigris-Euphrates river systems of lower Mesopotamia. Poppy juice was recommended as an analgesic and sedative in ointments in Egyptian hieroglyphs (Escoho-tado 1999). Over the years, poppy heads appeared in images in Babylon and in the Cretan-Mycenaean culture. Knowledge of opium was widespread throughout Europe by the end of the second millennium B.C. (Booth 1996). The use of opium was commonplace in ancient Greece. In India, Thailand, and other Asian countries, opium use became part of ritual and societal customs. Some parts of India used opium for social occasions to create and cement friendships. Record books show that in 1687 the Turks ate opium for pleasure, mixing opium with nutmeg, cinnamon, and other spices to disguise opium's bitter taste. In Europe, opium was mixed with liquids like wine and honey (Booth 1996). In China and the East Indies, opium was smoked, but first had to be concentrated.

In the 1660s, opium was first formally prepared as a medicine known as laudanum, a very expensive mix of other additives that kept it out of the reach of the general public. Soon after arrived the first inexpensive opium medicine called *Dover powder*, named after an English physician. The powder contained 20 percent opium and was sold in drugstores as a general analgesic, the same as aspirin is today. In Europe and America, laudanum was the main form in which opium was taken until the mid-nineteenth century. Estimates of opiate imports imply that opium was used widely in Britain, Western Europe, and America throughout the nineteenth century. It is estimated that consumption in Britain increased at an average rate of 2.4 percent per year between 1831 and 1859. In 1860, it is estimated that roughly 280,000 pounds were imported to Britain and 151,000 pounds were re-exported, more than half going to America (Booth 1996).

A German scientist, Frederich Serturner, isolated the active ingredient in opium in 1806 and named the drug morphine. The subcutaneous injection of morphine became popularized in 1853 with the perfection of the hypodermic syringe. It is believed that the unrestrained use of morphine by injection helped to fuel the drug's addiction, and by 1914 addiction was recognized and named. Morphine was used abundantly as a painkiller in the American Civil War, the Prussian-Austrian War, and the Franco-Prussian War. Soldiers often returned home addicted to morphine. At the same time the addictive nature of opium and morphine was coming to light, scientists seeking to develop a non-addictive alternative to morphine developed heroin in 1898. The word's origin is based on the German word *heroisch*, meaning heroic. But soon after its development heroin's addictive nature became known, and when the Council of Pharmacy and Chemistry of the American Medical Association included heroin for the first time in their annual publication, *New and Non-Official Remedies*, the entry for heroin included the warning that addiction is readily formed and can lead to "deplorable results" (Booth 1996).

International Actions against Drugs

As problems with opium smoking grew around the world at the turn of the twentieth century, the United States initiated discussions with several nations tied to the Far East in the hope that the countries could work together to reduce the flow and use of opium and other narcotics. These informal discussions took on substance as many countries were invited to attend the Shanghai Conference in 1909. Representatives from Austria-Hungary, China, Great Britain, France, Germany, Italy, Japan, the Netherlands, Persia, Portugal, Siam, Russia, and the United States attended. The conference put forth several nonbinding resolutions, the most significant being the recognition that opium should be limited to legitimate medicinal purposes. The gradual suppression of opium smoking was supported, along with recommendations that each country enact appropriate legislation.

The 1912 Hague Convention carried the spirit of international cooperation further by translating the recommendations from the Shanghai Conference into binding agreements. The same nations met at The Hague, with the exception of Austria-Hungary. The result was the International Opium Convention of 1912 which made international narcotic control a matter of international law. Although the recommendations were binding, the convention did not set up administrative procedures that would assist in the implementation of the agreement.

It wasn't until 1921 that the newly established League of Nations was delegated with the supervision and implementation of international agreements. The League of Nations soon formed the Advisory Committee on the Traffic of Opium and Other Dangerous Drugs to handle all agreements regarding dangerous drugs. Within a few years, the shortcomings of the Hague Convention became known. Adequate restrictions on production of dangerous drugs did not exist and countries were having difficulty suppressing the trafficking of drugs. At the urging of many nations, a conference in Geneva was held from November 1924 to February 1925. The main purpose of the Geneva Conference was to produce an agreement with two goals in mind: (1) limit the amount of morphine, heroin, and cocaine that could be manufactured, and (2) limit the amount of raw forms of these drugs—the poppy and the coca leaf. But countries withdrew from the conference as some nations refused to agree to making opium smoking illegal. Trafficking and consumption continued to increase. Another conference was held in Geneva in 1931 to consider more effective ways of controlling the illegal traffic of drugs. Known as the Narcotic Limitation Convention, it attempted to reach agreements that would limit the world manufacture of drugs to required medical and scientific needs. Then in 1936, the Convention for Suppression of Illicit Traffic in Dangerous Drugs attempted to put sanctions on drug trafficking, which previously had not existed. This was the first treaty that specifically addressed enforcement rather than control. But the problem was that countries did not have to implement the new provisions, except where they were consistent with their own laws.

By World War II, the rate of addiction in many countries had sharply decreased. However, U.S. authorities worried that as the war ended, illegal transport and consumption would rise, as it did following World War I. When the League of Nations dissolved and the United Nations was established, the Economic and Social Council of the United Nations adopted a resolution to establish the Commission on Narcotic Drugs. The Commission, composed of fifteen members from countries leading in the manufacture of opium or in countries where those drugs were a serious problem, was responsible for overseeing the implementation and progress of all international agreements related to dangerous drugs. In addition, the Commission was responsible for developing new agreements. In 1948 the Paris Protocol was signed, bringing synthetic drugs deemed harmful by the World Health Organization under international control. Then in 1953, the Opium Protocol was developed to place more restrictions on opium. In essence, the protocol made it illegal for any country other than Bulgaria, Greece, India, Iran, Turkey, Russia, and Yugoslavia to produce opium for export. Farmers had to be licensed to cultivate the poppy for opium, and the legal countries had to establish a national opium administration. Nations that were party to the treaty could continue to permit opium smoking by registered users for a limited time.

By 1961, membership in the United Nations Commission on Narcotic Drugs had increased to twenty-one nations. It was at this time, fifty years after efforts to stem the worldwide production and trafficking of dangerous drugs, that the Commission began to codify the various drug control treaties. The Single Convention of Narcotic Drugs (1961) replaced all earlier existing agreements with the exception of certain provisions of the 1936 Convention that suppressed drug trafficking. The Single Convention, adopted in March, 1961, was ratified by forty nations by December, 1964. However, the United States, who felt that the Single Convention was weak in some areas, did not ratify the Convention until three years later.

In 1971, the United Nations established the Convention on Psychotropic Substances. The Convention was developed to respond to the growing spectrum of drugs of abuse. Controls were introduced for a number of synthetic drugs that were not covered in the Single Convention of 1961. The 1971 Convention was mainly developed to cover three new drug classes: sedatives, amphetamine-type stimulants, and LSD-type hallucinogens.

A year later, the 1972 Protocol amending the 1961 Convention on Narcotic Drugs was created to respond to increased illicit cultivation of the opium poppy and cannabis, and the illicit production of heroin. The 1972 Protocol expanded the role of the International Narcotics Board and strengthened the obligations of the signatory countries. Historians have suggested that the 1972 Protocol did little to counteract the further increase in illicit cultivation, production, and manufacturing trends. By the late 1980s, the international community was shocked by the explosion of cocaine abuse. Illicit traffic of drugs had become an international criminal activity and governments began witnessing corruption as the result of increased ties between illicit drug trafficking and other organized criminal activities. Seeking to strengthen international relations to combat drug trafficking and abuse, in 1988 forty-three signatory United Nations members adopted the Convention against Illicit Traffic in Narcotic Drugs and Psychotropic Substances. The main provisions of the 1988 Convention included the control of shipments of precursor chemicals; reaffirmation of the nations' commitment to eradicate or reduce the raw materials used to manufacture drugs; the authorized seizure of drug-related assets; and permission to extradite and prosecute persons charged with drug violations. The 1988 Convention also provided a comprehensive legal framework for close international collaboration (Bayer and Ghodse 1999).

The Single Convention on Narcotic Drugs (1961), the Convention on Psychotropic Substances (1971), and the Convention against the Illicit Traffic in Narcotic Drugs and Psychotropic Substances (1988) remain the three major international drug control treaties. These treaties are seen as mutually supportive and complementary efforts to codify internationally applicable control measures.

References

Alexander, Bruce. 1990. *Peaceful Measures: Canada's Way Out of the War on Drugs.* Toronto: University of Toronto Press.

Bayer, I., and H. Ghodse. 1999. "Evolution of International Drug Control, 1945–1995." *Bulletin on Narcotics*, Volume LI. United Nations Office on Drugs and Crime.

Booth, Martin. 1996. *Opium: A History.* London: Simon and Schuster.

Escohotado, Antonio. 1999. *A Brief History of Drugs: From the Stone Age to the Stoned Age.* Rochester, Vt.: Park Street Press.

Grinspoon, Lester, and James B. Bakalar. 1976. *Cocaine: A Drug and Its Social Evolution.* New York: Basic Books.

Weil, Andrew, and Winifred Rosen. 1993. *From Chocolate to Morphine: Everything You Need to Know about Mind-Altering Drugs.* Boston: Houghton Mifflin Company.

3

Drugs Today

DRUG ABUSE IS RAMPANT TODAY. The United Nations Office on Drugs and Crime (UNODC) estimates that there are 200 million consumers of illegal drugs around the world (2003: 11). Broken down, there are 163 million consumers of cannabis, 14 million consumers of cocaine, and 15 million consumers of opiates (107). Opiates and cocaine remain the most problematic drugs across the globe.

Around the world, countries are attempting to tackle their drug problems through treatment programs, new policies, and new approaches to law enforcement. However, South America, Southeast Asia, and the Middle East still remain hotspots for illegal drug production and exportation. Nonetheless, the trafficking of drugs grew at a slower rate in 2001 than in the 1990s (UNODC 2003). This may be attributed to widespread efforts to detect and destroy illicit drug laboratories and cultivation areas, and to seize shipments before they reach their destinations. In 2001, the largest amounts of seized drugs throughout the world were, in order from greatest to least, cannabis herb in Mexico, cannabis resin in Spain, cocaine in the United States, and cocaine in Colombia (10).

Opiates

There are 15 million abusers of opium and heroin across the world. The UNODC reports that "two thirds of treatment demand is related to the abuse of opiates" in Asia, Europe, and Oceania (2003: 107).

Chapter 3

TABLE 3-1
Annual Prevalence Estimates of Opiate Abuse: 2000–2001

	Opiates		Heroin	
	Number of People (Millions)	*In % of Population Age 15 and Above*	*Number of People (Millions)*	*In % of Population Age 15 and Above*
Europe	4.56	0.70	3.23	0.50
West Europe	1.57	0.42	1.30	0.35
East Europe	2.99	1.08	1.66	0.60
Oceania	0.14	0.63	0.14	0.63
Asia	7.46	0.29	3.59	0.14
Americas	1.86	0.30	1.86	0.30
North America	1.50	0.48	1.50	0.48
South America	0.36	0.12	0.36	0.12
Africa	0.92	0.20	0.95	0.20
Global	14.94	0.35	9.47	0.22

Original Source: UNODC Global Illicit Drug Trends 2003, Chapter 1. Consumption: Opium/Heroin, 108.

In 2002, Afghanistan produced 76 percent of the world's illegal opium, followed by Myanmar (18 percent), Laos (2 percent), and Colombia (1 percent). Other production regions were Mexico, Pakistan, Thailand, and Vietnam (UNODC 2003: 10). The UNODC's *Global Illicit Drug Trends 2003* report indicates that since 1998, the production of illicit opium has remained relatively stable at approximately 4,400 metric tons per year (7). However, after Afghanistan banned the cultivation of opium in 2001, there has been a large decrease in the production of opium around the world. Other large heroin markets, stimulated by Afghanistan's opium production, have expanded to Central Asia, the Russian Federation, and Eastern Europe.

Cannabis

Cannabis abuse is also on the rise across the world and is consumed more than any other drug across the globe (UNODC 2003: 136). Among countries surveyed by the UNODC, 53 percent reported increases in cannabis abuse (139). Countries reporting large increases are in Africa and the Americas.

Approximately 163 million individuals are estimated to have abused cannabis in 2000 and 2001 (136). This is an increase of 16 million from 1998 to 2000.

TABLE 3-2
Annual Prevalence Estimates of Abuse of Cannabis

	Number of People (Millions)	In % of Population Age 15 and Above
Oceania	3.93	16.89
Africa	33.21	8.60
Americas	36.70	6.10
North America	23.54	7.53
South America	13.16	4.56
Europe	34.09	5.20
West Europe	23.21	7.16
East Europe	10.88	3.29
Asia	54.88	2.17
Global	162.81	3.88

Original Source: UNODC Global Illicit Drug Trends 2003, Chapter 1. Consumption: Cannabis, 136.

Cocaine

According to the UNODC (2003), approximately 14 million people abuse cocaine across the globe. The UNODC found increases in cocaine trends among 56 percent of the countries surveyed in 2001, which was down from the 62 percent who reported increases in cocaine trends in 2000 (132). Colombia was the largest potential producer of cocaine in 2002, followed by Peru and Bolivia (10). Seizures of heroin were higher in 2001 than in 2000, but 7 percent less than the number of seizures in 1998 (63).

TABLE 3-3
Annual Prevalence Estimates of Cocaine Abuse: 2000–2001

	Number of People (Millions)	In % of Population Age 15 and Above
Americas	9.08	1.50
North America	6.35	2.03
South America	2.74	0.94
Oceania	0.23	1.03
Europe	3.71	0.57
West Europe	3.43	1.06
East Europe	0.29	0.09
Africa	0.91	0.20
Asia	0.15	0.01
Global	14.08	0.33

Original Source: UNODC Global Illicit Drug Trends 2003, Chapter 1. Consumption: Coca/Cocaine, 129.

The Costs of Drugs

The consequences associated with drug abuse reach well beyond the realm of those involved in the production, trafficking, and consumption of illegal narcotics. The drug problem today has taken its toll on families, communities, schools, and work environments, and extends to problems involving physical and mental health, crime rates, and violence (UNODC 1995). For example, within the workplace drug abuse is associated with more frequent accidents, lower productivity, increased absenteeism, and the costs associated with testing employees (UNODC 1998: 17).

The economic costs of drug abuse are enormous. In Canada, for example, the costs associated with drug, alcohol, and tobacco abuse in 1992 were estimated to be 2.7 percent of the country's GDP (UNODC 1998: 15).[1] Costs associated with illegal drugs were approximately $US 1.1 billion, or $US 40 per capita (15). In 1992, the cost of drug abuse in Australia was estimated to be 4.8 percent of the country's GDP, and the cost of illicit drugs was 0.4 percent of GDP, or $1.2 billion (15). Efforts in Germany to tackle the drug problem in 1995 cost $120 per capita, or 0.4 percent of its GDP ($9.6 billion). In the United States, the costs associated with drug abuse in 1991 amounted to $76 billion when accounting for increased criminality, lost productivity, medical costs, and increases in the population infected with HIV/AIDS (16). By 1998 the overall cost of drug abuse to society was estimated to be $143.4 billion (ONDCP 2001).

Note

1. Canadian officials will release a new study in 2005 to update information about the costs of substance abuse in Canada.

References

Office of National Drug Control Policy. 2001. *The Economic Costs of Drug Abuse in the United States, 1992–1998.* Washington, D.C.: The Executive Office of the President, Office on National Drug Control Policy.

United Nations Office of Drugs and Crime. 2003. *Global Illicit Drug Trends 2003.* www .unodc.org/unodc/en/global_illicit_drug_trends.html (accessed October 24, 2003).

United Nations Office on Drugs and Crime. 1998. *Economic and Social Consequences of Drug Abuse and Illicit Trafficking,* Number 6. www.unodc.org/unodc/en/ publications/technical_series_1998-01-01_1.html (accessed December 3, 2003).

United Nations Office on Drugs and Crime. 1995. *The Social Impact of Drug Abuse, Number 2.* Originally prepared by UNDCP as a position paper for the World Summit for Social Development, (Copenhagen, 6–12 March 1995). www.unodc.org/ pdf/technical_series_1995-03-01-1.pdf (accessed December 3, 2003).

Part II

NORTH AMERICA

T HE NORTHERN CONTINENT OF THE WESTERN HEMISPHERE, North America
extends northward from the Colombia–Panama border, and includes
Central America, Mexico, the islands of the Caribbean Sea, the United States,
Canada, the Arctic Archipelago, and Greenland. This section of the book provides details on the United States, Canada, and Mexico. Central America is
discussed in the following section, titled "Central and South America."

The annual prevalence of cocaine abuse among those aged fifteen and over
in North America is 2 percent (UNODC 2003 129). Trends in cocaine consumption have stabilized in Mexico and Canada in 2001 after increases in
2000 (132). In 2001, it was estimated that 1.9 percent of individuals who are
twelve years or older in the United States used cocaine within the last year
(UNODC 2003: 132). Among high schools, there was an "annual prevalence
rate of 5 percent in 2002, down from 6.2 percent in 1999 and some 60 percent
less than in the mid 1980s. The UNODC also reports that opiate abuse has stabilized in North America (UNOCDC 2003)." In 2001, 38 percent of global
seizures of cocaine took place in North America (UNODC 2003: 63). North
America alone accounted for 4 percent of global heroin seizures.

4

The United States

Overview

THE UNITED STATES OCCUPIES MOST OF North America stretching across the continent between Mexico and Canada, and includes Hawaii in the Pacific and Alaska on the northwestern border of Canada. With 263.4 million people, the United States is the third largest nation in the world in population, behind only China and India. In area, it is the fourth largest country after Russia, Canada, and China.

Three-quarters of the population in the United States live in urban areas, and more than forty metropolitan areas have populations over one million. Approximately 83 percent of Americans are Caucasian, 12.5 percent are African Americans, 4 percent are Asian or Pacific Islander, and 0.8 percent are American Indian, Eskimo, or Aleut. Hispanic Americans make up 12.5 percent of the population.

The United States is a democratic nation headed by a president who holds executive power. The Congress, consisting of the House of Representatives and the Senate, exercises legislative power. The judicial power rests in the hands of the Supreme Court, which interprets the highest law of the land, the Constitution.

Drug Offenses and the Law[1]

In the United States, early drug legislation came from state laws. But the legislation over the years was gradual and fragmentary, due to the limited knowledge regarding drugs and their harm. State laws evolved in three general stages: first to control the use of drugs, then to control and restrict the sale of drugs, and finally to provide mechanisms for treating drug abusers and addicts.

The early state laws had no provisions for enforcement, and were directed toward the smoking of opium. In 1872, California passed the first anti-opium law, which declared that the administration of laudanum or any other narcotic constituted a felony. In 1881, California passed legislation that prohibited individuals from maintaining a commercial establishment where opium was sold or smoked. It was Nevada that passed the first legislation against opium smoking in 1877. The other western states soon followed with similar legislation, but these laws generally did not address narcotics other than opium. It was not until 1887 that Oregon passed legislation which provided for licenses to be issued to physicians and pharmacists for the sale of narcotics and which stated that no person could sell, give away, or possess any opium-derived drug or cocaine except by prescription of a licensed physician. Other states passed similar legislation soon after, but the impact of the states' legislation was often impeded by the lack of control each state had over the movement of illegal drugs into different jurisdictions. In addition, no provisions were made to ensure compliance with the laws. Wyoming, in 1913, passed the first legislation prohibiting the sale of marijuana. In 1874, Connecticut was the first state to pass legislation that declared a person who was unable to attend to his affairs an addict, and therefore be committed to a state asylum for "treatment" until he was cured of his addiction. Again, other states followed suit. Some states even legislated the compulsory treatment of the narcotic addict but treatment was barely adequate, and often facilities were not available.

By the 1930s, various organizations recognized that existing state legislation was ineffective. The National Conference of Commissioners on Uniform State Laws recommended the enactment of the Uniform Drug Act, developed by the Federal Bureau of Narcotics as an attempt to make the states' laws consistent with federal laws. The most significant effect of the law was that marijuana was identified as a narcotic. However the act did not enumerate a schedule of penalties for the violations defined. The majority of states enacted the Uniform Act, and some passed versions of the bill.

But by the late 1960s there was the public perception that state laws continued to be ineffective in combating drug abuse. There were more than fifty federal laws relating to narcotics and dangerous drugs. In 1969, President Richard Nixon recommended a Model State Control Substances Act that would help consolidate the federal laws and bring the states' laws into congruence with the model law.

Like the federal law, the Controlled Substances Act of 1970 classified all narcotics, marijuana, and other dangerous drugs into five schedules. Each schedule lists its own criteria, and the states could add, delete, or reschedule substances as new scientific findings emerged. In essence, it created a common standard of dangerousness to rank all drugs rather than focusing on specific substances. This occurred at the same time that the Foreign Assistance Act (1971) was passed to authorize assistance to countries to control drug production and trafficking. It also allowed for the suspension of military or economic aid to countries that failed to control production and trafficking of substances. Though the Controlled Substances Act is specific about what it prohibits, it does not specify sentences. However, in developing their laws, most states followed the penalties designated in the federal law.

Looking back in time as the federal government became involved in drug laws, it wasn't until the early 1900s that Congress enacted legislation to control a growing drug problem. But like the states, the federal government's development of drug laws was reactive and piecemeal. In 1909, federal legislation made it unlawful to import opium in any form or preparation, except for medicinal purposes. The legislation was amended in 1914 to restrict the exportation of opium and cocaine and their derivatives. Congress also enacted legislation that imposed a large tax on all opium manufactured in the United States for smoking purposes. Opium could not be imported; but could still be legally manufactured in the United States for smoking purposes.

The requirements of the International Hague Convention brought about the Harrison Act of 1914. Drug companies must now be registered and severe restrictions were placed on the distribution of opium-based drugs. With the passage of the law, drug addiction was seen as criminal, and not a medical problem. Physicians stopped treating addicts, and the public began to view users as immoral and prone to crime. At that time, the United States was estimated to have at least one million addicts. Most of these addicts were involved with opium or heroin. To further curtail the importation of crude opium, Congress enacted a new law that prohibited the "importation and use of opium for other than medicinal purposes." The Act expressly stated that crude opium could not be imported for the purpose of manufacturing heroin.

By the late 1920s, public pressure helped enact legislation that focused on treatment. The Porter Narcotic Farm Act of 1929 established two narcotic farms, one in Lexington, Kentucky, and one in Fort Worth, Texas, for the treatment of individuals "addicted to the use of habit forming narcotic drugs who have been convicted of Federal offenses." These two hospitals were specifically designed to treat federal prisoners who were addicts and anyone who volunteered for treatment. Results from studies of the hospitals were satisfactory, but the states did not enact similar legislation or create special treatment centers for their addict populations.

In 1930, the Bureau of Narcotics was established with the enactment of new legislation. The bureau was given the mandate to administer and enforce the Harrison Act with all amendments and other federal laws regarding controlled substances. It was this bureau that helped develop the Uniform State Narcotic Act, which nearly all the states passed.

The Marijuana Tax Act was passed in 1937. It required all individuals having legitimate business that involved marijuana to register with the government, and to pay a special tax. Cannabis, which was considered to have no known medical purpose at the time, could not be used for industrial, medical, or scientific purposes. Also in 1937, Congress passed an act that greatly increased penalties for second, third, and subsequent offenses against narcotic laws. If a defendant was found to be a prior offender the judge could sentence the individual to no more than twenty years or fine him or her no more than ten thousand dollars. That same year seizure and forfeiture laws were enacted. During the next decade, laws were passed to prohibit domestic production of the opium poppy, restrict and control the use of Demerol, define a new class of drugs called opiates, and restrict the use and manufacture of any opium derivative.

As drug use increased, the Bureau of Narcotics urged Congress to pass laws establishing strict sentences for drug law violators. In 1956, the Narcotic Control Act was passed which established mandatory minimum penalties for violations of narcotic and marijuana laws, and prohibited judges from suspending periods of incarceration. In addition, the law prohibited narcotic addicts and convicted drug offenders from traveling abroad, unless they registered with the U.S. Customs Office. The Act also mandated the Bureau of Narcotics to create a Division of Statistics and Records. It was envisioned that this division would receive records from federal, state, and local agencies pertaining to drug use and law breaking, and that they would provide information back to those agencies for law enforcement purposes.

Almost a decade later, in 1965, Congress passed legislation to control the growing illicit traffic in depressants, stimulants, and hallucinogenic drugs. The 1965 Drug Abuse Control Amendments were based on Congress's authority to control these drugs with regulations on interstate commerce. Since intrastate commerce in these drugs affects interstate commerce, regulation of both interstate and intrastate commerce was deemed necessary. Penalties were established for those who sold or delivered these drugs, but no penalties were delineated for possession or personal use. The penalties for violation of the Drug Abuse Control Act were similar for violations under the Federal Food, Drug, and Cosmetic Act. A first offense could bring a sentence of up to a year in prison or a fine up to one thousand dollars; for subsequent offenses, three years' imprisonment or a fine up to ten thousand dollars. An amendment to the Act in 1968 increased the punishment in all categories of offenses. For instance, the punishment for a first offense increased to a maximum of five years' imprisonment or a fine of no more than 10,000 dollars.

Drug abuse control as a presidential priority began in January 1968, when President Lyndon Johnson in his State of the Union address declared the drug problem to be serious and gave priority to the reduction and elimination of drug use and abuse. Johnson stressed the need to work closely with other nations and expand worldwide operations to enforce legislation to reduce the use, manufacture, and sale of drugs. One year later, President Richard Nixon called attention to the dramatic increase in juvenile drug arrests and noted the increase in incidence of heroin addiction and the use by college students of other drugs, such as marijuana, LSD, and amphetamines. In October 1970, the Controlled Substances Act became law. This law attempted to consolidate the myriad federal laws pertaining to drug control and drug abuse prevention. The law, developed with the assistance of physicians, scientists, and attorneys, covered all known dangerous drugs and provided different treatment options for each general type of drug. Not only did the law provide for the treatment and rehabilitation of addicts but it also called for increased research into the prevention of drug abuse, and was careful to distinguish between the drug addict, the user, and the trafficker. Penalties for traffickers were very severe, compared to the more mild penalties for addicts and users.

An important aspect of the Controlled Substances Act was that it required states to enact legislation that was uniform with the Act. But, states could set their own penalties, and add, delete, or reschedule substances as new findings came to light. A little more than a decade later, the federal government increased criminal penalties for drug offenses with the 1984 Crime Control Act. The Act also established a determinate sentencing system, and amended the Bail Reform Act to target pretrial detention of defendants accused of serious drug offenses. Two years later, the 1986 Anti-Drug Abuse Act established mandatory prison sentences for large-scale marijuana distribution, added designer drugs to the drug schedule, and contained provisions to strengthen international efforts to control drugs. The 1986 Act also devoted a larger share of federal drug control monies to prevention and treatment. The 1988 Anti-Drug Abuse Act continued efforts to increase treatment and prevention targeted at the reduction of drug demand. The Act added programs to treat intravenous drug abusers as part of AIDS control, and programs for women who use drugs, and for their children. At the same time, however, this Act also endorsed the use of sanctions aimed at drug users to reduce the demand for drugs.

The Crime Control Act came into effect two years later in 1990. This Act included provisions to expand drug control and education programs aimed at

schools, expanded regulations of precursor chemicals used in the manufacture of illegal drugs, and included measures establishing drug-free school
zones and drug enforcement grants.

A number of foreign policy initiatives also came out of the federal drug laws
and their amendments. The 1986 Anti-Drug Abuse Act required foreign assistance to countries be withheld if the president does not certify that those
countries have cooperated with the United States or have taken the appropriate steps to prevent drug production, drug trafficking, and drug-related
money laundering. An amendment to the 1986 Act made it unlawful to certify a country's compliance unless it had signed a treaty with the United States
that addressed drug control and embraced cooperation with U.S. drug enforcement agencies.

Extent and Patterns of Use

The majority of information regarding the extent and patterns of use in the
United States comes from two reliable studies that track self-reported drug
use. The Monitoring the Future Study, which assesses secondary school and
college students' use of drugs, has been conducted annually since 1975. The
National Household Survey on Drug Abuse (NHSDA) surveys a sample of the
population aged twelve years and over.

According to monthly prevalence estimates derived from the NHSDA, in
1994 an estimated 13 million Americans aged seventeen or older used illicit
drugs; 10 million used cannabis, and 1.4 million used cocaine. Table 4-1 shows
the 1999 prevalence of drug use for different age groups. By 2001, the prevalence estimates increased to 15.9 million, or 7.1 percent of the population of
the United States.

The 2002 Monitoring the Future Study reported that within the year prior
to the survey 5.0 percent had used cocaine, 2.3 percent had used crack cocaine, 1.0 percent had used heroin, and 36.2 percent used marijuana/
hashish (UNODC 2003).

Table 4-2 provides the lifetime, annual, and thirty-day prevalence rates of
any illicit drug, marijuana, cocaine, and heroin for eighth, tenth, and twelfth
graders as found in the Monitoring the Future Studies over the years.

The United States is the largest market for cocaine across the globe
(UNODC 2003: 8) and "is the main problem drug in America" (129). The
UNODC (2003) estimates that the number of cocaine users has stabilized over
the past several years and reports that the prevalence rates in 2002 were 15
percent lower than in 1998 and 60 percent lower than in 1985 (8). About 90
percent of the cocaine that is imported into the United States passes through

TABLE 4-1
Results from National Household Survey on Drug Abuse, United States, 1999

Drug/Prevalence	12 Years and Older	26 Years and Older	Ages 18–25
Any Illicit Drug			
Lifetime	39.7	39.2	52.6
Past Year	11.9	7.7	29.6
Past Month	6.7	4.4	17.1
Marijuana			
Lifetime	34.6	34.7	46.8
Past Year	8.9	5.4	24.8
Past Month	5.1	3.0	14.8
Cocaine			
Lifetime	11.5	12.7	11.9
Past Year	1.7	1.1	5.3
Past Month	0.7	0.5	1.7
Heroin			
Lifetime	1.4	1.4	1.8
Past Year	0.2	0.1	0.5
Past Month	0.1	0.1	0.2
Any Illicit Drug other than Marijuana			
Lifetime	24.1	23.3	33.3
Past Year	6.3	3.9	15.9
Past Month	2.9	1.9	6.4

Source: SAMHSA, Office of Applied Studies, National Household Survey on Drug Abuse, 1999 CAI.

or was produced in Colombia. Cocaine is often routed from Colombia to Mexico to the United States, or on boats through the Caribbean.

Most of the heroin in the United States is imported from Colombia and Mexico (UNODC 2003: 57). Of all global seizures of heroin in 2001, 38 percent took place in North America.

Law Enforcement

Since 1980, the drug offender inmate population has risen steadily. Between 1980 and 2001, the inmate population of drug offenders in state prisons has risen from 6 percent (19,000) to 20 percent (246,100) (see Table 4-3). The inmate population of drug offenders in federal prisons has risen from 25 percent (4,749) in 1980 to 54.7 percent (70,009) in 2002 (Table 4-4). The steady increase of incarcerations reflects the steady increase of drug-related arrests. The Federal Bureau of Investigation (FBI) reported 580,900 drug-related arrests (5.6 percent of all arrests) in 1980. In 2001, there were 1,586,902 drug arrests

TABLE 4-2

Results from The Monitoring the Future Surveys, United States, 1994–2000

Grade	8th Graders						
Year	'94	'95	'96	'97	'98	'99	'00
Any Illicit Drug							
Lifetime	25.7	28.5	31.2	29.4	29.0	28.3	26.8
Annual	18.5	21.4	23.6	22.1	21.0	20.5	19.5
30-Day	10.9	12.4	14.6	14.6	12.1	12.2	11.9
Marijuana							
Lifetime	16.7	19.9	23.1	22.6	22.2	22.0	20.3
Annual	13.0	15.8	18.3	17.7	16.9	16.5	15.6
30-day	7.8	9.1	11.3	10.2	9.7	9.7	9.1
Daily	0.7	0.8	1.5	1.1	1.1	1.4	1.3
Cocaine							
Lifetime	3.6	4.2	4.5	4.4	4.6	4.7	4.5
Annual	2.1	2.6	3.0	2.8	3.1	2.7	2.6
30-Day	1.0	1.2	1.3	1.1	1.4	1.3	1.2
Heroin							
Lifetime	2.0	2.3	2.4	2.1	2.3	2.3	1.9
Annual	1.2	1.4	1.6	1.3	1.3	1.4	1.1
30-Day	0.6	0.6	0.7	0.6	0.6	0.6	0.5

Grade	10th Graders						
Year	'94	'95	'96	'97	'98	'99	'00
Any Illicit Drug							
Lifetime	37.4	40.9	45.4	47.3	44.9	46.2	45.6
Annual	30.0	33.3	37.5	38.5	35.0	35.9	36.4
30-Day	18.5	20.2	23.2	23.0	21.5	22.1	22.5
Marijuana							
Lifetime	30.4	34.1	39.8	42.3	39.6	40.9	40.3
Annual	25.2	28.7	33.6	34.8	31.1	32.1	32.2
30-day	15.8	17.2	20.4	20.5	18.7	19.4	19.7
Daily	2.2	2.8	3.5	3.7	3.6	3.8	3.8
Cocaine							
Lifetime	4.3	5.0	6.5	7.1	7.2	7.7	6.9
Annual	2.8	3.5	4.2	4.7	4.7	4.9	4.4
30-Day	1.2	1.7	1.7	2.0	2.1	1.8	1.8
Heroin							
Lifetime	1.5	1.7	2.1	2.1	2.3	2.3	2.2
Annual	0.9	1.1	1.2	1.4	1.4	1.4	1.4
30-Day	0.4	0.6	0.5	0.6	0.7	0.7	0.5

Grade	12th Graders						
Year	'94	'95	'96	'97	'98	'99	'00
Any Illicit Drug							
Lifetime	45.6	48.4	50.8	54.3	54.1	54.7	54.0
Annual	35.8	39.0	40.2	42.4	41.4	42.1	40.9
30-Day	21.9	23.8	24.6	26.2	25.6	25.9	24.9

Grade			12th Graders				
Year	'94	'95	'96	'97	'98	'99	'00
Marijuana							
Lifetime	38.2	41.7	44.9	49.6	49.1	49.7	48.8
Annual	30.7	34.7	35.8	38.5	37.5	37.8	36.5
30-day	19.0	21.2	21.9	23.7	22.8	23.1	21.6
Daily	3.6	4.6	4.9	5.8	5.6	6.0	6.0
Cocaine							
Lifetime	5.9	6.0	7.1	8.7	9.3	9.8	8.6
Annual	3.6	4.0	4.9	5.5	5.7	6.2	5.0
30-Day	1.5	1.8	2.0	2.3	2.4	2.6	2.1
Heroin							
Lifetime	1.2	1.6	1.8	2.1	2.0	2.0	2.4
Annual	0.6	1.1	1.0	1.2	1.0	1.1	1.5
30-Day	0.3	0.6	0.5	0.5	0.5	0.5	0.7

Source: http://165.112.78.61/Infofax/HSYouthtrends.html, retrieved: 7/12/01, conducted by the University of Michigan's Institute for Social Research.

accounting for 11.6 percent of all arrests (Federal Bureau of Investigation 2001). Looking only at felony convictions, in 2000, 34.6 percent (319,700) of all felony convictions in state courts were for drug offenses (Durose and Langan 2003: 2). Of all felony convictions, 12.6 percent were for drug possession and 22 percent were for trafficking. The mean prison sentences in state prisons for drug offenses was 47 months in 2002, although prisoners were expected to serve only 49 percent of their sentences (5). The mean sentence for trafficking was fifty-two months, and the mean sentence for possession was thirty-four months.

When broken down by gender and race, 83 percent of those convicted of drug offenses in state courts were male (Durose and Langan 2003: 6). Of those convicted of drug offenses, 46 percent were white and 53 percent were black.

The Office of National Drug Control Policy (2003) reported that among state prisoners whose release was expected in 1999, 83.9 percent were involved with alcohol or drugs when they committed their offense, 58.8 percent had used drugs in the month prior to their offense, 45.3 percent had been on drugs while committing their offense, 24.8 percent had ever tried intravenous drugs, and 20.9 percent committed their offense in order to financially support their drug habit (2).

In 1989, 1.3 million pounds of drugs were seized by the FBI, DEA, U.S. Border Patrol, U.S. Coast Guard, and U.S. Customs Service (ONDCP 2003: 3). By 2001, this figure had risen to 2.9 million pounds. While in 1989, officials seized 51,625 pounds of hashish, only 433 pounds were seized in 2001. Further, 1,070,965 pounds of marijuana were seized in 1989. By 2001, this figure had more than doubled, reaching 2,673,535 pounds.

TABLE 4-3
Persons in State Custody by Most Serious Offense, United States, 1980–2001

Year	Drug	Violent	Property	Public Order
1980	19,000	173,300	89,300	12,400
1981	21,700	193,300	100,500	14,600
1982	25,300	215,300	114,400	17,800
1983	26,600	214,600	127,100	24,400
1984	31,700	227,300	133,100	21,900
1985	38,900	246,200	140,100	23,000
1986	45,400	258,600	150,200	28,800
1987	57,900	271,300	155,500	31,300
1988	79,100	282,700	161,600	35,000
1989	12,100	293,900	172,700	39,500
1990	148,600	313,600	173,700	45,500
1991	155,200	339,500	180,700	49,500
1992	168,100	369,100	181,600	56,300
1993	177,000	393,500	189,600	64,000
1994	193,500	425,700	207,000	74,400
1995	212,800	459,600	226,600	86,500
1996	216,900	484,800	231,700	96,000
1997	222,100	507,800	236,400	106,200
1998	236,800	545,200	242,900	113,900
1999	251,200	570,000	245,000	120,600
2000	251,100	589,100	238,500	124,600
2001	246,100	596,100	233,000	129,900

Source: Bureau of Justice Statistics. 2003. Number of persons in custody of state correctional authorities by most serious offense, 1980–2001.

Drug Policy

Generally, federal policy through the mid-1970s focused on a balanced approach of demand and supply, with budget allocations supporting this balance. After 1975, federal expenditures for prevention and treatment became second to enforcement of controls against drug trafficking. The Justice Department was responsible for enforcement, while the Department of Health Education and Welfare handled prevention and treatment. International drug control was the responsibility of the State Department. Priority being given to enforcement has continued during the last two decades. By fiscal year 1985, the Federal Drug Strategy called for $1.2 billion for enforcement, compared to $252.9 million for demand reduction. It was during this time that the federal strategy also shifted its focus toward cocaine, as research began to show that it was cocaine, not heroin, that was posing more of a health threat in the United States.

By 1985, the federal government had passed the responsibility for prevention to local communities, and urged them to utilize local resources with

TABLE 4-4
Federal Sentenced Prison Population, and Numberr and Percent
Sentenced for Drug Offenses, United States, 1970–2002

Year	Total	Drug Offenses	
		Number	Percent of Total
1970	20,686	3,384	16.3
1971	20,529	3,495	17.0
1972	20,729	3,523	16.9
1973	22,038	5,652	25.6
1974	21,769	6,203	28.4
1975	20,692	5,540	26.7
1976	24,135	6,425	26.6
1977	25,673	6,743	26.2
1978	23,501	5,981	25.4
1979	21,539	5,468	25.3
1980	19,023	4,749	24.9
1981	19,765	5,076	25.6
1982	20,938	5,518	26.3
1983	26,027	7,201	27.6
1984	27,622	8,152	29.5
1985	27,623	9,491	34.3
1986	30,104	11,344	37.7
1987	33,246	13,897	41.8
1988	33,758	15,087	44.7
1989	37,758	18,852	49.9
1990	46,575	24,297	52.2
1991	52,176	29,667	56.9
1992	59,516	35,398	59.5
1993	68,183	41,393	60.7
1994	73,958	45,367	61.3
1995	76,947	46,669	60.7
1996	80,872	49,096	60.7
1997	87,294	52,059	59.6
1998	95,323	55,984	58.7
1999	104,500	60,399	57.8
2000	112,329	63,898	56.9
2001	120,829	67,037	55.5
2002	128,090	70,009	54.7

Source: Sourcebook of criminal justice statistics online. Federal prison population, and number and percent sentenced for drug offenses. Table 6.51.

guidance and leadership support available from the federal government. The year 1984 saw the first effort in the form of a "national strategy" which came from the White House Drug Abuse Policy Office. The National Drug Enforcement Policy Board was created one year later to coordinate national drug policy and international issues related to drug policy.

By 1995, the federal drug control budget had surpassed $13 billion. To put it into perspective, this figure was almost 1 percent of the estimated U.S. government budget expenditure. In terms of social costs, however, the 1996 National Drug Control Strategy estimates that the annual social costs of drug abuse amount to over $65 billion (ONDCP 1996).

The ONDCP (2003) reports the estimated costs of drug abuse to society to be the following:

TABLE 4-5
Estimated Costs to Society of Drug Abuse, United States, 1992–2000 ($ millions)

Year	Health Care Costs	Productivity Losses	Other Costs	Total
1992	10,820	69,421	21,912	102,153
1994	11,279	82,685	24,440	118,404
1996	11,428	92,423	27,444	131,295
1998	12,862	98,467	32,083	143,412
2000	14,899	110,491	35,274	160,664

Between 1998 and 2002, the funds spent on federal drug control increased from $8,179 million to $11,485 million (UNODC 2003: 6). Spending on drug treatment, drug prevention, prevention research, treatment research, and international efforts increased, while domestic law enforcement spending decreased. For fiscal year 2004, a total of $11,679.3 million has been requested.

Recent drug policy and referendums in the United States have seen the government and the people at odds over how to approach the country's drug problem. The federal government has continued to support the War on Drugs with support for increased spending, more prisons, and strict sentencing guidelines. The federal government has also refused to consider the validity of medical marijuana and gained ground in this debate with the Supreme Court's unanimous ruling against an Oakland-based cannabis cooperative. But in the last six years, voters and local governments have begun to support alternative sentencing, such as drug treatment instead of incarceration, and a handful of states have passed bills allowing patients who qualify to cultivate, possess, and use marijuana for medical purposes without the threat of arrest by state or local authorities.

Between 1978 and 2000, thirty-five states have passed legislation that recognizes the therapeutic value of marijuana. Although these laws exempt individuals with prescriptions from local prosecution, these laws do not provide the patient with a legal means to obtain the drug. In 1996, California was the first state able to draft an effective medical marijuana ballot initiative and have it voted into law by the people. The law allowed for those who had received a "recommendation" from a doctor to legally possess, cultivate, and use marijuana to treat an illness. The word "recommendation" was crucial because physicians can be held criminally responsible under federal law for prescribing a controlled substance. The same year, Arizona voters approved a similar initiative that used the word "prescribe" instead of "recommend." Between 1996 and 2000, Alaska, Oregon, Washington, the District of Columbia, Maine, Colorado, and Nevada have all passed referendums similar to that of California. In 2000, Hawaii took a different approach and allowed for medical marijuana via the state legislature. The governor of Hawaii introduced the original bill to the state legislature and signed it into law on June 14.

On May 14, 2001, the Supreme Court ruled 8-0 in *U.S. v. Oakland Cannabis Buyers* that federal law "reflects a determination that marijuana has no medical benefits worthy of an exception" and that federal law does not provide a "medical necessity" exception, even to those patients who claim that marijuana is the only drug that alleviates the symptoms they have as a result of a serious or terminal illness (Lane 2001). This ruling provides the federal government with authority to prosecute cannabis clubs or physicians who recommend marijuana.

In November 2000, California voters passed Proposition 36, an initiative that allows first and second time nonviolent, simple drug possession offenders the opportunity to go into drug treatment, in lieu of jail. The plan aims at diverting 36,000 drug offenders. A program similar to Prop 36, but much more stringent, exists in Milwaukee, Wisconsin. Milwaukee has started a program that allows "young men with drug-related sentences of up to 11 years [to] participate in a highly structured regimen focusing on what they need to stay out of prison" (Cusac 2001). They are provided with an education, drug treatment, and counseling. If they are successful, within several months the men are allowed to obtain jobs in the community while spending their nights in a locked facility. The program is gradual and eventually allows for the participants to move out on their own or back home while still under the watch of a probation officer and, in some cases, an electronic ankle bracelet that monitors the location of the participant. There are many other examples of state and local jurisdictions implementing programs that divert drug offenders away from traditional sentencing. These include drug courts, boot camps, intensive treatment programs, and intense probation supervision.

Note

1. Discussion of the specific laws that follow should not be taken as comprehensive. In general, when pertinent to consumption issues and/or regulations concerning marijuana, cocaine, or opium, or its derivatives, provisions of the laws are discussed.

References

Beiser, Vince. 2001. "How We Got to Two Million: How did the Land of the Free become the world's leading jailer?" July 10, 2001. *Mother Jones.com Special Report.* www.motherjones.com/prisons/print_overview.html (accessed July 24, 2001).

Bureau of Justice Statistics. 2003. *Number of persons in custody of State correctional authorities by most serious offense, 1980–2001.* Washington, D.C.: Bureau of Justice Statistic. www.ojp.usdoj.gov (accessed October 8, 2003).

Cusac, Anne-Marie. 2001. "What's the Alternative: Society has to respond to lawbreakers, but it doesn't always have to lock them up." July 10, 2001. *Mother Jones.com Special Report.* www.motherjones.com/prisons/print_alternatives.html (accessed July 24, 2001).

Durose, Matthew, and Patrick A. Langan. 2003. *Felony Sentences in State Courts, 2000.* Washington, D.C.: Bureau of Justice Statistics.

Federal Bureau of Investigation. 2001. *Estimated Arrests 2001*, 233, Table 29. Washington, D.C.: Federal Bureau of Investigations. www.fbi.gov/ucr/cius_01/01crime4 .pdf (accessed October 8, 2003).

Harrison and Karberg. 2003. *Prison and Jail Prisoners at Midyear 2002.* Washington, D.C.: Bureau of Justice Statistics.

Johnson, Gary E. 2001. "Bad Investment: Take It from a Businessman: The War on Drugs Is Just Money Down the Drain." July 10, 2001. *MotherJones.com Special Report.* www.motherjones.com/prisons/print_investment.html (accessed July 24, 2001).

Lane, Charles. 2001. "Supreme Court Ruling Deals Blow to 'Medical Marijuana.'" *Washington Post,* May 15. www-tech.mit.edu/V121/N26/marij.26w.html (accessed July 26, 2001).

Marijuana Policy Project. 2001. "State-by-State Medical Marijuana Laws: How to Remove the Threat of Arrest." www.mpp.org/statelaw/body.html (accessed July 26, 2001).

Office of National Drug Control Policy. 2003. Drug Data Summary. Washington, D.C.: Executive Office of the President. Office of National Drug Control Policy. www.whitehousedrugpolicy.gov (accessed october 8, 2003.)

Office of National Drug Control Policy. 1996. The Presdient's National Drug Control Strategy, 1996. Washington, D.C.: Executive Office of the President, Office of National Drug Control Policy.

Sourcebook of Criminal Justice Statistics Online. *Federal prison population, and number and percent sentenced for drug offenses.* Table 6.51. www.albany.edu/sourcebook/ 1995/pdf/t651.pdf (accessed October 8, 2003).

Sourcebook of Criminal Justice Statistics Online. *Students reporting use of alcohol and drugs.* Table 3.69. www.albany.edu/sourcebook/1995/pdf/t369.pdf (accessed October 8, 2003).

United Nations Office on Drugs and Crime (UNODC). 2003. *Global Illicit Drug Trends 2003.* www.unodc.org/unodc/en/global_illicit_drug_trends.html (accessed October 24, 2003).

5

Canada

Overview

CANADA BORDERS THE NORTH ATLANTIC OCEAN on the east, the North Pacific Ocean on the west, the Arctic Ocean on the north, and the United States on the south. It has a population of 32,207,113 (July 2003 est.). The ethnic groups in Canada are those of British Isles origin (28 percent), mixed background (26 percent), French origin (23 percent), other European (15 percent), Amerindian (2 percent), and other, mostly Asian, African, and Arab (6 percent). The predominant religions are Roman Catholic (46 percent), Protestant (36 percent), and other (18 percent). The figures are according to the 1991 Census.

Canada is a federalist country that is divided into ten provinces and two territories. It is a parliamentary democratic government. The authority to make laws is divided between the Parliament and the provincial legislatures. The Constitution Act of 1867 established the division of power and authority between the federal and provincial levels of government. The federal, provincial, and municipal levels of government share the responsibility for the various parts of the criminal justice system. The federal police force is concerned mainly with the enforcement of federal statutes, such as the Customs Act and Narcotic Control Act. The Canadian Parliament has been given exclusive jurisdiction with regard to passing criminal laws and developing criminal procedures. The provinces have jurisdiction over the administration of justice in each province.

Canada's legal system utilizes an inquisitorial process in some proceedings such as a coroner's inquest or a Royal Commission Inquiry, but an adversarial process is used for both civil and criminal trials. Enacted in 1892, the Canadian Criminal Code, uniform across the country, is the basis for criminal law. But, in 1955, a totally new revised Criminal Code came into force.

Crimes are classified into two broad categories: those that are tried by summary conviction and those that are tried by indictment. The most serious crimes fall under the category of indictable offenses, and these crimes are punishable by at least two years imprisonment in a federal penitentiary. Summary offenses are less serious crimes. Local provinces can define these offenses and sentences can range from fines and probation, to a maximum of six months incarceration in a provincial prison. Offenses can also be hybrid offenses or dual offenses where the prosecutor has discretion to proceed by summary conviction or by indictment (Cohen and Longtin). Possession of drugs are considered hybrid offenses.

The age of criminal responsibility, as defined under the Young Offenders Act of 1985, is eighteen years old (Ekstedt and Griffiths 1988). The Parliament of Canada abolished the death penalty in 1976 (Ekstedt and Griffiths 1988).

Drug Offenses and the Law

Canada's legislative history relating to drug use begins in the late nineteenth century as opium use was rising. Many Canadians resented immigrant Chinese for working for lower wages, and they began to associate opium with Chinese immigrants. After a violent riot in 1907, British Columbia put pressure on the federal government to prohibit opium. The Opium Act was enacted in 1908; it prohibited the sale, importation, and manufacture of opium. Penalties ranged from a fifty-dollar fine to three years imprisonment. In addition, Parliament passed the Proprietary and Patent Medicine Act in 1908. This Act required that patent medicines containing heroin, morphine, opium, and other drugs must list their contents on the label and that the medicines could not contain more alcohol than was necessary as a solvent. Cocaine in medicines was also prohibited. Punishment for violations of these rules was a fine and loss of registration for the medicine involved. As these "prohibition" laws were enacted, public sentiment turned more punitive. The 1911 Opium and Drug Act soon followed, which banned cocaine and instituted penalties for the use of opium. In addition, it became a crime to be in the presence of someone smoking opium. One decade later, amendments to the 1911 Act upped the penalties: the maximum penalty became a seven-year imprisonment for the importation, manufacture, or sale of opium or other drugs mentioned in the Act. It became an offense be in a building that also contained narcotics unless the alleged offender could prove he had no knowledge of the presence of drugs.

The harshness of the penalties did not concern most Canadians because they were assured that the legislation would be used mainly against Chinese immigrants. Statistics show that from 1921 to 1922, 634 out of 853 convictions were of Chinese immigrants (Alexander 1990). In 1929, an even more punitive law was passed essentially creating the drug addict as a criminal typology. Addiction was now the venue of the police. Then came the Narcotic Control Act of 1961, which specified life imprisonment as the maximum penalty for trafficking or possession for the purpose of trafficking in drugs. Trafficking was defined broadly as any of the following: manufacture, sell, give, administer, transport, send, deliver, or distribute, or to offer to do any of those. Marijuana was included as a narcotic under the Act. For instance, if one person offers to give another person a marijuana cigarette, it would constitute trafficking, punishable by a maximum life sentence (Alexander 1990). The Act also gave the police great power in search and seizure cases.

In 1996, Canada enacted the Controlled Drugs and Substances Act (CDSA) to align their policies with the Single Convention on Narcotic Drugs, the Convention on Psychotropic Substances, and the relevant portions of the United Nations Convention against Illicit Traffic in Narcotic Drugs and Psychotropic Substances (United Nations Office on Drugs and Crime 2003). The Canadian law repealed the Narcotic Control Act and Parts III and IV of the Food and Drugs Act. The law restricted the production, importation, exportation, and distribution of certain substances to medical, scientific, and industrial uses. Further, it specified the actions which the police and courts may take to curb the illegal use of controlled substances. Many public health practitioners had hoped that this legislation would be linked to harm reduction policies as discussed in Canada's Drug Strategy, initiated in 1987 (Hathaway and Erickson 2003). However, the CDSA only contains a broad provision for rehabilitation with no guidelines for the exercise of judicial discretion.

Extent and Patterns of Use

According to the U.S. State Department, Canada had approximately 1,000,000 drug users as of 1998. These users include some 250,000 cocaine addicts and 40,000 heroin addicts (Bureau for International Narcotics and Law Enforcement Affairs 1999). The Research Group on Drug Use reports that in Toronto, there were 40 heroin deaths in 1990, 67 deaths in 1994, and 36 deaths in 1998.[1] Overall, Toronto experienced one hundred and fifty-five drug-related deaths that year. A Center for Addiction and Mental Health survey in 1998 showed that 1 percent of respondents used cocaine powder and 13 percent used cannabis. The Ontario Student Drug Use Survey found increases in teen drug

TABLE 5-1
Rates of Drug Use in Canada, 1994 (percent of all Canadians)

	Used at Least Once	*Used in the Previous Year*
Any Illicit Drug	24%	8%
Cannabis	23%	7%
Cocaine	4%	0.7%
Heroin, Speed, LSD	6%	1%

Source: Canadian Community Epidemiology Network on Drug Use [CCENDU] 2002 National Report.

use between 1997 and 1999. In 1999, 26 percent of junior high and high school students reported using cannabis. From 1997 to 1999, the percent reporting cocaine use increased from 2.7 percent to 6.4 percent.

Reported rates by respondents in Toronto for cocaine use in 1998 remained stable at about 1 percent for adults and 3 percent for students. Cocaine is the most common illicit drug for which users seek treatment. Requests for treatment involving cocaine abuse increased for Toronto and Ontario between 1996 and 1997. In 1997 there were twenty-seven drug-related deaths involving cocaine, compared to twenty-two such deaths in 1996. Heroin use was reported by less than 1 percent of Toronto adults and less than 2 percent of students. In 1997, there were thirty-six drug-related deaths in Toronto that included positive findings for heroin. This marked the third straight year that heroin-related deaths dropped after reaching a high of sixty-seven in 1994. Cannabis use by Toronto adults remained relatively stable in 1997 (11 percent) and 1998 (13 percent). Cannabis use among students rose from 9 percent in 1993, to 18 percent in 1995, and finally, 19 percent in the survey conducted in 1997. In 1997, only 1 of 132 drug-related deaths involved the use of cannabis (Research Group for Drug Use, 1999).

Adult cannabis use remained stable in 1999 at 10 percent while students in junior high and high school reported marijuana use at a rate of 26 percent, the highest rate since the survey started in 1974. In 1998, 18 percent of those being treated for addiction cited cannabis as a "problematic substance" (Research Group for Drug Use, 2000).

AIDS and IV Drug Use

Cocaine and heroin are the most commonly injected drugs. Approximately one-fifth of recent AIDS cases are due to intravenous drug use. This proportion is on the rise each year. While the extent of injection drug use is not known, one estimate says there are between 50,000 and 100,000 intravenous drug users in Canada (Canadian Community Epidemiology Network on Drug Use [CCENDU] 2002 National Report).

By the end of 1999, the Bureau of HIV/AIDS, STD, and TB received 16,916 reports of AIDS cases.[2] During that year it is estimated that 20.7 percent of adult AIDS cases were associated with injection drug use, a significant increase since 1990 when about 1.5 percent of adult AIDS cases were related to the use of injection drugs (Bureau of HIV/AIDS, STD and TB, Ontario). Drug use resulting in AIDS among women has been on the increase. Prior to 1990, 7.3 percent of women and 1.1 percent of men with AIDS contracted the virus through injection drugs. By 1999, these figures increased to 31.7 percent among women and 16.1 percent among men.

Law Enforcement

National policy has focused on drug abuse treatment, while law enforcement has focused its efforts on gang-related and organized drug smuggling operations. Canada has been a popular target for international drug smugglers. Not only are drugs brought into the country for consumption, but also Canada's long-standing open border policy with the United States makes it a popular transshipment point for drugs that will eventually end up in U.S. markets. Law enforcement agencies have recently acknowledged a growing trend of Asian-sourced heroin entering North America through Canadian ports. These major ports of entry include Vancouver, Montreal, and Halifax.

In 1999 the Canadian government enacted legislation that required mandatory reporting for suspicious transactions in the financial sector. The lack of such legislation had made Canada an attractive venue for international drug-money laundering. Canada has also taken steps to increase the capability of its law enforcement agencies to detect suspicious transactions and investigate money-laundering schemes.

While efforts have been made to curb organized drug smuggling, Canadian courts have been reluctant to impose tough prison sentences on local drug users and producers, opting for fines instead. This trend reflects the widespread view that drugs are a "victimless" crime and should be dealt with mainly as a national health concern. Courts have questioned the legality of police "sting" operations and acquitted suspects caught in the act of drug consumption citing privacy grounds.

In 1990, the police recorded 7,153 incidents of cocaine trafficking, at a rate of 27 per 100,000 (Canadian Crime Statistics 1990, 1991).[3] Canadian police departments reported a total of 87,945 drug offenses in 2000. The overwhelming

TABLE 5-2
Number of Police-Reported Incidents by Type of Drug, Canada, 1996 to 2000

	1996	1997	1998	1999	2000
Marijuana	47,234	47,933	50,917	60,011	66,171
Cocaine	11,478	11,468	12,183	11,963	12,812
Heroin	1,287	1,235	1,323	1,323	1,226
Other drugs*	5,730	5,957	6,509	6,845	7,736
Total	65,729	66,593	70,922	80,142	87,945

* "Other drugs" include other illegal substances such as PCP, LSD, and ecstasy as well as controlled substances such as barbiturates and anabolic steroids.
Source: R. Logan, "Crime Statistics in Canada, 2000," *Juristat*, Statistics Canada, Canadian Centre for Justice Statistics, 85-002-xie, Vol. 21, No. 8, 2001, 11.

majority of these offenses involved marijuana, with 68 percent of them for possession.

For statistical purposes, the Canadian Centre for Justice Statistics divides drug offenses into the categories of trafficking/importation/cultivation and possession. It is a federal crime to traffic (e.g., manufacture, sell, give, administer, transport, send, deliver, distribute, or to attempt such actions), import, export, cultivate, or possess drugs listed under the Narcotic Control Act and under the Food and Drugs Act. The Narcotic Control Act (1985) lists the following drugs to be illegal under Schedule 1: Opium, coca, cannabis sativa, phenylpiperidines, phenazepines, amidones, methadols, phenalkoxsams, thiambutenes, moramides, benzazocines, ampromides, benzimidazoles, phencyclidine, fentanyl, tilidine, carfentanil, and alfentanil. The drugs listed under the Food and Drugs Act are generally those which must be controlled, are available only for medical use, are legally restricted, or are used for nonmedical purposes (Canadian Centre on Substance Abuse, 2000).

An analysis in 1996 estimated that substance abuse inflicted approximately $18.45 billion in costs in 1992, or 2.67 percent of Canada's gross domestic product (Single et al. 1996). Of the total costs, 40.8 percent was re-

TABLE 5-3
Statistics for Drug-Related Law Enforcement, Canada, 1998, 1999

	1999	1998
# of Drug-Related Arrests	12,541	7,531
Cannabis Seized	4.289 metric tons (mt)	5.955 mt
Cocaine Seized	500 kg	1.22 mt
Heroin Seized	51 kg	121 kg

Source: Bureau for International Narcotics and Law Enforcement Affairs, U.S. Department of State, International Narcotics Control Strategy Report, 1999.

lated to alcohol, 51.8 percent was related to tobacco, and 7.4 percent was associated with illegal drugs. This figure takes into account costs associated with workplace losses (direct or indirect), law enforcement costs, health care, prevention and research, loss of productivity, administrative costs, and other direct costs.

Drug Policy

Through the 1980s, the government of Canada focused on law enforcement as the key response to drug abuse. But, as Canada recognized the limitations in this approach, the federal government implemented its new National Drug Strategy in May 1987. The strategy was to provide $210 million over five years, with over 70 percent allocated to prevention and treatment, including education and rehabilitation, information, and research (Hathaway and Erickson 2003). The provinces and territories were made directly responsible for following through on the development of a strong rehabilitation and treatment program, although the federal government provided matching funds for treatment and rehabilitation. The strategy also targeted the subpopulations of young people, the aboriginal Indian and Inuit people, prison-inmates, and health professionals. The government provided funding for an augmented research program and to improve the national narcotics database. Although the strategy emphasized demand-side measures, as opposed to supply-side measures, many Canadian scholars believed that these were the years that marked Canada's entry into a drug war similar to that of the United States. Statistics on drug offenses show that the proportion of drug offenders in Canadian prisons grew from 9 percent in 1987 to 14 percent in 1991 (Erickson 1992). Possession offenses accounted for over half of all drug charges (Williams, Chang, and van Truong 1994).

Recently, there have been some policy developments with regard to cannabis and heroin. On July 31, 2001, Canada passed legislation to allow patients to use cannabis to treat certain illnesses if they obtain written permission from a physician. The legislation allows patients to possess and process marijuana. The law does not set limits on the amount of marijuana a patient can possess, allowing the doctor to make recommendations on a case-by-case basis. The general rule will be that a patient may possess a thirty-day supply of marijuana in accordance with the amount determined by the physician. Also, patients will have to renew their licenses every twelve months instead of every six months. And finally, it allows for individuals who are not physicians to assist patients but outlaws obtaining marijuana from street dealers and "compassion clubs," which previously distributed marijuana to those patients who had approval from their physician (Rooney 2001). With regard to processing marijuana, patients may process the marijuana themselves or designate a representative to grow it on their behalf. The regulations will: 1) Establish a maximum number of indoor and outdoor plants dependent on the patient's daily dose; 2) Authorize the receipt and possession of seeds; 3)Allow for the storage and transportation of marijuana; 4) Enable up to three licenses to produce at one address; 5) Allow for site inspections and criminal record checks for designated representatives.

In November of 2000, Vancouver Mayor Philip Owen announced that his city would take new and different steps in an attempt to curb the open heroin markets in the Downtown Eastside and reduce the amount of crime and drug overdoses plaguing the city (Bula 2000). Mayor Owen's plan contains recommendations that are aimed at strengthening equally the areas of prevention, treatment, legal enforcement, and harm reduction. The plan is modeled after the four-pillar approach that has been implemented in some European cities. The plan includes the formation of drug courts that would divert users from jail into treatment programs, special treatment beds for juvenile users, day centers for drug users outside of the Downtown Eastside, the testing of illicit street drugs to prevent overdoses, more police to go after large-scale drug dealers, and two controversial measures. The first controversial measure would expand the needle exchange program and decentralize its services. The second measure aims to create a task force to investigate the possibility of a scientific, medical project to develop safe injection sites (Bula 2000). A month after the plan was announced a survey conducted in Vancouver showed support for the legalization of marijuana was 57 percent. Sixty-one percent supported the medical use of heroin for drug treatment (*Vancouver Sun* 2001).

In 2000, the Canadian Senate formed the Special Committee on Illegal Drugs to hear expert testimony on the use of nonmedical drugs. The Committee produced a report in September 2002 calling for a regulatory form of legalization of cannabis that would stipulate conditions for obtaining licenses to produce and sell cannabis. Criminal penalties for illegal trafficking as well as export of cannabis would remain intact. The report also recommended amnesty for any person convicted of possession of cannabis under current or past legislation. In addition to the Senate Committee, Canada's multi-party group of legislators, the House of Commons, formed its own special committee to examine drug legislation. Justice Minister Anne McLellan said on May 18, 2001, that she is "quite open" to debate on the legalization of cannabis. Prime Minister Jean Chretien, on the other hand, stated that decriminalization "is not part of the government's agenda" (Dunn 2001). Chretien was joined by the Canadian Police Association in denouncing the decriminalization of marijuana. On May 27, 2003, the Liberal government put forth a new act that proposes to decriminalize the possession of fifteen grams or less of marijuana and one gram or less of hashish. Possession of marijuana would result in a $150 to $400 fine, but no criminal record would result. If the law were passed, it would not result in amnesty for those previously convicted.

Notes

1. Statistics from the Research Group on Drug Use, 2000: www.city.toronto.on.ca/drugcentre/rgdu00/rgdu1.htm.

2. These figures are from the website: www.womenfightaids.com.

3. The definitions of crimes are based on administrative definitions which are constructed by the Canadian Centre for Justice Statistics to aid Canadian Police in reporting crime statistics to the Uniform Crime Report Survey and have legal standing under the Canadian Criminal Code. When offenses are reported, attempted offenses are included in the counts.

References

Alexander, Bruce. 1990. *Peaceful Measures: Canada's Way Out of the War on Drugs.* Toronto: University of Toronto Press.

Andrade, John. 1985. *World Police and Parliamentary Forces.* New York: Stockton Press.

Annual Report, Adult Correctional Services in Canada (#85-211), 1990–1991, Canadian Centre for Justice Statistics. Statistics Canada. December 1991.

Archibald, Bruce P. 1988. "Police and Citizens' Powers to Arrest and Detain" in *From Crime to Punishment: An Introduction to Criminal Law System,* ed. by Joel E. Pink and David Perrier. Toronto: Carswell.

Bayley, David H. 1991. "Managing the Future: Prospective Issues in Canadian Policing." *User Report to the Ministry of the Solicitor General of Canada.*

Bryden, Joan. 2001. "Chretien Says 'No' to Legalizing Marijuana." *Vancouver Sun,* May 29. www.mapinc.org/drugnews/v01.n968.a09.html (accessed August 3, 2001).

Bula, Frances. 2000. "Mayor Philip Owen unveils today his sweeping plan for city's drug crisis." *Vancouver Sun,* November 21, A1, Front. www.cfdp.ca.general.htm (accessed August 3, 2001).

Bureau for International Narcotics and Law Enforcement Affairs, U.S. Department of State, International Narcotics Control Strategy Report, 1999, reported on www.womenfightaids.com.

Canadian Centre on Substance Abuse. 1999. www.ccsa.ca/Profile/cp99high.htm.

Canadian Centre on Substance Abuse. 2002. Canadian Community Epidemiology Network on Drug Use (CCENDU) 2002 National Report. Drug Trends and the CCENDU Network. Ottawa, Ontario: Canadian Centre on Substance Abuse.

Canadian Medical Association Journal (CMAJ). 2001. "Marijuana: federal smoke clears, a little." CMAJ 164 (10): 1397. www.cfdp.ca/cmaj.htm (accessed August 2, 2001).

Cohen, Debra, and Sandra Longtin. No date. World Factbook of Criminal Justice Systems: Canada. www.ojp.usdoj.gov/bjs/pub/ascii/wfbcjcan.txt (accessed August 2, 2001).

Cohen, Tom. 2001. "Canada Law Allows Medical Marijuana." *San Jose Mercury News,* July 31. www.mapinc.org/newscfdp/v01/n1395/a05.html (accessed August 2, 2001).

Cohen, Tom. 2001. "Rules Broaden Use of Medical Marijuana." *Associated Press,* August 1. www.mapinc.org/newscfdp/v01/n1402/a06.html (accessed August 2, 2001).

Dunn, Mark. 2001. "No Plans to Reduce Penalty for Pot." *Toronto Sun,* May 29. www.mapinc.org/drugnews/v01.n962.a06.html (accessed August 3, 2001).

Dunfield, Allsion. 2001. "Clark Supports Decriminalizing Marijuana". *Globe and Mail Update,* May 23. www.cfdp.ca/general4.htm (accessed July 27, 2001).

Ekstedt, John W., and Curt T. Griffiths. 1988. *Corrections in Canada,* 2nd ed. Toronto: Butterworths.

Erickson, P. G. 1992. "Recent Trends in Canadian Drug Policy: The Decline and Resurgence of Prohibitionism." *Daedalus,* 121(summer), 247–77.

Freeze, Colin, and Carolyn Abraham. 2001. "Marijuana Regulation Draws Fire." *Globe and Mail,* July 31, A1. www.mapinc.org/newscfdp/v01/n1396/a09.htm (accessed August 2, 2001).

Hathaway, Andrew D., and Patricia G. Erickson. 2003. "Drug Reform Principles and Policy Debates: Harm Reduction Prospects for Cannabis in Canada." *Journal of Drug Issues,* 33(2), 465–96.

Harvey, Bob. 2001. "Support Grows for Legalizing Marijuana: 5 years ago, one-third of Canadians favoured making drug legal; today about half do" *The Ottawa Citizen,* May 22. www.cfdp.ca/general4.htm (accessed July 27, 2001).

Health Canada. 2001. "Rock to unveil proposed regulations governing the possession and production of marijuana for medical purposes." Health Canada Online; 2001-34. www.hc-sc.gc.ca/english/archives/releases/2001/2001_34e.htm (accessed August 2, 2001).

Logan, Ron. 2001. Crime Statistics in Canada, 2000, *Jurisdat,* Statistics Canada, Canadian Centre for Justice Statistics, 85-002-xie, Vol. 21, No. 8, 2001, p. 11.

MacKinnon, Mark. 2001. "Minister 'Quite Open' to Marijuana Debate". *Toronto Globe and Mail,* May 19. www.cfdp.ca/general4.htm (accessed July 27, 2001).

McKenzie, Diane. 1997. *Canadian Profile: Alcohol, Tobacco, and Other Drugs.* Ontario: Canadian Centre on Substance Abuse.

Public Health Agency of Canada. 2003. Estimates of HIV Prevalence and Incidence in Canada, 2002. www.phac-aspc.gc.ca/publicat/ccdr-rmtc/03vol29/dr2923ea.html (accessed December 10, 2003).

Research Group for Drug Use (RGDU). 2000. *Drug Use in Toronto—2000.* Retrieved July 27, 2001. www.city.toronto.on.ca/drugcentre/rgdu00/rgdu1.htm.

Research Group for Drug Use (RGDU). 1999. *Drug Use in Toronto—1999.* www.city.toronto.on.ca/drugcentre/rgdu99/rgdu1.htm (accessed July 27, 2001).

Rooney, David. 2001. "Legal Paths to Pot." *Edmonton Sun*, August 1. www.mapinc
.org/newscfdp/v01/n1399/a03.html (accessed August 2, 2001).

Single, Eric, Lynda Robson, Xiaodi Xie, and Jürgen Rehm. 1996. "The Costs of Substance Abuse in Canada." In collaboration with Rachel Moore, Bernard Choi, Sylvie
Desjardins, and Jim Anderson. www.ccsa.ca/docs/costhigh.htm (accessed September 11, 2002).

Solicitor General Portfolio Corrections Statistics Committee. 2002. *Corrections and
Conditional Release Statistical Overview.* www.sgc.gc.ca/publications/corrections/
pdf/StatsNov2002_e.pdf (accessed October 8, 2003).

United Nations Office on Drugs and Crime (UNODC). 2003. Global Illicit Drug
Trends 2003. www.unodc.org/unodc/en/global_illicit drug trends.html (accessed
October 24, 2003).

Vancouver Sun. 2001. "Vancouver Residents Soften Views on Drugs." *Vancouver Sun,*
January 31. www.cfdp.ca.general.htm (accessed August 3, 2001).

Williams, B., K. Chang and M. van Truong. 1994. *Canadian Profile 1993: Alcohol and
Other Drugs.* Toronto: Addiction Research Foundation.

Women Fight Aids.com. www.womenfightaids.com/epi-drug.html.

6

Mexico

Overview

MEXICO'S GOVERNMENT AND LEGAL SYSTEM are similar to those of the United States. It is a federal republic with three branches of government: executive, legislative, and judicial. Mexico is comprised of thirty-one administrative states.

Mexico borders the United States on the north and Guatemala on the south. Twenty percent of its roughly 98.9 million inhabitants (UNODC, Regional Office, Mexico 2003) belong to pure Indian groups, but the majority of Mexico is made up of descendants of the Mestizaje, a blend of Spanish and Indian. Indian groups are concentrated in the country's poorest states, such as Chiapas, Oaxaca, and Yucatan.

Crimes in Mexico are deemed *serious* or *nonserious* (Portillo n.d.). Severity is determined not only by a codification of the crime, but by its punishment. The age of criminal responsibility in Mexico is generally eighteen. Children who are ages sixteen and seventeen can be prosecuted as adults in certain areas, such as Veracruz, Durango, Coahuila, Oaxaca, and Guanajuato (see Portillo n.d.).

Judges use their discretion to determine appropriate sentencing, which is based on the defendant's criminal history, special circumstances, the seriousness of the offense, the defendant's involvement in the offense, the nature of the crime, the circumstances under which the offense occurred, the offender's socioeconomic status, the offender's behavior after committing the crime, and the damages done unto the victim (Portillo n.d.). Possible sanctions include: prison, treatment, community service, job loss, and financial losses. Furthermore, the death penalty may be applied in cases involving wartime traitors, certain homicides, piracy, arson, kidnapping, and road assault (Portillo n.d.). However, Mexico has not executed an offender since 1937.

Drug Offenses and the Law

The federal government is the only government body that can prosecute drug crimes, which include "production, transportation, traffic, sale, supply (even free), prescription, import, export, assets, financial supply, supervision and publicity oriented towards drug consumption; contribution, or deviation of chemical precursors, essential chemical products or machinery for growing, extraction, production, preparation and narcotics assembly" (Portillo 2003).

First-time drug users are not legally sanctioned. The personal consumption of a small quantity of drugs is not subject to legal sanctions, although the individual is placed in treatment. The Federal Penal Code specifies sanctions for individuals caught with or transporting more than a small quantity of drugs.

Enacted on December 24, 1997, the Federal Law for the Control of Chemical Precursors, Essential Chemical Substances and Machinery for Manufacturing Capsules, Tablets and/or Pills sets forth a guideline that "controls the production, manufacture, sale, acquisition, import, export, transport, storage and distribution of precursors and other essential chemicals, as well as the equipment necessary for the manufacture of tablets, pills and capsules" (UNODC, Regional Office, *Mexico* 2003: 30).

The Federal Law for the Official Norms for Prevention, Treatment and Control of Addictions was enacted on April 12, 2000 and set "minimum standards" for issues addressing addiction, prevention, treatment, and investigations (UNODC, Regional Office, *Mexico* 2003: 31).

Extent and Patterns of Use

Mind-altering substances were used in Mexico before the Spanish inhabited the continent. Spanish missionaries working to convert the Indians were opposed to the use of plants for religious rituals. The Spaniards attempted to quell the Indian religious traditions because they were contrary to Christian practices. The Indians believed that the use of the natural substances did not pose a threat to the individual because the powers within the plant could be controlled by the drug use (Dobkin De Rios 1990). The values that sustained substance use for spiritual and religious uses are in many ways still maintained today, having been mixed with other influences throughout history.

Spaniards introduced *cannabis indica*, but *cannabis sativa* already existed in parts of the country. The first reports of using marijuana in rituals came in the eighteenth century (Rosovsky and Romero 1996). Opium and morphine were reported in the Mexican medical literature, but there is no evidence that usage of these drugs became problematic. A review of the historical literature also shows no evidence that coca leaves or cocaine were problems for Mexico until recent years.

Drug use has increased greatly in the last fifty years, due to globalization and the opening of markets, the introduction of foreign products, and the need for rapid industrialization (Rosovsky and Romero 1996). Mexico has been described as a "drug producing and transit country" (UNODC, Regional Office, *Mexico*, 2003: 7) that exports cannabis and heroin to the United States and Canada.

Since 1974, research has been conducted on drug use among Mexican students. The Mexican Institute of Psychiatry (Instituto Mexicano de Psiquiatria), together with the Ministry of Public Education (Secretaria de Educacion Publica), surveyed youth in 1976, 1986, and 1991. The results of the 1991 National Survey on Drug Use among Students showed that of the 3,501 junior high and high school students sampled, drug use prevalence remained low with 8.2 percent reporting ever using a drug, excluding alcohol and tobacco; 4.4 percent had used within the prior year, and 2 percent had used during the thirty days prior to the survey (Medina-Mora et al. 1993). Ninety-five percent of the sample was younger than eighteen (44.2 percent were thirteen and under) and all the respondents were in school (Juarez et al. 1998). Mexico has made some effort to research drug use among nonschool youth, as a growing number of school-age youth are working on the streets to support themselves and help their families. Medina-Mora et al. (1982) found that 10 percent of street youth reported marijuana use and 1.5 percent used it daily; 27 percent of street youth reported using inhalants and 22 percent inhaled solvents daily.

In 1988, Mexico conducted the first National Household Survey on Addictions. The survey, a random sample of 12,557 individuals between the ages of twelve and sixty-five living in urban areas, found that 4.3 percent reported having used at least one drug in their life, excluding alcohol and tobacco (7 percent of males; 2 percent of females). One year prevalence was 1.7 percent (SSA 1989). Thirty-day prevalence was 1 percent of males and 0.5 percent of females, and the most widely used illicit drug was marijuana, followed by tranquilizers, stimulants, and inhalants. The use of marijuana began between eighteen and twenty-five years old. Individuals from Mexican states along the U.S. border reported the highest proportions of drug use, which was double the national average. (U.S. lifetime prevalence in 1988 is 37 percent for males; in Mexico it is 4 percent.) The study also found that 25 percent of the heroin users had obtained the drug for the first time in the United States and 58 percent in the northern regions of Mexico. Overall, the intravenous drug use rate is very low in Mexico. This finding is supported by the small proportion of reported AIDS cases who have been infected through intravenous drug use.

Another source of information on drug use prevalence for youth and adults comes from the Information Reporting System on Drugs that has been operating since 1987 with data collection beginning in 1996. Maintained by the Mexican Institute of Psychiatry (MIP), the system integrates data gathered from a number of health and criminal justice agencies around the country (Ortiz et al. 1989). This source of data serves as a method to estimate trends. In June 1994 there were 564 analyzed cases, of which the main drugs used were reported to be marijuana (70.4 percent), inhalants (54 percent), and cocaine (26.1 percent). A similar percentage was reported for use of marijuana in 1986. However, the increase in cocaine use has been dramatic—only 1.6 percent said they had ever used it in 1986, but by 1994 the proportion had grown to 26.1 percent (as reported in Rosovsky and Romero 1996: 1676).

A more recent survey, conducted in 1998, assessed the prevalence of drug use among individuals age eighteen to sixty-five in urban homes (UNODC, Regional Office, Mexico 2003: 8; see *Secretaria de Salud, "Observatorio Epidemiologico en Drogas 2001"*). The study found that among the participants, the lifetime prevalence for marijuana was 5.9 percent, for cocaine 1.7 percent, and for heroin 0.5 percent. When asked about drugs that the participants had used more than fifty times, the prevalence rates were 1.0 percent for marijuana, 0.3 percent for cocaine, and 0.1 percent for hallucinogens and heroin. Overall, 6.4 percent of the male respondents had consumed any form of a drug during their lifetime, while the same was true for 1.1 percent of the women. When asked if they had consumed any drug more than fifty times in their lifetime, the rate at which men responded was 2.9 percent, while only 0.2 percent of female respondents responded affirmatively (UNODC, Regional Office, *Mexico* 2003, Table 11, 24).

Among school-age children surveyed in Mexico City,[1] the percent of respondents who reported having tried amphetamines, tranquilizers, marijuana, cocaine, crack, hallucinogens, inhalants, heroin, and other drugs once in their lifetime increased between 1997 and 2000. Further, respondents who had consumed the aforementioned drugs, except for inhalants, within the year prior to the surveys increased between 1997 and 2000 (UNODC, Regional Office, *Mexico* 2003, Table 9, 22).

TABLE 6-1
Reported AIDS Cases by Year, Mexico (By Any Cause)

1994	1995	1996	1997	1998	1999
4129	4106	3810	3550	3498	1094

AIDS and IV Drug Use

UNAIDS keeps a small amount of statistics about Mexican HIV/AIDS patients who contracted the disease through intravenous drug use. As a whole, the trend of contracting HIV/AIDS through IV use is diminishing in Mexico. In 1995, 6 percent of the intravenous drug users tested in the city of Chihuahua were HIV positive. In 1997, 1 percent of the intravenous drug users in Tijuana were HIV positive. The total number of reported AIDS cases diminished in Mexico between 1994 (the peak year) and 1999. The number of AIDS sufferers who contracted the disease through intravenous drug use has likewise diminished (UNAIDS 2000).

Law Enforcement

While law enforcement efforts have led to the arrests of drug cartel leaders from Tijuana, Ciudad Juarez, and the Gulf, drug trafficking has not decreased and there have been increases in seizures of cocaine, opium, and ecstasy (UNODC, Regional Office, Mexico 2003: 7).

Drugs are smuggled into Mexico through a variety of means, such as air, fishing vessels, airdrops, and human couriers (UNODC, Regional Office, Mexico 2003: 14). In 1999 an estimated 60 percent of South American cocaine sold in the United States entered via Mexico. Mexican cartels have become major producers and distributors of precursor chemicals for cocaine and amphetamine refinement. Mexico produces about 2 percent of the world's opium supply, but virtually all of it is destined for U.S. markets. While Mexico is also

TABLE 6-2
Reported AIDS Cases by Year, Mexico (IV Drug Users)

1996	1997	1998	1999
24	14	13	10

Source: Epidemiological Fact Sheets [on HIV/AIDS and sexually transmitted infections], The UNAIDS/WHO Working Group on Global HIV/AIDS and STI Surveillance, Mexico, 2000 Update.

TABLE 6-3
Persons Arrested for Trafficking and Possession, Mexico, 1996–2001

1996	1997	1998	1999	2000	2001
11,283	10,742	10,289	10,732	11,409	23,232

Source: UNODC, Regional Office, *Mexico*. 2003. Country Profile: Mexico, Table 6, 18.

a major producer of marijuana, its crop eradication force is highly sophisticated and one of the best in the world. Toward the end of the 1990s, Mexico's
rate of drug seizure also increased sharply.

Corruption in Mexico's law enforcement agencies and military continues to
be a major problem. From April 1997 to December 1999 more than 1,400 of
3,500 federal police officers were fired for corruption charges; 357 officers
have been prosecuted. Army personnel and federal officers have been arrested
or dismissed for violations such as keeping seized drugs, faking destruction of
drug caches, offering protection to known cartel members, abuse of power,
and links to cartel activity. At the same time, Mexican law enforcement has
made some notable arrests in 1999 including mid-level traffickers, cartel
money launderers, and inter-cartel power brokers.

Drug Policy

Mexican drug policies were formulated in the 1970s as concern about drug
use grew due to increased reporting of widespread drug use in the United
States. New policies and programs were elaborated and the creation of agencies dedicated to the understanding and treatment of drug use included a center for treatment of juveniles, a center for research, and a council to coordinate involvement throughout the Mexican states. Rosovsky and Romero
(1996) report that Mexico's policies reflect the normative system: Mexico's
legal frame is based on how people should act, it does not really integrate the
reality of values, customs, and norms.

Schools and health agencies have conducted several educational campaigns,
but with little or no evaluation of their impact. Mexican researchers question

TABLE 6-4
Cultivation and Production Statistics, Mexico, 1999, 1998, 1997

	1999	1998	1997
Opium	43 metric tons	60 mt	46 mt
Marijuana	6,700 metric tons	8,300 mt	8,600 mt

Source: UNODC, Regional Office, *Mexico*. 2003. Country Profile: Mexico, Table 4, 10.

TABLE 6-5

Drug Seizures, Mexico, 1996–2001

Drugs Seized (kg)	1996	1997	1998	1999	2000	2001
Cannabis leaf	1,015,756	1,038,470	1,062,144	1,471,960	2,050,402	1,953,900
Cannabis seeds	5,099	3,968	4,949	5,847	10,354	—
Hashish	9	115	2	—	—	—
Cocaine	28,833	34,950	22,598	34,622	23,196	33,427
Crack	27	3	—	—	—	—
Poppy seed	1,155	587	703	750	1,036	1,126
Opium	196	343	105	801	469	576
Heroin	363	115	121	260	299	261

Original Source: UNODC, Regional Office, Mexico. 2003. *Country Profile: Mexico,* Table 2, 8.

Table 6-6
Arrests for Drug Trafficking, Mexico, 1999

Total	10,464
Mexicans	10,261
Foreigners	203

Source: Bureau for International Narcotics and Law
Enforcement Affairs, U.S. Department of State, International Narcotics Control Strategy Report,
1999.

the benefit of broad, single goal campaigns within such an ethnically and cul-
turally diverse society (Rosovsky and Romero 1996).

Health agencies' priorities have been to prevent the initiation of drug use
and to rehabilitate addicts; wheras the justice sector is focused on stemming
the production and trafficking of drugs. Recent legislation allows individuals
not to be prosecuted for carrying only the amount of drugs necessary for personal use.

In 1999, President Ernesto Zedillo committed $500 million over the next
four years to implement a national security plan. Policy initiatives included
integrating several existing law enforcement agencies into a new Federal Preventative Police to focus on crime prevention and public security. Several
amendments to the Constitution called for the streamlining of requirements
to obtain arrest warrants and dismiss corrupt government officers. Proposed
legal reforms were intended to create specialized courts with "faceless judges"
to prevent cartels from targeting or intimidating judicial officers. Changes
have also been made in the financial sector to allow detection of suspect transactions and money laundering.

The Administration of Vicente Fox Quezada, elected president in July 2000,
"has shown a willingness to increase its efforts against drug trafficking, corruption and money laundering" (UNODC, Regional Office, *Mexico* 2003: 10).

Currently, the General Attorney's Office (PGR) and the Ministry of Health
administer national drug control policies (UNODC, Regional Office, *Mexico*
2003: 32). Other involved bodies include the Ministry of the Marines, Ministry
of Treasury, Ministry of Foreign Affairs, Ministry of Family Development, and
The Ministry of Public Education (UNODC, Regional Office, *Mexico* 2003: 32).

Note

1. Original Source: Villatoro, J., Medina-Mora, M.E., Cardiel, H., Alcántar, E.,
Fleiz, C., Navarro, C., Blanco, J., Parra, J., Néquiz, G. *Consumo de Drogas, Alcohol y
Tabaco en Estudiantes del Distrito Federal; "Reporte Estadístico."* SEP, IMP, México

Table 6-7
Cultivation of Opium and Production of Opium, Mexico, 1990–2002 (in hectares)

1990	1991	1992	1993	1994	1995	1996	1997	1998	1999	2000	2001	2002
5,450	3,765	3,310	3,960	5,495	5,050	5,100	4,000	5,500	3,600	1,900	4,400	2,700

Source: United Nations Office on Drugs and Crime, Global Illicit Drug Trends Report 2003, Chapter 1: Trends and Production, 16.

1997, and Villatoro, J., Medina-Mora, M.E., Rojano, C., Fleiz, C., Villa, G., Jasso, A., Alcántar, M.I., Bermudez, P., Castro, P. *"Reporte Estadístico."* INP-SEP. Mexico 2001.

References

Bureau for International Narcotics and Law Enforcement Affairs, U.S. Department of State, International Narcotics Control Strategy Report. 1999.

Dobkin De Rios, M. 1990. *Hallucinogens: Cross-Cultural Perspectives.* Great Britain, Australia: Prism Unity Press.

Juarez, Francisco, Elena Medina-Mora, Shoshana Berenzon, Jorge A. Villatoro, Silvia Carreno, Elsa K. Lopez, Jorge Galvan, and Estela Rojas. 1998. "Antisocial Behavior: Its Relation to Selected Sociodemographic Variables and Alcohol and Drug Use among Mexican Students." *Substance Use and Misuse* 33(7): 1437–1459.

Medina-Mora, M. E., A. Ortiz, C. Caudillo, and S. Lopez. 1982. "Inhalacion deliberada de disolventes en un grupo de menores mexicanos [Deliberate Inhalation of Solvents in a Group of Mexican Children]. *Salud Ment.* 5(1): 77–86.

Medina-Mora, M. E., E. Rojas, F. Juarez, and S. Berenzon, et al. 1993. Consumo de sustancias con efectos psicotropicos en la poblacion estudiantil de ensenanza media y media superior de la Republica Mexicana [Substance with Psychotropic Effects Consumption in Student Population of Middle and High School in the Mexican Republic]. *Salud Ment.* 16(16): 2–8.

Ortiz, A. et al. 1989. Development of an Information Reporting System on Illicit Drug Use in Mexico. *Bulletin of Narcotics* 41: 41–52.

Portillo, Ernesto. n.d. *World Factbook of Criminal Justice Systems: Mexico.* Washington, D.C.: Bureau of Justice Statistics. www.ojp.usdoj.gov/bjs/pub/ascii/wfcjsmx.txt (accessed October 8, 2003).

Rosovsky, Haydee, and Martha Romero. 1996. "Prevention Issues in a Multicultural Developing Country: The Mexican Case." *Substance Use and Misuse* 31 (11 &12): 1657–1688.

SSA[Secretaria de Salud (Ministry of Health)]. 1989. Encuesta Nacional de Adicciones (National Survey on Addictions). Direccion General de Epidemiologia Instituto Mexicano de Psiquiatria.

SSA[Secretaria de Salud (Ministry of Health). 2001. *"Observatorio Epidemiologico en Drogas 2001.*

Toro, Maria Celia. 1995. *Mexico's "War" on Drugs: Causes and Consequences.* Boulder, Colo.: Lynne Rienner Publishers.

UNAIDS. Joint United Nations Programme on HIV/AIDS. 2000. AIDS epidemic update: December 2000. Geneva, Switzerland: UNAIDS/World Health Organization.

United Nations Office on Drugs and Crime (UNODC) Regional Office. 2003. *Mexico.*

Part III

CENTRAL AND SOUTH AMERICA

T HIS SECTION OF THE BOOK provides details on three countries in Central and South America: Brazil, Colombia, and Costa Rica.

According to the United Nations Office for Drug Control and Crime Prevention, over 98 percent of coca leaf cultivation takes place in Colombia, Peru, and Bolivia (UNODC 2000: 29). Prior to 1990, Colombia cultivated less coca than Peru and Bolivia, but by 1999, Colombia produced two-thirds of the world's coca.

Of all global seizures of cocaine in 2001, 45 percent occurred in South America (UNODC 2003: 63). The seizures of cocaine in Colombia, Peru, and Bolivia accounted for 41 percent of all global seizures in 2000 (64). By 2001, this percent decreased to 29. However, seizures in other areas, such as Ecuador, Brazil, Mexico, the United States, and Canada increased. The annual prevalence of cocaine abuse among those aged fifteen and over in South America is 1 percent (129).

In 2001, Colombia, Venezuela, Panama, Chile, and Argentina experienced increases in opiate abuse (UNODC 2003: 127). However, in 2003, the UNODP reported that the abuse rate of opiates in South America was below the worldwide average (107). Among those twelve years and older in the Americas, 0.2 percent abused heroin occasionally in 2001 (UNODC 2003: 127). However, this percent increases to 0.5 when chronic heroin abusers are taken into consideration.

The Inter-American Drug Abuse Control Commission (CICAD) under the Organization of American States (OAS) has put together a series of projects to monitor problems associated with drug use, which include the construction of a uniform database on drug use and trafficking indicators, drug information and outreach, and development of policies for the Inter-American Drug Information System (IADIS).

TABLE III-1

Arrests for Drug Trafficking and Possession, The Americas, 1989–1997

Region	1989	1990	1991	1992	1993	1994	1995	1996	1997
South America	26,946	28,408	44,413	40,882	42,829	50,661	55,978	55,585	61,102
Central America	1,512	1,496	1,621	2,186	2,117	3,103	3,708	3,927	4,059
The Caribbean	6,382	14,098	13,676	10,997	11,762	10,731	14,384	12,057	12,420
North America	n.a.	n.a.	43,511	64,561	50,668	42,010	46,300	50,938	54,059

Source: Inter-American Drug Abuse Control Commission, Statistical Summary, 1998.

TABLE III-2
Arrests for Drug Trafficking and Possession, Selected South American Countries, 1989–1997

Country	1989	1990	1991	1992	1993	1994	1995	1996	1997
Argentina	6,289	4,377	5,949	10,019	10,936	11,708	13,980	12,432	16,066
Peru	2,254	2,464	3,210	4,099	5,007	6,459	10,303	12,139	14,316
Venezuela	8,601	9,207	9,207	14,063	12,299	11,093	9,741	8,722	6,349
Chile	—	2,748	7,676	4,392	4,769	10,826°	11,173	11,500	13,041
Bolivia	912	900	1,114	1,298	1,450	2,632	2,424	3,312	3,428
Colombia	3,607	2,501	6,389	2,190	2,554	2,152	2,885	2,866	2,244
Ecuador	2,833	3,286	2,907	1,465	1,779	1,869	2,104	2,525	3,692

Source: The Inter-American Drug Information System (IADIS.

IADIS provides analysis of the number of persons arrested for drug trafficking and possession in each OAS member country. CICAD has made a
great effort to standardize the definitions to achieve comparability across
member countries. Data are provided for the regions of North America, South
America, Central America, and the Caribbean.

References

InterAmerican Drug Abuse Control Commission, Statistical Summary, 1998.
United Nations Office on Drugs and Crime (UNODC). 2000. *World Drug Report.*
United Nations Office on Drugs and Crime (UNODC). 2003. *Global Illicit Drug
    Trends 2003.*

7

Brazil

Overview

BRAZIL IS LOCATED IN EASTERN SOUTH AMERICA, and is bordered by all of the South American countries except for Ecuador and Chile. It borders the Atlantic Ocean.

With a population of 177 million, Brazil is the fifth largest nation in the world and the largest in Latin America. Its six major ethnic groups make it one of the most diverse nations in the world. The ethnic groups are white, including Portuguese, German, Italian, Spanish, and Polish (55 percent); mixed white and black (38 percent); black (6 percent); and other, Japanese, Arab, Amerindian (1 percent). The main religion is Roman Catholic (80 percent). The languages spoken in Brazil are Portuguese (the official language), Spanish, English, and French. Major industries operating in Brazil are concentrated in transportation, communication, weapons, aircrafts, nuclear power production, and energy (Library of Congress 1997). The country is a large exporter of goods such as tin, iron, manganese, steel, sugar, coffee, cocoa, soybeans, and orange juice.

Brazil operated under military rule from 1964 to 1985 but is now a democratic nation, with a popularly elected president, a legislative branch consisting of a popularly elected Senate and Chamber of Deputies, and a judicial branch, whose eleven tribunal members are appointed by the president. Its Congress represents fifteen different political parties. These governmental branches are set forth by the Constitution of 1988, or the "citizen constitution."

There are five codes of law in Brazil: civil, commercial, civil procedure, penal, and penal procedure (Scuro). The Penal Code in Brazil was first adopted in 1940 and then subsequently underwent many revisions. There are two sections, the first of which differentiates misdemeanors from felonies and specifies citizens' responsibilities under the code of law. The second section defines criminal behavior and describes crimes against persons, property, custom, public welfare, and public trust.

Drug Offenses and the Law

Felonies are defined as "crimes against life," which include intentional homicide, abortion, crimes against religious sentiment and respect for the deceased, crimes against family, crimes against public peace and public trust, crimes against public administration, crimes against property—and immaterial property—and crimes against social mores (Scuro n.d.). Misdemeanors include crimes involving weapons, contraceptives, negligence, gambling, begging, and animal cruelty.

Sanctions received are thought of as "conditions for the devolution of freedom" that focus on "presumed social adaptability" of the offender (Scuro n.d.). Persons who are aged eighteen and older are subject to the Penal Code, whereas children between ages twelve and seventeen may be handled under the Statute of Children and Adolescents.

Sanctions for drug offenses fall under Law 6368 and range from three to fifteen years incarceration, along with fines. These offenses are "intentional acts involving the cultivation, production, manufacture, extraction, preparation, offering for sale, distribution, purchase, sale, delivery on any terms whatsoever, brokerage, dispatch, dispatch in transit, transport, importation and exportation of internationally controlled drugs" (Scuro n.d.). The punishment for purchasing drugs for personal use ranges from six months to two years in prison (UNODC *Brazil* 2003: 2).

Sentencing in Brazil involves consideration of aggravating or mitigating circumstances and can specify the goals of punishment, such as incapacitation, deterrence, or rehabilitation (Scuro 2003). Maximum sentences range up to thirty years. The death penalty can only be imposed during times of war and "as a response to aggression by a foreign national" (Scuro n.d.).

Extent and Patterns of Use

Four studies conducted by the Brazilian Information Centre on Psychotropic Substances over the past decade, found that among primary and secondary students, those who responded to "use 6 times or more during the month" increased by "325 per cent for marijuana and 700 per cent for cocaine," as reported by the UNODC (UNODC *Brazil* 2003: v).

Among persons age fifteen and older, the average prevalence rate of opiate abuse was 0.1 percent, and for cannabis 5.8 percent (UNODC 2003: 334, 339). In 1999, the percent of cocaine abusers among the same population was 0.8 (337). The three most common reasons for using drugs in 1997 and 1999 were, respectively, "To escape from problems with family and parents" (28 percent) and "To be accepted by a group of friends" (UNODC *Brazil* 2003: 28).

A household survey of 8,589 persons ages eighteen to sixty-five, as reported by the UNODC Regional Office in Brazil (2003: 9), revealed that cannabis was the most prevalent drug abused (6.9 percent). Among males, cannabis (10.6 percent), cocaine (3.7 percent), and orexigen (3.2 percent) were the most prevalent drugs that were abused. Among women, the most prevalent drugs were orexigen (5.3 percent), benzodiazepines (4.3 percent), and cannabis (3.4 percent).

The number of IUD-related AIDS cases has decreased significantly from 14.8 cases per 100,000 inhabitants in 1996 to 12.4 in 2000 (UNODC *Brazil* 2003: v).

In addition, drug-related homicides are of a concern, and the World Health Organization has estimated that "for every person killed, 25 to 40 receive injuries that require hospital treatment" (UNODC *Brazil* 2003: 2).

Law Enforcement

The UNODC Regional Office in Brazil reports a total of 11,703 federal arrests for crimes involving trafficking, preparation, cultivation, sales, or induction to drug use and/or psychological dependence-causing substances from 1997 to 2001 (UNODC *Brazil* 2003: 16). During the same time period, there were 1,373 federal arrests for acquiring, keeping, or carrying drugs for personal use.

There have been recent increases in levels of drug trafficking, much of which operates out of the Amazon. Brazil is a major producer of marijuana, and most of its production is for domestic use. Furthermore, Brazil is a large importer of cocaine (UNODC *Brazil* 2003: 2). In 2000, 3 percent of all cocaine seizures in the Americas took place in Brazil (UNODC 2003: 64). In 2001, 3 percent of all worldwide cannabis seizures occurred in Brazil (74). Cannabis is produced for domestic consumption (UNODC *Brazil* 2003: 21). Drugs are often dispersed to private residents via couriers, who are generally teenagers (UNODC *Brazil* 2003: 2). These children earn anywhere from US $300 to $500 per month, which often exceeds their parents' income.

Drug Policy

Brazil has adopted a consistent policy in the field of drug control and enforcement. Its first priority has been to curb drug abuse and the demand for narcotic drugs within its borders. It has also pursued a policy of close cooperation with other countries in the western hemisphere and the world at large to combat illicit traffic in narcotic drugs.

Brazil is party to the major international agreements relating to the control of narcotic drugs. In May 1995 Brazil was elected to the United Nations Commission on Narcotic Drugs, which reports to the Economic and Social Council. Brazil has actively participated, at the regional level, in the work of the Inter-American Commission on Drug Abuse Control of the Organization of American States. Brazil takes the position that drug prevention and enforcement depend increasingly on broad international cooperation.

Brazil is also party to various bilateral agreements on the implementation and coordination of drug control policies. Those agreements provide for cooperation in drug abuse prevention and rehabilitation and for the exchange of information on national legislation, and jurisprudence. Beginning in the 1970s, Brazil entered into agreements with, among others, Germany, Portugal, and the United Kingdom as part of its policy of intensifying the fight against narcotic drugs. An agreement was signed with the Russian Federation in 1994 and, the following year, the mutual cooperation agreement with the United States was renewed for an additional period. Similar bilateral agreements are currently under discussion with Italy, Romania, and the Republic of South Africa.

Brazil has taken steps to improve enforcement along its borders and, to that effect, has developed a series of high-level bilateral cooperative programs with its neighbors in South America. Partnership and joint responsibility is the key to the successful outcome of these programs, which call for operational links with the competent authorities of neighboring countries.

Brazil played a key role in the adoption by the Community of Portuguese-Speaking Countries of an agreement on cooperation in the field of drug control. It has also presented an antidrug initiative to the Member States of the Zone of Peace and Cooperation of the South Atlantic that recently met at the ministerial level in Midrand, South Africa. The Brazilian government is taking steps to update and improve national legislation on drug abuse control as part of a comprehensive effort to curb the demand for narcotic drugs. The National Narcotics Council is the focal point and main executive organ of the national system of drug law enforcement, which includes drug abuse prevention, treatment, and rehabilitation as well as monitoring and enforcement actions. New legislation, which became effective in 1995, further regulated the production and sale of chemical substances used in the manufacture of narcotic drugs, like cocaine, and created formal investigative procedures to curtail drug-related organized crime. Draft legislation is currently under consideration to define legal criteria and norms to ensure the control and monitoring of drug-related money laundering.

Brazil's drug demand reduction measures are coordinated by the National Anti-drug Secretariat (SENAD), through which different levels of government can work together (UNODC *Brazil* 2003: 3, 37). SENAD also manages the National Anti-drug Fund, which financially supports the National Anti-drug System (37). Drug treatment efforts are carried out through SENAD, the Ministry of Health, Sector for Alcohol and Drugs, and the Ministry of Health, CN/DST, and the AIDS National Coordination for Sexual Diseases and AIDS (39).

References

Library of Congress. No Date. *A Country Study: Brazil.* Washington, D.C.: Library of Congress, Federal Research Division. www.lcweb2.loc.gov/frd/cs/brtoc.html (accessed October 24, 2003).

Scuro, Pedro. n.d. *World Factbook of Criminal Justice Systems: Mexico.* Washington, D.C.: Bureau of Justice Statistics. www.ojp.usdoj.gov/bjs/pub/ascii/wfcjsbr/txt. (accessed October 8, 2003).

United States Department of State, Bureau of Western Hemisphere Affairs. 2003. *Background Note: Brazil.* www.state.gov/r/pa/ei/bgn/1972.htm; www.unodc.org/pdf/brazil/brazil_country_profile.pdf; www.216.239.37.104/search?q=cache:61b7_acci_MJ: www.unodc.org/pdf/brazil/brazil_country_profile.pdf+%22brazilian+information+centre+on+psychotropic+substances&hl=en&ie=UTF-8.

United Nations Office on Drugs and Crime (UNODC). 2003. *Global Illicit Drug Trends 2003.* www.unodc.org/unodc/en/global_illicit_drug_trends.html (accessed October 24, 2003).

8

Colombia

Overview

COLOMBIA, A SOUTH AMERICAN COUNTRY with a population of 44 million, is a republic dominated by the executive branch. After many political struggles throughout the 1800s, a federal and centralized system emerged (Vasquez and Vargas de Roa n.d.).

Colombia is situated in the northwest corner of South America along the Pacific Ocean and the Caribbean Sea and its inhabitants include 50 percent mestizo (part Indian, part white), 20 percent mulatto (part African, part white), 25 percent white, four percent of African origin, and 1 percent South American Indian. Almost 80 percent of the population lives in urban areas.

In 1980, the current penal system, based on "liability due to culpability or blameworthiness," was set into motion (Vasquez and Vargas de Roa n.d.). The current legal system is based on Spanish law. In 1992–1993 the government enacted a new criminal code modeled after U.S. procedures. The Penal Code and Penal Procedure Code were both amended in 2000 under Law 599. The legislative branch is composed of a bicameral Congress, while the judicial branch's highest order of review takes place in one of four coequal judicial organs depending on the nature of the case. The age of criminal responsibility in Colombia is eighteen.

Colombia is well known for its predominance in the world of drug trade. Factors that facilitate Colombia's notoriety include the traditional import and export of contraband, a deeply entrenched system of money laundering, and a geographical location that aids shipment of illegal drugs out of the country

(Thoumi 1995). Guerilla movements control parts of the country making violence a main means of resolving conflicts.

The bulk of cocaine available worldwide is produced in South America. Colombia is the largest processor of cocaine and the largest producer of the coca plant, followed by Peru and Bolivia. From 1993 to 1999, the domestic cultivation of cocaine increased significantly, providing nearly 75 percent of the world's supply of cocaine (UNODC 2003a: 8). In 2001, Colombia provided nearly 100 percent of the cocaine found in Central America, the Caribbean, and North America. The United Nations (192) reports that by the end of 2002, 102,000 hectares of coca were cultivated in areas covering 0.09 percent of the entire nation (195). However, this was a 30 percent reduction from yearend 2001, and a 37 percent reduction from 2000, suggesting a decrease in cultivation levels.

Colombia is also a major cultivator of opium poppy in the central and southern mountainous areas of Cauca, Nariño, Huila, and Tolima (191).

The cultivation, production, and trafficking of drugs greatly impacts the political, social, and economic life of Colombia. Colombian drug cartels are well organized and well armed with influence reaching into the government. Entire swaths of the southern Colombian countryside remain under the control of insurgent paramilitary groups and local guerilla forces. Although the insurgents do not have the military strength or popular support to overthrow the Colombian government, they prospered greatly during the 1990s from the drug trade. Coca and opium cultivation and production flourish in the re-

TABLE 8-1
Coca Cultivation in Colombia 1994–2002

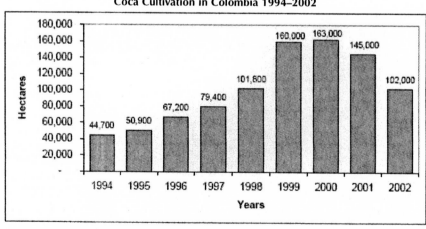

Source: United Nations Office of Drugs and Crime, *Global Illicit Drug Trends, 2003, Chapter 2: Statistics, Coca Production,* 192 [http://www.unodc.org/pdf/report_2003-06-26_1.pdf].

gions under their control, as they protected cartel crops in return for arms and money.

Colombia remains the world's largest cocaine producer. About three-quarters of the world's cocaine hydrochloride (HCI) is processed in Colombia from coca plants cultivated locally and in neighboring countries. Colombia has relied primarily on aerial fumigation to destroy illegal crops. This has become more difficult due to the southward movement of farming. The farther south the crops move, the deeper into rebel territory fumigation aircraft must fly making them vulnerable to ground fire. Despite the Colombian government's efforts and a steady increase of funding from the United States, drug production and cultivation increased during the 1990s. Furthermore, the rate of drug seizures for most illicit drugs decreased.

Drug Offenses and the Law

Drug offenses listed in Article 32, which is entitled Planting, Preservation or Funding of Plantings, may be sanctioned by four to twelve years of imprisonment and fines up to US $50,000. Persons that are convicted of offenses in Article 33, Dealing, Manufacture, or Possession of Narcotics, may receive anywhere from one to twenty years of imprisonment. Fines range from 2 to 50,000 monthly minimum salaries. Additional Articles describe other drug-related offenses, such as encouraging the use of narcotics and providing drugs to minors (Vasquez and Vargas de Roa n.d.).

Possession of illegal drugs for personal use is legal in Colombia since a court ruling in May of 1994 that decriminalized possession of small quantities. The court felt that past law infringed on a person's constitutional right to self-development and expression. But the Colombian government raised a series of decrees banning drug use later that same month in an attempt to show their displeasure with the court's ruling. The decrees ban drug use almost everywhere except in the home. In general, imprisonment is reserved for offenses related to drug trafficking. Generally, the maximum sentence for drug trafficking is twelve years, but the sentence may be reduced within two years under certain circumstances, such as confession of the crime, collaboration, or good behavior while in prison (UNODC 2003).

Approximately one-fifth of the 30,000 prisoners in Colombia in 1995 were incarcerated for drug-related offenses. Almost 90 percent of persons convicted for drug offenses in 1994 were between the ages of twenty-five and twenty-nine. Of all convictions in that year, over 70 percent involved cocaine. Sentencing in Colombia is based on a two-part decision made by a judge. The ruling contains a reasons section, which summarizes the charges and evidence, and a decision section, which must correspond with the ruling section. Decisions must logically follow that which is specified in the reasons section (Vasquez and Vargas de Roa 2003). Primary punishments include imprisonment and fines. Other punishments may prohibit the defendant from consuming alcohol, participating in certain arts or professions, and may terminate a defendant's position in public office. In 1972, Law 17 stated that "no capital punishment shall be restored in those States that have abolished the same."

Extent and Patterns of Use

The National Narcotics Bureau examined drug consumption in 1996 by surveying persons between the ages of twelve and sixty in twenty-nine major urban centers in Colombia (UNODC 2003b: 21). Excluding alcohol, findings indicate that the lifetime (ever used) prevalence was the greatest for cannabis (5.4 percent), followed by inhalants (4.6 percent), cocaine (1.6 percent), basuco (1.5 percent), stimulants (0.2 percent) and heroin (0.1 percent).

A national survey among university students found a lifetime prevalence (ever used) for cannabis of 8.1 percent. When asked about their drug use in the previous week, students reported extremely low levels of use—only 1.3 percent reported using cannabis in the previous week. Survey results also showed that although there is little heroin use among students, it seems to be increasing.

The National Survey on Drug Consumption among persons ages ten to twenty-four in 2001 revealed that the lifetime prevalence (excluding alcohol and tobacco) was greatest for cannabis (8.9 percent) (UNODC, Office for Colombia and Ecuador 2003: 22).[1] The drugs with the next highest lifetime prevalence were cocaine (4.5 percent) and tranquilizers (2.2 percent). The drugs that were consumed the most within the year prior to the survey (last-year prevalence) were cannabis (6.2 percent), cocaine (3.0 percent), tranquilizers (1.7 percent), and ecstasy (1.7 percent).

The UNODC reports that 4.5 percent of persons ages ten to twenty-four in 2001 had abused cocaine, 2.2 percent had abused ecstasy, 1.1 percent had abused amphetamines, and 1.1 percent had used heroin (UNODC 2003: 133). These figures, which rose from 1999, are seen in Table 8-2.

Overall, it appears that cannabis, cocaine, and heroin abuse is increasing while the abuse of basuco has decreased (UNODC, Office for Colombia and Ecuador 2003: 23). Those seeking treatment in 1998 were most likely to have been abusing, aside from alcohol, cocaine (28.1 percent) and cannabis (13.4 percent) (UNODC, Office for Colombia and Ecuador 2003: 22).

TABLE 8-2
Drug Abuse among
Ages 10 to 24, Colombia, 1999 and 2001

	1999	2001
Cocaine	3.6%	4.5%
Ecstasy	1.8	2.2
Amphetamines	0.7	1.1
Heroin	0.8	1.1

Original Source: United Nations Office of Drugs and Crime, *Global Illicit Drug Trends 2003,* Chapter 1, Trends: Consumption—Coca/Cocaine, p. 133.

Efforts to eradicate cocaine in Colombia led to the dismantling of 316 clandestine laboratories in 1999, 647 in 2000, 1,574 in 2001, and 587 in 2002 (UNODP 2003: 65). Seizures of cocaine in Colombia in 2002, which accounted for 88 percent of all cocaine seizures in the Andean region that year, increased by 70 percent. This dismantling effort in 2000 and 2001 ultimately decreased the demand for coca by farmers (65).

Table 8-3 shows cultivation levels for 1991 through 1999, by 2001 cultivation levels (potentially harvestable area after eradication) of opium was 6,500 hectares, and 144,807 hectares for coca bush (UNODC, Office for Colombia and Ecuador 2003: 5). Production in 2001 had reached 88 metric tons of opium and 236,035 metric tons of coca leaf. The potential manufacturing of heroin had reached 8.8 metric tons and 617 metric tons of cocaine in 2001.

Law Enforcement

Table 8-4 shows law enforcement efforts in Colombia throughout the 1990s. The amount of cannabis that was seized by law enforcement officials decreased from 329 metric tons in 1991 to 65 metric tons in 1999 (Bureau for International Narcotics and Law Enforcement Affairs 1999). Seizures of other drugs decreased as well from 1991 through 1999, with seizures of cocaine HCl decreasing from 77.07 to 22.73 metric tons and seizures of total HCl/base decreasing from 86.35 to 31.73 metric tons. The total number of arrests for drug-related offenses increased from 1991 to 1999, although the number of foreigners who were arrested decreased during that time period. We also see that the number of cocaine/base labs that were destroyed decreased from 239 in 1991 to 156 in 1999, although the number of destroyed morphine/heroin labs increased from 5 to 10 between 1991 and 1999.

TABLE 8-3
Drug Cultivation and Harvesting, Colombia, 1991–1999, in Metric Tons

	1991	1992	1993	1994	1995	1996	1997	1998	1999
Coca									
Potential Harvest	37,500	37,100	39,700	44,700	50,900	67,200	79,500	101,800	122,500
Eradication	972	959	793	4,900	8,700	5,600	19,000	—	43,246
Estimated Cultivation	38,472	38,059	40,493	49,610	59,650	72,800	98,500	—	—
HCl Potential (metric tons)	60	60	65	70	230	300	350	435	520
Opium									
Potential Harvest	1,344	20,000	20,000	20,000	6,540	6,300	6,600	6,100	7,500
Eradication	1,156	12,858	9,821	3,906	3,760	6,028	6,972	—	—
Estimated Cultivation	2,500	32,858	29,821	23,906	10,300	12,328	13,572	—	—
Potential Opium	—	—	—	—	65	63	66	61	75
Cannabis									
Potential Harvest	2,000	2,000	5,000	4,986	4,980	5,000	5,000	5,000	5,000
Eradication	0	49	50	14	20	—	—	—	—
Estimated Cultivation	2,000	2,049	5,050	5,000	5,000	5,000	5,000	5,000	5,000
Potential	1,650	1,650	4,125	4,138	4,133	4,150	4,150	4,150	4,150

Source: Bureau for International Narcotics and Law Enforcement Affairs, U.S. Department of State, International Narcotics Control Strategy Report, 1999.

TABLE 8-4
Law Enforcement Statistics, Colombia, 1991–1999

	1991	1992	1993	1994	1995	1996	1997	1998	1999
Seizures (Metric tons)									
Heroin/Morphine	-	0.05	0.261	0.181	0.419	0.183	0.261	0.317	0.504
Opium	-	0.43	0.261	0.128	0.078	0.036	0.120	0.100	0.183
Cannabis	329	206	549	2000	166	235	136	69	65
Base/Basuco	9.28	5.81	10.40	32.00	19.50	17.50	10.00	29.30	9.00
Cocaine HCl	77.07	31.92	21.76	30.00	21.50	23.50	34.00	54.70	22.73
Total HCl/Base	86.35	37.73	32.16	62.00	41.00	41.00	44.00	84.00	31.73
Arrests									
Nationals	—	—	—	—	1,646	1,482	1,478	1,879	—
Foreigners	—	—	—	—	99	79	68	82	—
Total	1,170	1,700	2,562	2,154	1,745	1,561	1,546	1,961	—
Labs Destroyed									
Cocaine/Base	239	224	401	560	396	861	213	311	156
Morphine/Heroin	5	7	10	9	11	9	9	10	10

Source: Bureau for International Narcotics and Law Enforcement Affairs, U.S. Department of State, International Narcotics Control Strategy Report, 1999.

Drug Policy

In the mid-1990s, Colombia made drug use prevention and treatment more of a national priority than it had been in previous decades. A National Plan for Drug Control was revised and approved in 1995. The plan now includes objectives aimed at reducing the causes and effects of drug abuse. Historically, the focus on drugs has remained solely on the control of production and trafficking, with the Colombian government dispersing US $1.5 billion dollars from 1995 to 1999 (UNODC, Office for Colombia and Ecuador 2003: 24). The government's expenditure for demand reduction is generally supported by local governments, neighborhood organizations, and international cooperation. For instance, the United Nation's Drug Control Program has provided millions of dollars—3.5 million in 1993, 4.7 million in 1994, and 5.3 million in 1995—for alternative development and demand reduction programs. In addition, a small portion of the monies supported drug control measures.

Colombian drug control policy is developed by the National Narcotics Council and the National Narcotics Bureau. Their strategy is to enable collaboration between state and local bodies, NGOs, and communities in order to reduce the causes of drug use, commercialization, drug abuse, and drug trafficking (UNODC, Office for Colombia and Ecuador 2003: 33). Other participating members are the Anti-Narcotics Police, PLANTE, the Public Prosecutors Office, the Ministry of Education, the Comptroller of Banks, and other administrative agencies.

Below is a list of the government's achievements with regard to prevention from 1998 to the present, as listed by the UNODC (*Country Profile: Colombia*, 2003, 35–36):

- Strengthening the political and administrative endorsement for prevention by governmental and nongovernmental organizations at the national, departmental, and municipal levels. This favors the institutionalization and the sustainability of prevention process.
- Developing a communication strategy through the publication and distribution of educative material, as well as producing and broadcasting radio and TV programs.
- The participation of training processes in prevention with different population groups, especially with the educational communities throughout the country. Many of these have included prevention programs in their Institutional Educational Project (*PEI*).

Note

1. Original Source: National Survey on Drug Consumption among young people aged between ten and twenty-four years. RUMBOS, 2001.

TABLE 8-5

Government Expenditures in Drug Control (US$ millions), Colombia

	1995	1996	1997	1998	1999	2000	2001	Total
Alternative development	9.5	31.5	56.8	34.7	11.2	9.2	17.0	169.9
Supply reduction	179.0	181.0	215.5	160.5	124.8	216.0	88.8	1,165.6
Judicial and institutional strengthening	55.9	83.5	88.3	96.4	63.7	66.4	38.2	492.4
Demand reduction	9.2	15.5	17.8	19.5	17.7	17.3	9.6	106.6
Environmental management	0.6	3.4	3.4	3.1	2.3	0.6	1.0	14.4
International policy	0.1	0.1	0.1	0.1	0.2	0.1	0.1	0.8
Total	254.3	315.0	381.9	314.3	219.9	309.6	154.7	1,949.7

Source: UNODC, Office for Colombia and Ecuador. 2003. *Country Profile:* 24.

References

Bureau for International Narcotics and Law Enforcement Affairs, U.S. Department of State. 1999. International Narcotics Control Strategy Report.

Drug Enforcement Administration (DEA). 1997. The National Narcotics Intelligence Consumers Committee (NNICC) Report, 1996: The Supply of Illicit Drugs to the United States. Washington, D.C.: Department of Justice.

Thoumi, F. 1995. *Political Economy and Illegal Drugs in Colombia.* Boulder, Colo.: Lynne Rienner Publishers.

United Nations Office on Drugs and Crime (UNODC)a. 2003. *Global Illicit Drug Trends, 2003,* Chapter 2: "Statistics, Coca Production," 192. www.unodc.org/pdf/report_2003-06-26_1.pdf.

United Nations Office on Drugs and Crime (UNODC)b. Office for Colombia and Ecuador. 2003. *Country Profile: Colombia.* www.unodc.org/unodc/index.html (accessed October 10, 2003).

Vasquez, Rafael Campo and Rosa Margarita Vargas de Roa. n.d. *World Factbook of Criminal Justice Systems: Republic of Colombia.* Washington, D.C.: Bureau of Justice Statistics. www.ojp.usdoj.gov/bjs/pub/ascii/wfcjsco.txt (accessed October 8, 2003).

9

Costa Rica

Overview

COSTA RICA, LOCATED IN CENTRAL AMERICA between Panama and Nicaragua, has approximately 3 million inhabitants. Approximately 94 percent of the population in Costa Rica is white (including Mestizo). Other ethnic groups include blacks, Amerindians, and Chinese. The predominant religion is Roman Catholic, followed by Evangelical, Jehovah's witness, and Protestants. The country declared its independence from Spain in 1821. Since then, the judiciary, El Poder Judicial, has been in operation. Their legal system is based on a Roman-Germanic Style of law.

Crimes are generally divided into two categories: the more serious are the "delitos" or felonies and the less serious misdemeanor crimes are known as contraventions. The penal system is guided by the 1949 Constitution, the Penal Code of 1970, the Penal Procedural Code of 1996, and the 1996 Penal Juvenile Justice Law (Rico n.d.). Sentences are decided upon by judges through majority rule voting, who may deliberate for up to two days. Judges take into consideration the seriousness of the crime and the defendant's personality when determining an appropriate sentence. There are many offenses that can lead to imprisonment, as well as fines equivalent to the defendant's salary during a specified length of time. The death penalty was abolished in 1977.

The *World Factbook on Criminal Justice Statistics* estimates that in the early 1990s the average combined total inmate population was 2,500. By 2001, the population was estimated to be 11,152, an incarceration rate of 279 per 100,000 inhabitants (Rico n.d.).

Drug Offenses and the Law

Costa Rica created its first domestic drug laws in 1923, and by 1927 a board was established to monitor drug control. A 1927 decree regulated the import, export, and sale of opium, and the following year decrees were issued regulating heroin and marijuana. In the latter case, the use and possession of heroin and marijuana were regulated, in addition to the import, export, or sale of the substances. No distinction was made between marijuana and other drugs. Fines and prison terms for drug violators became stiffer with the passage of a new law in 1930. Growers faced three to six months in prison and dealers and users were subject to fines or prison confinement up to two months.

A new Health Code was issued in 1949 that continued to group marijuana with cocaine, heroin, and opium. Growers of any of the natural drugs now faced prison sentences from six months to one year and workers in cannabis fields could be imprisoned up to six months. Users, instead of being imprisoned, now could be sent to treatment at the National Hospital for the Mentally Ill. Possession of drugs was considered to be the same as selling drugs, and punishment ranged from six months to three years imprisonment.

The Single Convention on Drugs and Narcotics of 1961 was approved by the Costa Rican government in 1972. A special police force was created whose main responsibility was to reduce the number of drugs available and the number of drug users. By 1974 another Health Code was approved that increased the penalties for growing and selling marijuana, coca, and poppies, but reduced the punishment for users of the drugs. Users were given treatment, while growers, importers, exporters, transporters, and drug dealers of any level were given from five to ten years imprisonment.

Today, sanctions for drug offenses are found in the 1991 Law on Narcotics, Psychotropic Substances, Non-authorized Drugs and Related Activities (Rico n.d.). Up to twenty years in prison may be given to a person involved in international trafficking, distribution, trading, supplying and manufacturing, cultivating, producing, transporting, and storing illegal substances. Fines that are equivalent to 60 to 180 days salary are imposed for publicly consuming drugs.

Drug crimes, trafficking and possession are considered serious in Costa Rica. The country utilizes the same definition of illegal drugs as that of the United States. Penalties for felonies are roughly greater than one year and under twenty-five years. Misdemeanor offenses carry penalties of less than one year in jail. A recent change to the Constitution forbids a combined sentence of more than fifty years in prison.

TABLE 9-1
Drug Seizures, Costa Rica, 1995–2000 (kg)

	2000	1999	1998	1997	1996	1995
Cannabis	1,139	1,628	469	107	35	810
Cocaine	5,894	2,060	7,387	7,863	1,871	1,168
Heroin	8	2	14	26	18	11

Source: Inter-American Observatory on Drugs, Statistical summary, 2001.

Extent and Patterns of Use

Although hemp was being used in Costa Rica for fiber in the mid to late 1800s, there is little indication that marijuana was being used for its psychotropic effects until the turn of the century (Carter 1980). Even in 1913, when Costa Rica signed its first international treaty regarding drugs, there was no mention of cannabis by the Costa Rican government.

Before the 1960s, use of marijuana was generally confined to a small minority of adult, working-class males, but during the late 1960s and early 1970s, use of the drug spread to the middle and upper classes, largely among university students and some secondary school students. Estimates in the late 1970s indicate that at least 25 percent of all university students had tried marijuana (Carter 1980).

Law Enforcement

Costa Rica is primarily a transshipment point for smuggling cocaine from South America to the United States (U.S. Department of State 2004). While authorities have detected small amounts of cultivated marijuana, there is negligible illicit drug production and cultivation in Costa Rica. In 1999 and 2000 authorities eradicated twelve and fourteen hectares of cannabis, respectively. Law enforcement efforts and national policy focuses on augmenting narcotics anti-trafficking forces and detecting suspicious money-laundering transactions in the banking sector.

TABLE 9-2
Drug Arrests from, Costa Rica, 1993–2000.

1993	1994	1995	1996	1997	1998	1999	2000
189	344	550	704	487	909	846	4953

Source: Inter-American Observatory on Drugs, Statistical Summary of Drugs, 2001.

TABLE 9-3
Number of Arrests for Trafficking and Possession, Costa Rica, 1993–1997

	1993	*1994*	*1995*	*1996*	*1997*
Total Arrested	189	544	550	704	487
Arrested for Trafficking	169	511	529	673	443
Male	134	357	328	481	325
Female	35	154	201	192	118
Arrested for Possession	20	33	21	31	44
Male	17	16	18	31	31
Female	3	17	3	0	13

Source: Inter-American Observatory on Drugs, Statistical Summary, 2001.

Drug Policy

Costa Rica's policies regarding drugs began in the early 1900s when it was party to the International Conference on Opium. The conference influenced domestic legislation, and the government began a campaign in 1929 to reduce growing drug use and trafficking. The policies had three priorities: establish general drug control, provide treatment for users, and imprison the drug dealers.

Little was heard from the Costa Rican government regarding drugs until media accounts in the late 1960s and early 1970s raised concern that marijuana use was growing rapidly, spreading into schools, and reaching youth of all ages. In addition, officials began to assert a relationship between marijuana and crime in general, often citing research conducted in the United States. Police officers and narcotics agencies increased their efforts to arrest individuals and confiscate drugs, and the effects were considerable. It is estimated that 26 percent of male users were detained by the police between 1973 and 1975 (Carter 1980). The public began to regard all drug use, and marijuana use in particular, as very damaging. Marijuana use was perceived as the main drug problem. Indeed, almost all hard drug-related arrests in this period were of foreigners, not Costa Ricans (Carter 1980).

Today, Costa Rica focuses domestic drug policies on the prevention of drug use among school age youth. Costa Rica utilizes the Drug Abuse Resistance Education (DARE) program modeled after its U.S. counterpart (U.S. Department of State 2004).

References

Carter, William E. (ed.) 1980. Cannabis in Costa Rica: A Study of Chronic Marijuana Use. Philadelphia: Institute for the Study of Human Issues, Inc.

Inter-American Observatory on Drugs. 2002. Statistical Summary on Drugs 2001: Costa Rica. Inter-American Drug Abuse Control Commission (CICAD), Organization of

TABLE 9-4

Reported Offenses, Persons Prosecuted and Convicted, Convicted Prisoners, Costa Rica, 1980–1986

	1980	1981	1982	1983	1984	1985	1986
Offenses Reported to the Police							
Total	Na	Na	Na	21,779	22,340	23,248	23,320
Drug possession	Na	Na	Na	37	36	37	48
Other drug	Na	Na	Na	69	79	75	66
Apprehended or arrested							
Total	—						
Drug possession	—						
Other drug	—						
Persons Prosecuted							
Total	Na	Na	Na	34,297	Na	35,442	Na
Drug possession	Na	Na	Na	419	393	360	414
Other drug	Na	Na	Na	341	314	236	298
Offenders Convicted							
Total	Na	Na	5552	6094	6273	5525	6426
Drug possession	Na	Na	20	20	22	5	34
Other drug	Na	Na	94	122	114	81	101
Convicted Prisoners							
Total	1150	1327	1470	1464	Na	Na	1715
Drug possession	13	14	22	16	Na	Na	50
Other Drug	149	179	193	169	Na	Na	134

Source: Inter-American Observatory on Drugs, Statistical Summary, 2001.

American States. www.cicad.oas.org/cicad/resumen2001/costa_rica.pdf (accessed October 21, 2003).

Rico, Jose Maria. n.d. *World Factbook of Criminal Justice Systems: Costa Rica.* Washington, D.C.: Bureau of Justice Statistics. /www.ojp.usdoj.gov/bjs/pub/ascii/wfcjscr.txt (accessed October 8, 2003).

Rico, Jose Ma; Luis Salas. La Justicia Penal en Costa Rica. Editorial Universitaria Centroamericana. Edited by Florida International University. 1988

U.S. Department of State. 2004. International Narcotics Control Strategy Report, May 2004: Canada, Mexico and Central America. Washington, D.C.: United States Department of State, Bureau for International Narcotics and Law Enforcement Affairs. http://www.state.gov/g/inl/rls/nrcpt/2003/vol1/html/29833.htm (accessed June 1, 2004).

Part IV

WESTERN EUROPE

THE COUNTRIES DISCUSSED IN THIS SECTION include Great Britain (England, Scotland, Wales), France, Italy, Spain, and the Netherlands. On average, the countries of Western Europe have been experiencing a steady decline in drug use in recent years (UNODC 2003). Prevalence estimates of problem drug use in most Western European countries ranged between 2 and 10 cases per 1,000 among members of the general population aged 15–64.

In 2002, there was a decline in the number of drug-related deaths in several West European countries (UNODC 2003: 8). Nonetheless, new markets in Europe are being stimulated by South American cocaine traffickers and most West European countries reported increases in rates of cocaine abuse in recent years (8).

The 3.7 million Europeans who abuse cocaine, 90 percent of whom reside in Western Europe, reflect 25 percent of the world's cocaine abusers (129). The annual prevalence of cocaine abuse among those aged fifteen and over in Western Europe is 1 percent (129). In 2001, 33 percent of countries surveyed by UNODC reported increases in the consumption of cocaine (133).

However, with regard to heroin abuse, in recent years, heroin abuse rates were either stable or declining in most Western European countries.

The average prevalence rate of cannabis abuse in Europe is 5.2 percent, and in Western Europe it is 7.2 percent (UNODC 2003: 136). Among those seeking treatment for drug abuse in Europe, 13 percent have abused cannabis (136). (UNODC 2003: 107).

With regard to drug seizures, in 2001, Europe accounted for 33 percent of global heroin seizures (53). Western Europe alone accounted for 26 percent of these global seizures. These seizure rates appear to have remained stable from prior years. About 25 percent of global opiate seizures take place in Europe, and in 2001, 81 percent of European opiate seizures were in Western Europe (UNODC 2003: 52).

In 1998, 8 percent of the global seizures of cocaine came from Western Europe, but by 2001, this had risen to 17 percent (8). Of all global seizures of cocaine in 2001, 17 percent occurred in Europe, of which 99 percent took place in Western Europe (63).

References

United Nations Office on Drugs and Crime (UNODC). 2003. *Global Illicit Drug Trends 2003.* www.unodc.org/unodc/en/global_illicit_drug_trends.html (accessed October 24, 2003).

10

Great Britain

Overview

Great Britain is located in the north Atlantic Ocean and lies northwest of continental Europe. Politically, Great Britain consists of England, Scotland, and Wales, as well as a number of small islands. The population is 60,094,648 (July 2003 est.). The ethnic groups are English (81.5 percent), Scottish (9.6 percent), Irish (2.4 percent), Welsh (1.9 percent), Ulster (1.8 percent), West Indian, Indian, Pakistani, Black Caribbean, Black African, and other (2.8 percent). The religions are Anglican and Roman Catholic (40 million), Muslim (1.5 million), Presbyterian (800,000), Methodist (760,000), Sikh (500,000), Hindu (500,000), and Jewish (350,000). The languages spoken are English, Welsh, and Gaelic. (*Columbia Electronic Encyclopedia* 2004)

England has an uncodified constitution that is a blend of statute law, precedent, and tradition dating back to the 1100s. Legislation may be put forth by government ministers or departments. Parliament, which is made up of the House of Lords and the House of Commons, may annul such legislation. England is a member of the European Union which entails adherence to European Community law. European Community law takes precedence over both legislation and common law. England's legal system is an adversarial one. All cases first appear in magistrates' courts, which are also known as "courts of first instance." The magistrates' courts decide if the nature of the offense is appropriate for that court and whether the parties consent to try the offense in that court. The court may decide not to try the offense in the magistrates' courts, but to commit the accused for trial in the Crown Court.

Crimes are classified by their seriousness. Offenses also may be classified according to the procedure by which a case is brought to trial (in a magistrates' court only, by indictment, or triable-either-way in a magistrates' or the higher Crown Court).

Today, Great Britain is experiencing drug use-related problems similar in many ways to that of the United States. Young people are coming into contact with drugs at a younger age than before. There is a wider range of drugs available and although heroin use remains a minority activity, there is probably more heroin available than ever before at a very low price.

Great Britain's geographical location keeps it from being a drug transit route, but it is a major destination for drugs grown and manufactured elsewhere. Heroin flows into England from the Near and Far East, the former Soviet Union, and Colombia. Colombia also supplies Great Britain with cocaine. Cannabis mainly comes from the Near and Far East as well as North Africa.

Although Britain has had its problems with cocaine, it did not experience the crack explosion. But, the drug has found a level in the drug-using community where it causes substantial problems for users and their families. The good news is that rates of HIV among drug injectors are in decline and, in general, strategies put into place to reduce the spread of HIV such as needle exchanges and distribution of free condoms have been successful.

Drug Offenses and the Law

During the early part of the twentieth century Great Britain's concerns regarding the abuse of opium, cocaine, and cannabis led to the beginning of a series of international conventions and domestic laws. Many of these restrictions were eventually consolidated into the Misuse of Drugs Act of 1971. This Act, which is still current, is consistent with the UN Drug Conventions of 1961 and 1971.

The Home Office compiles statistics on convictions and drug seizures from police and customs involving action taken against people who have committed drug offenses controlled under the Use of Drugs Act of 1971. By the 1970s the following drugs were controlled: cannabis, amphetamine, amyl nitrite, mushrooms, LSD, ecstasy, glue, benzodiazepines, cocaine, anabolic steroids, methadone, heroin, and crack. In 1985, the Misuse of Drugs Regulations expressly laid out the circumstances in which it is lawful to import, export, produce, supply, possess with intent to supply, and possess drugs. Use of drugs itself remains uncontrolled.

The severity of penalties for drug violations is associated by the class (A, B, or C) into which the drug falls. Offenses involving those in Class A, such as heroin, attract the highest penalties. Penalties include life imprisonment for production and supply. Class B drugs (such as cannabis) attract a maximum penalty of fourteen years, and Class C drugs (such as Temazepam) can lead to a maximum sentence of five years. As in many other countries, offenses involving possession result in lesser maximum penalties.

The regulations of 1985 also divide the drugs into schedules. Schedule 1 includes drugs that have little or no acknowledged therapeutic use. The drugs in the other schedules are subject to lesser regulations and are considered to have legitimate medical uses.

Great Britain is also party to the 1988 UN Convention against Illicit Traffic in Narcotic Drugs and Psychotropic Substances. After 1988, the Criminal Justice Act fulfilled the U.K. obligations under the Vienna Convention of 1988 in relation to provisions for the monitoring and control of substances used in the manufacture of illicit drugs. The Customs and Excise Office, which handles Misuse of Drugs Act violations, has the discretion to offer a settlement in lieu of court proceedings for the illegal importation of small amounts of cannabis.

Other important legislation regulating activities relating to drugs include the Intoxicating Substances (Supply) Act of 1985, which makes it an offense for a person to supply to another person under eighteen years old substances which (or the fumes of which) he believes are likely to be inhaled for the purpose of causing intoxication. The Road Traffic Acts (1972, 1991) made it an offense to drive, attempt to drive, or be in charge of a motor vehicle when unfit to drive because of alcohol or drugs. The 1991 Act added the offense of causing death by careless driving when under the influence of drink or drugs. The Children Act of 1989 made it possible for the removal of a child from the family environment if it can be proved that the child has suffered harm (the priority, however, is to keep families intact whenever possible). Harm can be caused by a drug-using parent or a drug-using environment. The Community Care Act of 1990 puts responsibility on local authorities to assess the needs of, and arrange for residential and other services for drug abusers.

In 1995, the Drug Trafficking Act of 1994 came into effect, replacing the Drug Trafficking Offenses Act of 1986 and later amendments. This law allows for the seizure of any property representing the proceeds of trafficking following conviction for drug trafficking. The law applies to England and Wales, but similar provisions were formulated in Scotland and Northern Ireland (ISDD 1999).

The Crime and Disorder Act of 1998 introduces new community penalties that require drug treatment and testing for those convicted of a crime committed in order to maintain drug use. An offender must voluntarily give his or her consent, but once consent is given, drug testing is mandatory. The orders are being tested as a pilot program until early 2000, at which time the program may be implemented nationwide (ISDD 1999).

Other recent legislation regarding illicit drugs includes: enabling authorities to immediately close clubs and similar venues where there are serious problems involving drug abuse and mandatory minimum sentences for persistent drug dealers. A new mandatory minimum sentence of seven years imprisonment is being introduced for traffickers in Class A drugs such as heroin, cocaine, and ecstasy, who are convicted on a third or subsequent occasion.

Extent and Patterns of Use

With the development of stronger strategies to reduce drug use, Great Britain has begun to develop a more central repository for data regarding drug use and abuse. Local assessments and surveys from England, Scotland, Northern Ireland, and Wales have contributed to a better understanding of the current patterns and trends of use and abuse. The Web site of Britain's Institute for the Study of Drug Dependence (ISDD), linked to the European Monitoring Centre on Drugs and Drug Addiction (EMCDDA) site has listed the following as the main sources of ongoing epidemiological information available: Home Office Addicts Index, the Regional Drug Misuse Database, National Office of Statistics Mortality Data, Home Office Addicts Register, Public Health Laboratory, and St. George's Hospital Medical School. These sources have been brought to the attention of the EMCDDA, and as the European Union strives to develop common indicators across EU countries, these sources may serve as some guidance to the other countries.

The nature of the drug-abusing population seeking treatment can be found using the Home Office Addicts Index (discontinued as of 1997) and the Regional Drug Misuse Databases (RDMD). Morbidity and mortality data are made available by the National Office of Statistics Mortality Data; Home Office Addicts Register; Public Health Laboratory data on HIV/AIDS; Hospital Episode statistics; and St. George's Hospital Medical School solvent mortality statistics. Prevalence of drug use data are collected in the British Crime Survey and Exeter University Schools Health Unit data, in addition to other public opinion surveys.[1] Drug law enforcement data are made available by the Home Office (covering police and Customs & Excise) and the National Criminal Intelligence Service although information from the latter is largely confidential.

Drug use emerged as a social problem in the 1960s. Heroin use was spreading from inner city London to residential counties and other cities such as Liverpool and Manchester. As in the United States, cannabis and LSD became popular with university students embracing the hippie culture. Heroin use increased through the 1970s and when smokable heroin became readily available in the 1980s, large numbers of young adults who had stayed away from heroin because of the needle, turned to the drug.

The British Crime Survey (BCS), carried out by the Home Office, measured drug use patterns and attitudes toward and experience of crime through self-report. Information was collected through a nationally representative sample of people living in households in England and Wales. In 1994 over 14,000 individuals participated in the crime survey and a subset of nearly 10,000 were asked to complete the drug self-report section. Twenty-eight percent of the 1994 BCS sample admitted to lifetime use of drugs. This was nearly two-thirds more than the 1992 BCS. One-year prevalence in the 1994 survey was 10 percent and use in the last month was 6 percent. Some caution must be involved in comparisons between the 1992 and 1994 surveys because changes were made in interviewing techniques. But, even with the changes, officials attest that the absolute numbers of drug users have risen. Although the proportion of lifetime users who have used drugs in the last year has remained stable, just over one in three with lifetime experience of drugs will have taken a drug in the last twelve months (Pease and Cox n.d.). Lifetime use was highest among sixteen to nineteen year olds (46 percent). The twenty to twenty-four year olds were close behind at 44 percent and falling to 33 percent among thirty to thirty-four year olds and to 13 percent among forty-five to fifty-nine year olds (Ramsay and Percy 1996).

In 1992, a household survey, known as the Four City survey, was administered to 5,000 people aged sixteen and over in four urban centers in England and Scotland. Each of the four cities had a general sample of 1,000 people, and an additional group of 250 young people thought to be most at risk from drug use. Lifetime prevalence across the main sample was 19 percent, and one year prevalence was 8 percent. One month prevalence was only asked for cannabis; roughly 16 percent of those ever using cannabis, used in the last month. With regard to age, use peaked in the early twenties at 41 percent, but there were more users in the sixteen to nineteen year old category (use in the last year was highest for sixteen to nineteen year olds at 26 percent) (Leitner, 1993).

University of Exeter Schools' Unit studies surveyed 18,000 school students in 1995. This survey, coordinated by Dr. John Balding, began in the mid 1980s. At the time, it was the largest school-based survey of its kind. The survey is not random, however, and underreporting may also result from youth not wanting teachers—who administer the survey—to see their survey responses. In addition, the studies are school-based, and therefore prevalence rates will miss those youth who were not in school on those days, and the dropouts. But even with some methodological problems, the survey results are similar to those generated by more representative studies as shown below. Of the youngest youth—those twelve to thirteen years of age—nine percent reported ever using drugs or inhalants. The percentage increased to 30 percent for fourteen to fifteen year olds and 37 percent for fifteen and sixteen year olds. Comparisons of these data to earlier years show more youth using drugs at an earlier age (Balding 1996).

Similar numbers were found in a 1995 survey by Millar and Plant (1996) at Edinburgh University and the Drug Realities Survey by the Health Education Authority (1996). Millar and Plant surveyed 7,700 fifteen and sixteen year olds using a representative drawn from both state and private schools throughout the United Kingdom. Overall, 42 percent had taken a drug at some point in their life. The Drug Realities' survey was administered to 5,000 eleven through thirty-five year olds drawn representatively throughout England in 1995. The results showed approximately 30 percent of fourteen to sixteen year olds reported ever having used drugs.

Data from the British Crime Survey, conducted in both 1994 and 1996, surveyed the personal use of drugs among a total of 22,128 adults. The participants were asked about their use of several drugs within the past year and within the past month. In 1994 and 1996 respectively, 25.9 percent and 26.6 percent of the respondents reported "*any use*" of any drug, 16.5 and 16.9 percent reported "*past use only,*" 9.4 and 9.7 percent reported "*used in past year,*" and 5.4 and 5.8 percent reported "*used in past month*" (MacDonald 1999: 589). Respondents were also asked about the class of drugs they had used. Class A drugs include cocaine, crack, ecstasy/MDMA, heroin, LSD, magic mushrooms, and methadone/physeptone, while Class B drugs include amphetamines and cannabis. Class C drugs are tranquilizers/Temazepam. In 1994 and 1996, respectively, 9 percent and 9.3 percent of the respondents had ever used Class A drugs in their lifetime, whereas 24.8 and 25.7 percent had ever used Class B or C drugs in their lifetime. Within the past year, 2.1 and 9.7 percent had used Class A drugs, and 0.8 and 1.1 percent had used Class A drugs within the past month. Respondents in 1994 and 1996, respectively, reported that within the past year 9.2 and 9.5 percents had used Class B/C drugs, and 5.3 and 5.7 percents had used Class B/C substances within the past month.

Clearly, there is a rise in the number of adults who had ever used any type of drug between 1994 and 1996, as well as increases in the percent who had used Class A, B, or C substances ever, within the past year, and within the past month (MacDonald 1999: 589).

In terms of gender, the Four City Survey (Leitner et al. 1993) found about two male drug users for every female, but in recent years this proportion seems to have fallen. Both the 1994 BCS and the 1995 HEA survey found that four men to every three women admitted to having used drugs once in their lifetime. More specifically, the 1994 BCS found that half of all men between sixteen and twenty-nine had taken drugs, and that only a third of women had (36 percent). However, in the sixteen to nineteen age group, women were matching men's drug consumption almost drug for drug. As for under-sixteens, both the Edinburgh University survey and Balding's series have found that school-age drug use is remarkable in its similarity between the sexes.

When ethnicity was examined, the Four City survey found that over half the white respondents in one location's booster group had taken drugs while only a third of black respondents had. white and Afro-Caribbean lifetime drug use was identical, at 29 percent, with Indian use standing at 11 percent and Pakistani/Bangladeshi at 15 percent. Afro-Caribbean adults over twenty-nine had a higher rate of lifetime use than Whites in the same age group (25 percent compared to 22 percent), although Afro-Caribbeans in the younger age group (sixteen to twenty-nine) had a rate of lifetime use that was substantially lower than that of whites (34 percent compared to 43 percent) (Leitner et al. 1993).

In addition to survey data, the Home Office Addicts Index had been a key indicator of drug abuse in Great Britain. All doctors were required by law to notify the Home Office when they believe or know that a patient is addicted to certain drugs. The legal criterion for identifying an addict was that the addict has an overpowering desire to continue taking one or more of the thirteen opiates and their substitutes or cocaine. These drugs are listed as "notifiable" drugs in the Misuse of Drugs Act and its regulations.[2] The Addicts Index was discontinued because a number of regional health authorities were dissatisfied with the limited nature of the Index (ISDD 1999). Officials report that the numbers of notified addicts represent one-fifth to one-third of all opiate addicts (ISDD 1994).

According to the Addicts Index, the number of addicts notified almost doubled between 1990 and 1994. But, in 1995, there were 37,164 notified addicts, an increase of only 9 percent from the previous year. Forty percent of these addicts were newly registered (14,735), a proportion which has remained relatively static over the years (Home Office 1996).

Roughly half of all addicts are in their twenties (the average age of persons notified for the first time was 26.4 years in 1994). The number of under twenty-one year olds is increasing (15.6 percent for males in 1990, 16.8 percent for males in 1994; and 20.6 percent for females in 1990 and 22.7 percent for 1994) (Home Office 1996).

Heroin accounted for 24,530 notifications in 1995, two-thirds of all notifications, and 10 percent more than in 1994. For methadone, 17,409 people were notified to the Home Office as addicted to the drug in 1995, 47 percent of all notifications. Notifications for cocaine addiction increased by 8 percent in 1995 to 3,357, although in 1994 and 1993 they increased by 26 percent each year. In the early 1990s, hospitals and treatment centers were responsible for the majority of notifications, but this number has decreased as notifications from prison and police doctors increased from 11 percent in 1991 to 17 percent in 1995.

The UNODC (2003) reports that from 1998 to 2000, the rate of heroin abuse nearly tripled (see British Crime Survey data) and that seizures of heroin and heroin arrests increased as well (118).

Law Enforcement

In 1995, there were 113,000 drug seizures in the United Kingdom (Great Britain and Northern Ireland). Of that number, 93,600 individuals were sentenced, cautioned, or dealt with by compounding. Compounding, which was introduced in 1982, involves paying a fine in lieu of prosecution for cases involving the import of small quantities of cannabis resin or herbal cannabis for personal use. The number convicted for drug offenses in 1995 is double the number estimated to have been convicted in 1989. Over a third of those sentenced or cautioned were under twenty-one. Cautioning is gaining ground as a sentencing option. Cautioning creates a criminal record without punishment on the first offense. If the offense is repeated, it is treated as a second offense. In 1985, 3,600 people were cautioned for drug offenses compared to almost 49,000 in 1995. This implies an effort to divert minor offenders from the court process, and also a reduction in stringency in drug enforcement of minor crimes. Table 10.1 displays the number of persons found guilty, cautioned, or dealt with by compounding for cocaine, cannabis, and heroin, and all drugs combined. One can see that cannabis accounted for the greatest number of offenses (83 percent of all drug offenses) in 1994. Possession of cannabis accounted for 94 percent of all cannabis offenses (not shown). Males represented over 90 percent of the cases in 1994 and the average age of offenders was between twenty-four and twenty-five years old. The

TABLE 10-1
Persons Found Guilty, Cautioned, or Dealt with by Drug Type and Year, United Kingdom

Type of Drug	1990	1991	1992	1993	1994
Cocaine	860	838	913	1671	1804
Cannabis	40,194	42,209	41,353	56,417	72,392
Heroin	1,605	1,466	1,415	2,164	2,791
All drugs	44,922	47,616	48,927	69,735	86,961

Source: Home Office, 1995.

average sentence length for those sentenced for drug crimes was approximately two years.

Drug Policy

With the advent of AIDS in the 1980s, the British government focused some of their efforts toward "harm reduction" in the medical sense. Initiatives such as the provision of sterile drug injecting equipment and condoms were introduced. There was also a relaxation of drug substitution prescribing policies (which had become increasingly more stringent through the 1970s) whereby prescriptions of substitute drugs like methadone were available to some addicts over a longer period of time.

In 1993, the four countries of the United Kingdom recognized that a more demand reduction-focused drug strategy was in order to quell the rise of addiction and casual drug use. New strategies are now in place that respond to national needs. The strategies for each of the countries are fundamentally similar, though they vary to meet local needs.

After reviewing the current drug policies in England, the Central Drugs Coordination Unit held discussions with health, police, and other professionals regarding drug use and its related problems. These discussions led to the publication of a consultation document in October 1994, that eventually formed the basis of England's current strategy, which was published in May 1995 (*Tackling Drugs Together*). The statement of purpose focused on the following:

> vigorous law enforcement, accessible treatment and a new emphasis on education and prevention to increase the safety of communities from drug related crime; reduce the acceptability and availability of drugs to young people; and reduce the health risks and other damage related to drug misuse through multiagency coordination at national and local levels.

An important part of the strategy was to build aspects of drug education into the National Curriculum to be followed by all primary and secondary schools in England and Wales.

In 1998, the British government created what was called "the first cross-cutting strategy to tackle drugs in an integrated way" (Drug Strategy Directorate 2002: 6). The strategy involves an array of educational and informational programs with the intention of:

- Identifying vulnerable youth through support and specialized services
- Expanding and improving drug education through communication efforts
- Imposing more severe penalties for dealing Class C drugs

- Expanding prevention and treatment efforts
- Including parents and guardians in treatment and support efforts
- Integrating and improving treatment within the youth justice system
- Reducing the supply of illegal substances by increasing drug seizures, working with EU candidate countries, establishing agencies such as the Concerted Inter-Agency Drugs Action Group and the National Crime Squad (7–9)
- Cracking down on international trafficking by working with the Afghan government, collaborating with other countries, studying the drug supply chain, targeting middle markets, strengthening police efforts

These strategies will usher Great Britain into the twentieth century in its efforts to provide "universal programmes of education and information [which] will give all young people and their families the information and skills they need to protect themselves from the risks and harms of all drugs" (7).

Notes

1. Other studies include the Four City Survey 1992 (Leitner et al. 1993); Drug Realities (Health Education Authority, 1996); and Drug Futures (Parker, Measham and Aldridge 1995).
2. Home Office Addicts Index in 1997 has been discontinued because doctors no longer have to notify the Home Office if they attend to a drug addict.

References

Balding, J. 1996. *Young People in 1995.* Exeter: Exeter University.

Columbia Electronic Encyclopedia, 6th ed. 2004. New York: Columbia University Press.

Drug Strategy Directorate. 2002. *Updated Drug Strategy 2002, Executive Summary.* www.drugs.gov.uk/ReportsandPublications/NationalStrategy/1038840683 (accessed December 20, 2003).

Health Education Authority. 1996. Drug Realities—National Drugs Campaign Survey. London: HEA.

Home Office of Research and Statistics Department. 1995. "Statistics of Drug Seizures and Offenders Dealt With," United Kingdom, 1994, *Statistical Bulletin,* Issue 24/95.

Home Office. 1997. *Statistics of Drug Addicts Notified to the Home Office, United Kingdom, 1996.* Home Office Statistical Bulletin, 22/97. London: RSD.

Home Office. 1996. *Statistics of Drug Addicts Notified to the Home Office, United Kingdom, 1995.* Home Office Statistical Bulletin, 15/96. London: RSD.

Home Office. 1995. *Statistics of Drug Addicts Notified to the Home Office, United Kingdom,* 1994. Home Office Statistical Bulletin, 17/95. London: RSD.

Institute for the Study of Drug Dependence (ISDD). 1999. [Online] ISDD Homepage, www.isdd.co.uk/ (accessed July 23, 1999).

Institute for the Study of Drug Dependence (ISDD). 1999. *Drug Abuse Briefing,* 7th ed. London: Institute for the Study of Drug Dependence.

Institute for the Study of Drug Dependence (ISDD). 1994. *Drug Misuse in Britain 1994,* London.

Leitner, Maria, Joanna Shapland, and Paul Wiles. 1993. Drug Usage and Drugs Prevention: The Views and Habits of the general Public. Home Office: RSD. (Four City Survey).

MacDonald, Ziggy. 1999. "Illicit Drug Use in the UK." *British Journal of Criminology* 36(4), Autumn: 585–608.

Miller, P., and M. Plant, 1996. "Drinking, Smoking and Illicit Drug Use among 15 and 16 Year Olds in the United Kingdom." *British Medical Journal:* 313, 394–397.

Parker, Howard, Fiona Measham, and Judith Aldridge. 1995. *Drugs Futures: Changing Patterns of Drug Use Amongst English Youth.* London. Institute for the Study of Drug Dependence.

Pease, K, and G. Cox, no date. *World Factbook of Criminal Justice Systems: England and Wales.*

Ramsay, M., and A. Percy, 1996. Drug Misuse Declared: Results of the 1994 British Crime Survey." Home Office: RSD.

Ramsay, M., and J. Spiller, 1997. Drug Misuse Declared: Results of the 1996 British Crime Survey." Home Office: RSD.

United Nations Office on Drugs and Crime. 2003. *Global Illicit Drug Trends 2003.* www.unodc.org/unodc/en/global_illicit_drug_trends.html (accessed October 24, 2003).

11

France

FRANCE IS A REPUBLIC WITH EXECUTIVE, legislative, and judicial branches. The legal system is based on indigenous concepts of civil law. There is judicial review of administrative but not legislative acts.

France, with a population of 60,424,213 people, borders the Bay of Biscay and the English Channel, between Belgium and Spain southeast of the United Kingdom, and borders the Mediterranean Sea, between Italy and Spain. Ninety-two percent of the population is French (a mix of Celtic, Latin, Germanic, and Slavic origin), 3 percent are North African, and 2 percent are German. The remainder are Slavic, Indochinese, and Basque. Eighty-three to 88 percent of France's population is Roman Catholic, 2 percent are Protestant, 5 to 10 percent are Muslim, 4 percent are unaffiliated, and 1 percent is Jewish. French is the official and widely spoken language. But some speak regional dialects and languages such as Provencal, Breton, Alsatian, Corsican, Catalan, Basque, and Flemish (CIA World Factbook, France 2004). The largest of the Western European nations, it is also one of the four Western European trillion-dollar economies. France has a diversified industrial base and substantial agricultural resources. The government retains considerable influence over key segments of each sector, with majority ownership of railway, electricity, aircraft, and telecommunication firms.

France serves as a transshipment point for and consumer of South American cocaine and southwest Asian heroin.

Drug Offenses and the Law

Possession of drugs is a criminal offense, and France makes no legal distinction between hard or soft drugs (Drugtext Information Services 1995). Further, there is no legal difference between "possession for personal use and trafficking," such that possession can be prosecuted as trafficking (European Monitoring Centre for Drugs and Drug Addiction [EMCDDA] 2003). Drug trafficking is often met with stiff fines. Using drugs can result in a fine or up to one-year imprisonment. An individual caught for the first time using marijuana is usually given a warning. Those convicted for using drugs are subject to a sentence of imprisonment up to one year and a 25,000 franc fine. The Decree law of 1990 lists illegal substances (EMCDDA Web site 2003):

- List 1: Heroin, cocaine, cannabis, methadone, opium, etc.,
- List 2: Codeine, propiram, etc.,
- List 3: Psychotropic substances of the 1971 Vienna Convention such as amphetamines, MDMA, LSD, etc.,
- List 4: Substances not internationally controlled such as MBDB, 4-MTA, Ketam, Nabilone, THC, etc.

France stresses a therapeutic, treatment-based approach to drug use as an alternative to criminal justice sanctioning. This is similar to Greece, Luxembourg, Portugal, Finland, and Sweden. A law passed in 1999 provides alternatives to prosecution. A "penal agreement" may result in the waiving of prosecution in certain circumstances that involve minor offenses.

When convicted, drug dealers that are dealing to feed their addiction are generally given a sentence that does not exceed five years; organized drug traffickers can receive a maximum of thirty years, and the leaders a life sentence (EMCDDA 2003).

France serves as an important depot for drugs traveling to other European countries. Although authorities believe there is negligible production or cultivation of illicit drugs, France is an important transshipment country, particularly for heroin originating in southwest Asia, cocaine originating in South America, and cannabis originating in Morocco.

Extent and Patterns of Use

A 1993 census of treatment admissions (majority for heroin abuse) estimated that there are roughly 160,000 addicts in France's population of 60 million, which equals a rate of 2.8 addicted persons per 1,000 people. The rate of addicted users for those between the age of fifteen and fifty-four is 5.0 per 1,000 (EMCDDA 2003).

An estimated seven million have consumed at least one drug in their lifetime, and two million people have used drugs in the last year.

Between 1988 and 1998 France conducted roughly thirty surveys that include measures on attitudes toward drugs or drug use frequency. The majority of these studies were conducted by the French Center for Health Education (CFES). The 1996 through 1998 studies each surveyed roughly 1,000 individuals, with the exception of the 1997 school survey that reached almost 10,000 respondents. Over the years CFES found that although most all illicit substances are still perceived as dangerous, the perception of danger decreased from 69 percent to 54 percent for cannabis during the period 1992 and 1995. The perceived danger of cocaine also fell slightly (the question was: "According to you, which of the following drugs are dangerous?" [Reif and Melich 2000]). In 1996, 38 percent of those polled responded that they felt cannabis consumption had no serious health implications. But, the majority of French remain in favor of making no distinction between soft drugs and hard drugs (64 percent in 1993 and 61 percent in 1997).

The French people overwhelmingly consider drug addicts to be ill, though some surveys have shown that respondents feel that the notions of ill and delinquent can coexist. Support for alternative treatments in the 1996 and 1997 surveys was fairly strong—39 percent for heroin maintenance and 55 percent for medical marijuana. Only 6 percent of those surveyed in 1997 felt that imprisoning a drug addict would enable him/her to get off of drugs for good.

Individuals with more education, urban residents, and women have the most tolerant attitudes toward drug use (OFDT 1999). Seventy-seven percent of the French public considered that there was an increasing number of addicts in France. When broken down by whether the respondent had any contact with drugs, the percentages are different: 81 percent of those who have never had any contact with drugs responded that they thought the number of addicts was increasing and only 65 percent of individuals who had contact with drugs felt there was an increase in the number of addicts (OFDT 1999).

With regard to trends, heroin consumption seems to be stabilizing, although polydrug use is increasing. Cocaine use and crack use are not very widespread, though users report cocaine use in association with use of the other drugs. Crack use itself has increased considerably since 1990, but it is mainly contained to Paris and the French West Indies. There has been considerable increase in ecstasy and hallucinogen use, particularly among youth.

In 2000, one in five people in France had tried marijuana. First-time experimentation occurs for a majority of these people in adolescence. Among young people, marijuana use is largely casual, though use becomes more intense and regular with age. According to one study, 60 percent of nineteen-year-old boys had tried marijuana, and more than one in three use it regularly and heavily.

Cocaine use appears to have risen in recent years. The number of cocaine seizures that took place in France during 2001 increased by 58 percent (UNODC 2003: 66). In 2000, one in five people in France had tried cocaine. The highest levels of experimentation are generally in the eighteen to forty-four age group, especially the thirty-five to forty-four year age group (1.6 percent for women and 4 percent for men). Among young people (under eighteen), experimentation ranges from 1 percent to 3 percent.

Heroin use and experimentation begins at around age fourteen. For the eighteen-to forty-four-year-old group, 0.4 percent of women and 1.7 percent of men have tried heroin. For school age youth (fourteen to eighteen years), 0.8 percent of girls and 1.4 percent of boys claimed to have tried heroin. Heroin continues to be the most problematic drug in terms of forcing the user to seek health care or rely on social services. The vast majority of opiate users seeking social services are on substitute treatment. As of early 2001, about 84,000 people were undergoing substitute treatment.

In the 1980s, France experienced increasing rates of heroin abuse, which subsequently fell in the late 1990s (UNODC 2003: 115). Between 1995 and 2000, drug-related deaths decreased by over 75 percent (115).

Law Enforcement

In 1995, policing authorities handled 35,390 drug cases, although it has been estimated that the total number of drug abusers was 150,000 (Drugtext Information Services 1995). From these cases, 64,432 people were arrested for drug use or drug trafficking. The most frequent cause for arrest was drug use, accounting for approximately 90 percent of drug cases in 1995 (62,325 arrests). The remaining 10 percent were arrested for local or international trafficking. Eighty percent of the drug use cases were for light use. The overall number of arrests for drug use doubled from 1990 to 1995. The overwhelming majority of the increase can be accounted for by an increase in the number of arrests for cannabis.

The number of individuals arrested for drug use that did not go through judicial proceedings but were sentenced to receive therapeutic treatment was 8,630 in 1995. This number was up from 7,678 individuals in 1994 and 6,149 individuals in 1993. Of the 8,630 individuals sentenced to treatment in 1995, 6,072 actually received that treatment (OFDT 1997). The percentage of convicted individuals sentenced for drug use out of all drug-related offenses, has diminished steadily over the last five years.

Of the number arrested for drug trafficking, the majority are for trafficking in heroin (47 percent), followed by cannabis (42 percent) and cocaine (6 percent). Before 1983, the most frequently cited substance in drug trafficking related arrests was cannabis. Since that time the number of arrests for cannabis and cocaine trafficking has tripled, and the number of arrests for heroin trafficking doubled.

With regard to the type of sentence for persons convicted of drug-related crimes, 42 percent of offenders receive imprisonment but have their full sentence deferred; another 36 percent receive imprisonment of a partially suspended sentence; 15 percent receive fines; 3 percent receive educational measures; 2 percent receive a treatment substitution sentence; and 2 percent receive no sentence. Looking at who received imprisonment, the breakdown is as follows: of 12,277 imprisonments for drug-related offenses in 1995, 7,801 were for trafficking, 1,026 for sale and supply, 864 for use, and 2,586 for other drug related offenses (OFDT 1997).

Drug Policy

France's drug policy stems from a law enacted in 1970. This law had three main objectives: (1) to prohibit drug use, or lay out the principle of prohibition; (2) to repress drug trafficking; and (3) to ensure free treatment of substance abusers. Essentially the law established that drug use was harmful. Before the 1970 law, drug use was only prohibited in public places. In 1986, a law was created to promote swift justice for those accused of selling or supplying drugs. Other measures adopted in 1987 attacked drug trafficking and laid out sentences for those who supplied drugs to children. By 1996, laws had been passed that criminalized certain offenses involving organized crime and drugs, laundering money, and transporting drugs via the sea. France's current policies revolve around abstinence and detoxification of current users. Although public security is a great concern and is mirrored in the drug policy, public health has been a growing issue since the spread of AIDS began in the 1980s.

An interministerial commission was established in 1982 that coordinates the actions of ministries involved in observing and preventing drug addiction, treating substance abusers, training field workers, and conducting research, effectively allowing for a very comprehensive plan of action and the development of a specialized system of prevention and treatment. In 1987, France put forth a decree authorizing the sale of syringes, essentially introducing the first arm of a "harm reduction" policy. By 1993 a triennial governmental plan was adopted that established a series of short- and long-term measures to fight drug trafficking and combat abuse. The plan advocated a strong harm-reduction policy. Drug substitute treatments as an alternative to regular drug treatment were developed for the first time. This approach focused on educating the public through mass media, using schools and families to provide role models for children, and increasing local efforts to bridge different sectors of the community (Drugtext Information Services 1995).

In general, France supports treatment of drug abuse as a sanction and as an alternative to stiff penalties. Current policy aims to maintain a balance among repression, prevention, treatment and rehabilitation (OFDT 1997). As early as 1979, France had provided treatment for drug addicts through reception centers, which offered outpatient and psychotherapy services, special hospitals, foster families, and special care centers (Drugtext Information Services 1995). A General Delegation is responsible for forming drug policies in France (Drugtext Information Services 1995). In 1984, ECU 33.6 million was spent on preventing drug addiction and caring for addicts. By 1990, this figure increased to ECU 61 million.

References

CIA. *World Factbook: France.* 2004. www.odcl.gov/cia/publications/faetbook/fr.html.

Drugtext Information Services. 1995. *France.* www.drugtext.org (accessed October 3, 2003).

European Monitoring Centre for Drug and Drug Addiction (EMCDDA). 2003. European Legal Database on Drugs. Country Profile: France. www.eldd.emcdda.eu.int/databases/eldd_country_profiles.cfm?country=FR (accessed October 24, 2003).

Observatoire Francais Des Drogues Et Des Toxicomanies[OFDT] (1999). "Tendances No. 1: The French and Drugs: Perceptions, Opinions and Attitudes from 1988 to 1998." www.ofdt.fr/aiiglais/ofdt,,,eturec,/tenan<-).htini. (accessed July 26, 1999).

Observatoire Francais Des Drogues Et Des Toxicomanies[OFDT] (1997). National Report on the State of the Drug Phenomenon: France, 1997 Update. www.ofdt.fr,/anglais,/.html. (accessed July 26, 1999).

Reif, Karlheinz, and Anna Melich. 2000. Eurobarometer 37.0 and 37.1. European Drug Prevention Program [Computer File]. Conducted by INRA Europe on the request of the European Commission. ZA Second Edition. Cologne: Germany. Zentralarchiv fur empirische Sozialforschung [producer and distributor 2000]. Ann Arbor, Mich.: Inter-University Consortium for Political and Social Science Research 2000. ICPSR 9956.

United Nations Office on Drugs and Crime. 2003. *Global Illicit Drug Trend 2003.* www.unodc.org/unodc/en/global_illicit_drug_trends.html (accessed October 24, 2003).

12

Italy

Overview

ITALY'S LOCATION IN THE CENTRAL Mediterranean strategically gives it dominance in terms of southern sea and air approaches to Western Europe. Italy has roughly 58,057,477 inhabitants and has become a ranking industrial economy on the scale of the United Kingdom and France. It is homogenous and approximately two-thirds of Italians live in cities. Italian is the official language, although in some areas the use of the local language on official documents and in education is authorized. In 1992, Rome came to the realization that it may not qualify to participate in EU plans for economic and monetary union later in the decade; thus, it began to address large fiscal imbalances. As a result, the government adopted fairly stringent budgets, abandoned its inflationary wage index system, and started to scale back its generous social welfare programs, including health care benefits (CIA 2004).

In Italy's republic-style government, criminal laws are contained in the Penal Code and many other statutes. All laws are required by the Constitution of the Italian Republic (Art.73) to be published in the Gazzetta Ufficiale dello Stato, which is the Official Gazette of the State. The country is divided into twenty administrative districts which have the power to make laws, providing they do not conflict with the Constitution. But, only the state has jurisdiction over substantive and procedural penal law. The Minister of Justice is in charge of the organization and functioning of the criminal justice system (Marongiu and Biddau n.d.).

The basic principles of the Penal Code and the Constitution are as follows: (a) no penalty without a law (nulla poena sine lege) and no crime without a law; (b) legal responsibility rests solely on the acting individual; (c) rules of penal law are not retroactive; (d) no one can be sentenced without a fair trial; (e) no one can be considered guilty until a final sentence has been pronounced; (f) penalties cannot consist in treatment contrary to the sense of humanity and must tend to the rehabilitation of the offender; and (g) personal freedom is inviolable and no one shall be deprived of it except under specific provisions of the law (Constitution, Art.27). The principals of Italian Penal Code originated with the French Enlightenment influence. After Italy was unified in 1861, the Sardinian Penal Code of 1859 became Italy's Code until a more general Code was promulgated in 1889. Another Criminal Code was enacted on October 19, 1930 (Codice Rocco) which remains the basic statute in the field of substantive criminal law with the exceptions of a few amendments. Amendments have broadened the alternatives to incarceration and modified the terms of pretrial detention.

The basics of Italy's justice system was determined by the Code of Criminal Procedure enacted in 1930. The Code has been amended several times until a significantly different Code of Penal Procedure was developed in 1988 and came into force in 1989. The new code shifts Italy's procedural system of justice from an inquisitorial system to the more modern adversarial system.

An interesting feature of Italy's justice system is that the accused does not have the right to plead guilty to a lesser offense once he is charged with a crime. This is the principle of obbligatorieta dell'azione penale, which removes any discretion during the prosecution stage.

Essentially, selective enforcement does not exist because the alleged defendant must be processed through the system with the crimes for which he was charged.

The Penal Code divides criminal offenses into two categories: *delitti*, which are serious offenses and *contravvenzioni*, which are less serious offenses. A distinction is also made through the severity of punishment and type of prison facility. *Delitti* crimes can carry a penalty of fifteen days to twenty-four years imprisonment, and as much as thirty years or life imprisonment in special cases. For *contravvenziom* crimes, the penalty is five days to three years imprisonment. Fines can amount to roughly 500,000 U.S. dollars for serious drug offenses (Penal Code, Art.22,23.25).

A more detailed classification of the Code generally classifies each crime under a specific heading: (a) crimes against the nation such as espionage, assassination of the president, terrorism; (b) crimes against public authority such as corruption, bribery, embezzlement of public property by an officer; (c) crimes against judicial authority like perjury; (d) crimes against religious feelings and against the feelings of pity toward the dead; (e) crimes that breach the peace; (f) crimes against public safety such as arson; (g) crimes against the public (forgery and counterfeiting); (h) crimes against the public economy, industry, and commerce; (i) crimes against public morality like rape and prostitution; (j) crimes; against the family such as incest; (k) crimes against the person/violent crimes and (1) crimes against property. Note that Italy's Penal Code considers the violent crimes of robbery, extortion, and ransom kidnapping as property crimes because their main intent is to gain property.

Drug Offenses and the Law

In 1993, personal use of drugs was decriminalized. Through a national referendum, Italians voted for a new law that does not permit imprisonment for drug-related activities involving personal use only. Only administrative sanctions, such as revoking a driving license or passport, can be imposed for cases involving personal use. Judicial authorities make the determination as to whether the possession of drugs is for personal use or for sale (European Monitoring Centre for Drugs and Addiction [EMCDDA] 2003).

Although personal use of drugs has been decriminalized, illicit activities such as import, acquisition, or possession for personal use can result in administrative sanctions, such as suspension of a driving license or passport. Penalties remain severe for producing, selling, or trafficking drugs. Illegal drugs include opium and its derivatives, cocaine and its derivatives, amphetamine, synthetic drugs, cannabis, and hashish. Individuals convicted of minor drug trafficking generally receive six months to six years and/or a fine; those convicted of more serious drug drafficking will receive from two to twenty years and/or a fine. Convicted members of drug trafficking organizations receive a minimum of ten years, and the leaders of organized trafficking groups are subject to a minimum of twenty years (EMCDDA 2003).

Extent and Patterns of Use

National prevalence estimates are derived from a 1992 census of treatment admissions (majority for opiate abuse), combined with criminal justice data and public health data. There are roughly 190,000 to 313,000 addicts in Italy's population of 56 million which equals a rate of 3.3 to 5.5 addicted persons per 1,000 people. The rate of addicted users for those between the age of 15 and 54 is 5.9 to 9.7 persons per 1000 (EMCDDA 2003). Compared to France (2.8 in 1993), Sweden (1.6–2.3 in 1992), and the Netherlands (1.6–1.8 in 1993), Italy's rate of drug use prevalence for all ages is highest even at the lower bound estimate.

In 1995, the Swedish Council for Information on Alcohol and other Drugs (CAD) surveyed school youth in twenty-five European Union countries on drug use patterns (the survey is known as ESPAD) and found that, in Italy, 19 percent of fifteen to sixteen year olds had used cannabis in their lifetime (compared to 11.9 percent in France, 19.4 percent in Spain, 41 percent in the United Kingdom, 6.8 percent in Sweden) and 3 percent had used cocaine (compared to 1.1 percent in France, 1.7 percent in Spain, 3 percent in the United Kingdom, and 0.5 percent in Sweden). Two percent reported using heroin in their lifetime, on the high end of the fourteen countries.

However, since the 1990s, heroin abuse has been noted to be severe in Italy. The UNODC (2003) states that "Italy had, in absolute numbers, the largest heroin abusing population of all Western European countries over the 1998-2000 period" (113). The UNODC also notes that between 1992 and 2001, the demand for treatment for heroin abuse increased, accounting for 91 percent of the demand for drug abuse treatment in 1992 (113). Italy also experienced a 50 percent decline in drug-related deaths from 1996 to 2001 (UNODC 2003: 113). But there has not been a reduction in heroin abuse between 1996 and 2000 (114).

Law Enforcement

The number of crimes reported by police to the judiciary are collected by the Institute of Statistics (ISTAT). The 1992 figures are taken from an ISTAT press release, March 17, 1993 (Istituto Nazionale di Statistica). Excluding homicide, ISTAT sources do not specify whether attempts are included.

In 1992, police recorded 42,164 incidents of drug offenses, up from 30,691 in 1990 (and up from 31,079 in 1988). These drug offenses include growing, manufacturing, selling, or distributing drugs. The rate per 100,000 population in 1991 was 69.99.

Drug Policy

Italy practices a harm-reduction approach in terms of treatment policies, with the overall goal of reducing the harm of suffering that drug-dependent individuals experience. The government has launched educational programs that target school-age children (Drugtext Information Services 1995). Courts can offer alternative measures for drug abusers who voluntarily agree to treatment. Sentences up to four years are suspended, and instead individuals are given probation for five years. Upon successful completion of probation, the case is closed. Italy is also strongly committed to international efforts on drug regulation and control. It is the largest single donor to the United Nations International Drug Control Program.

In 1990, Italian Law No. 162 directed funds from the national budget for the prevention and treatment of drug abuse. An annual budget of US$140 million was allocated among the Health, Interior, Education, Defense, and Justice Ministries. An additional US$80 million was provided to the Ministry of Public Works to finance the construction and improvement of treatment centers. The number of cocaine seizures that took place in Italy decreased by 23 percent in 2001 (UNODC 2003: 66).

References

Antolisei, Francesco. *Handbook of Penal Law. General Section*, tenth edition. (Milano: Giuffre'). (Manuale di Direitto penale, Parte Generale, Decima Edizione).

Central Intelligence Agency (CIA). 2004. *World Factbook*. www.odei.gov/cia/publications/factbook/it.html.

Code of Penal Procedure, See: Official Gazette, Code of Penal Procedure (supplement), n. 254, October 29, 1930 and Official Gazette, Code of Penal Procedure.

Drugtext Information Services. 1995. *Italy*. www.drugtext.org (accessed October 3, 2003).

European Monitoring Centre for Drugs and Drug Addiction (EMCDDA). 2003. European Legal Database on Drugs. Country Profile: Italy. www.eldd.emcdda.eu.int/databases/eldd_country_profiles.cfm?country=fr (accessed October 24, 2003).

Fourth United Nations Survey of Crime Trends and Operations of Criminal Justice Systems. 1992. Crime Prevention and Criminal Justice Branch Centre for Social Development and Humanitarian Affairs, United Nations Office at Vienna; Statistical Office, United Nations, New York.

Istituto Nazionale di Statistics. ISTAT, Annuario Statisto o: Delilti denunciati all'Autorita giudiziaria dalle forze del l'ordine (Polizia di Stat o, carabinieri a Guardia di Finanza) per specie del delitto, anni 1986–1992.

Kerper, Hazel B. 1972. *Introduction to the Criminal Justice System*. Criminal Justice Series. St. Paul, Minn.: West Publishing Company.

Marongiu, Pietro, and Mario Biddau. n.d. *World Factbook of Criminal Justice Systems* U.S. Department of Justice, Bureau of Justice Statistics. www.ojp.usdoj.gov/bjs/pub/ascii/wfbcjita.txt. (accessed October 3, 2003.)

National Institute of Statistics. 1992. Fourth United Nation Survey of Crime Trends and Operations of Criminal Justice System. National Institute of Statistics, General Director's Secretary's Office. Rome, October 30, 1992. (Instituto Nazionale di Statistica, Segreteria del Direttore Generale).

National Institute of Statistics. *Yearbook of Statistics: Individuals Admitted to Prison, Years 1986–1992.* (Istituto Nazionale di Statistica (ISTAT), Annuario Statistico Italiano. Roma: Entrati negli istiuti penitenziari).

National Institute of Statistics. *Italian Yearbook of Statistics, 1991.* "Crimes Reported by the Police to the Judicial Authority According to the Type of Offense, Years 1987–1991." Rome.

United Nations Office on Drugs and Crime. 2003. *Global Illicit Drug Trends 2003.* www.unodc.org/unodc/en/global_illicit_drug_trends.html (accessed October 24, 2003).

13

Spain

Overview

SPAIN IS LOCATED IN SOUTHWESTERN EUROPE, encompassing a total area of 505,990 kilometers. It is bounded on the northeast by France; on the east by the Mediterranean Sea; on the West by Portugal and the Atlantic Ocean; and on the north by the Bay of Biscay. It has a population of approximately 39 million inhabitants. There is no official religion in Spain, although a large majority of Spanish citizens are Catholic. It has a government that consists of seventeen regional governments and a central government. The central government administers all the police functions and has responsibility for the penal system. Catalonia, however, has their own regional police and their own penal system. In addition, the Basque region also has their own police.

Similar to many other European countries, Spain has three branches of government—executive, legislative, and judicial. The legal system is called a European Continental legal system, requiring that behavior be defined as criminal and that the penal law assign a penalty to that behavior before it can be prosecuted. Spain's penal system originated during the Middle Ages with a newer, more moderate Penal Code developed in 1848. A more recent Penal Code was drafted in 1993 (Canivell 2003). The judicial system is adversarial in nature and all hearings are made public.

Spain's legal system distinguishes between serious (*delitos*) and less serious (*faltas*) offenses. Serious offenses are indictable and less serious offenses are nonindictable. Indictable offenses include offenses against state security, fakes and falsifications, offenses against the administration of justice, offenses against sanitation and health, behavior causing risk but not actual damage, offenses by public officers, offenses against individuals (which include the violent crimes such as homicide, aggravated assault and battery, and illegal abortions), sexual offenses, offenses against reputation (libel and slander), offenses against freedom and personal security, property offenses, and offenses committed recklessly and without intent. Drug offenses are included as indictable offenses under the category of offenses against sanitation and health.

The less serious, nonindictable offenses include public order offenses and minor property offenses (theft under US $200). The death penalty was abolished in 1978. Historically, Spain's past is very different from its European neighbors. Spain's ties to Latin America have influenced its patterns of drug use, particularly in that it has become a marketplace for Colombian cocaine. In addition, Spain's unrestrictive attitude toward immigration, coupled with its proximity to Northern Africa, makes it relatively easy to get drugs into the country. But, in 1990, Spain (and Italy) required visas for short-term visitors from North Africa.

Spain has acquired a reputation as Europe's most important drug center (Reeg 1992). During Spanish dictator General Franco's era in the 1960s and 1970s, the public attitude toward drugs was one of intolerance. Only those protesting their repressive state used drugs. But when Franco died in 1975, the public began to take full charge with their sense of freedom. At the same time, Spain was experiencing rapid economic development.

Drug Offenses and the Law

Spanish drug law remained weak until 1983's Criminal Drug Law. The old law (Article 344 of the 1944 Penal Code) had left great discretion to judges when sentencing drug offenders. The law did not distinguish among producing, transporting, possessing, selling, or trafficking. Progressive for its time, the 1983 Criminal Drug Law distinguished between "soft" and "hard" drugs by means of ranges of penalties. Traffickers convicted of trafficking soft drugs like cannabis, would only be sentenced for one to six months. But those convicted of trafficking in the hard drugs—heroin, cocaine, and amphetamines—could get a sentence from six months to six years. Possession of any illicit drug was removed from the list of punishable offenses except when associated with trafficking. To distinguish between possession for personal use and possession associated with trafficking the Supreme Court set that anything over 40 grams for cannabis and 1.5 grams for heroin was considered for the purpose of trafficking.

Another progressive feature of the 1983 law was that it specified crimes that were considered more dangerous than drug trafficking. These were: (1) distribution of drugs to person under eighteen years of age, (2) committing an offense in an educational, military, or penal institution, (3) trafficking in drugs as a member of a larger drug distribution organization and (4) trafficking in quantities of "notorious importance." Notorious importance was taken to be quantities over a certain amount.

Five years later, in 1988, Spain again reformed that law, believing that the 1983 revision had proven ineffective in combating drug use and trafficking. The distinction between hard and soft drugs remained in place, but the 1988 reform extended the punishable conduct included in the basic offense in the trafficking of drugs as well as creating a list of aggravated cases. Overall, the law brought an increase in penalties and gave new legal powers to combat the growing involvement of organized crime. For instance, for trafficking of soft drugs the penalty went from one to six months imprisonment to four months to four years with the new law. This harsher handling of drug trafficking also stemmed from the public's enlightenment about the corruption of politicians and law enforcement officials. As the public realized that government officials were using monies from the drug trade to supplement their income, the public began to demand harsher penalties overall for violations of the drug laws. However, there remained a leniency for lighter offenses in that probation was introduced as an alternative to incarceration for those cases that would have received under two years incarceration on a first offense.

With regard to sanctions, growing, processing, trafficking, promoting, and facilitating the consumption of "toxic, stupefacient or psychotropic drugs," as well as simple possession with the intent to engage in such behavior, can bring on a sentence of two to eight years in prison and a maximum fine of 100 million pesetas (US $666,000) if the drug can cause important harm to personal health. In all other cases, the prison sentence can be set between four months and four years and the fine can be a maximum of 50 million pesetas (US $333,000). Penalties become more severe for members of any type of organized crime—temporary or permanent—dedicated to the trafficking of drugs. Penalties are also more severe for health service personnel found guilty of supplying drugs to minors or to persons in drug treatment (Penal Code, Articles 344 and 344 bis). Personal use of drugs does not constitute an illegal activity if the individual's drug "stock" does not exceed what can be used in three days.

Drug trafficking is sanctioned by one to three years imprisonment, and a fine of twice the drug's value, if the narcotics do not cause severe health damage, under Article 368 of the Criminal Code (European Legal Database on Drugs 2003: 14). If the narcotics do cause significant health problems, then the sanction may be increased to three to nine years imprisonment, and a fine may be imposed of three times the value of the drug. Article 369.3 provides for more serious sentences for trafficking large quantities of drugs, such as increasing fines. The Criminal Court of the Supreme Tribunal focused on the need to distinguish large trafficking operations from situations involving smaller quantities (14).

According to the European Legal Database on Drugs (2003), "the aggravating circumstances of the notably large quantity is now applicable when the quantity involved exceeds 500 times the daily dose of a drug user" (14). Five hundred times the usual dosage for cocaine is 750 grams, for heroin 300 grams, and for hashish 2.5 kilograms (14).

Extent and Patterns of Use

In 1985 it was estimated that around 4 percent of Spain's population were regular cannabis users—1.2 to 1.8 million people. Estimates also put the number of heroin users at between 80,000 and 125,000, and 60,000 to 80,000 for cocaine users (Rodriguez and Anglin 1987). These estimates, if true, would be one of highest use rates in Europe. Looking at the mortality rates, 250 persons in 1988 died of heroin use.

During the 1980s, the prevalence of heroin abuse in Spain exceeded nearly every other country in Europe (UNODC 2003: 111). However, the rate of heroin abuse has receded dramatically over the past ten years (111). Between 1992 and 2000, deaths related to heroin use decreased by over 50 percent (112).

Table 13-1 shows an increase in cocaine abuse among the general population between 1995 and 2001.

During the 1990s, Spain, along with the Netherlands, had the highest number of cocaine seizures in Europe (UNODC 2003: 66). In 2000, Spain accounted for 21 percent of all cocaine seizures in Europe, and in 2001, this figure surpassed 50 percent (66). Together, Spain and the Netherlands reported 70 percent of all cocaine seizures that occurred in 2001 (66).

TABLE 13-1
Prevalence of Cocaine Abuse among
General Population (15–64 years), Spain

1995	1997	1999	2001
1.8%	1.5%	1.5%	2.6%

(*Source:* United Nations Office of Drugs and Crime, *Global Illicit Drug Trends 2003*, Chapter 1, "Trends: Consumption—Coca/Cocaine," 133.)

Law Enforcement

The arrest rate for drug trafficking in 1985 was 12.9 per 100,000. Two years later, it increased to 22.5 per 100,000. In 1991, 28,581 persons were detained for all drug offenses. This includes 13 percent who were non-Spanish (653 Moroccans, 565 Colombians, and 234 Italians).

Drug Policy

In December 1999, the Parliament approved the "Drug Strategy for 2000-2008" prepared by Spain's National Drug Plan Office (PNSD). This comprehensive plan confronts the drug phenomenon in three major areas. First, the plan allows the government to take more latitude in conducting undercover operations against drug traffickers. Law enforcement can authorize wiretaps and monitor communications without notification. The government can sell seized assets in advance of a conviction, and police informers would gain greater legal protections. Furthermore, it calls for the creation of a comprehensive registry of vehicles used by traffickers. The strategy also creates the "System for Assistance and Social Integration of Drug Addicts." This program implements several levels of treatment for drug addicts through state-run medical care. Finally, the strategy recognizes the need to cooperate with European neighbors to curb money laundering and chemical precursor exchange. Such cooperation means joint counternarcotics operations with Portugal, France, Italy, the United Kingdom, and Germany.

Domestically, Spanish city neighborhoods tend to gauge the battle against drugs based on the presence or absence of street-level drug pushers. Authorities estimate that drug-related activity accounts for 80 percent of urban crime. The PNSD continues to reach out to minority and youth audiences through media campaigns. Rehabilitation efforts are geared toward minors and implement methadone and needle exchange programs. There is also a campaign focusing on diseases called the Plan Nacional del Sida (National Plan on AIDS). Programs also offer alternative penalties to drug-addicted offenders, extending detoxification and rehabilitation methods to the prison system.

References

Canivell, Joaquin Martin. no date. World Factbook of Criminal Justice Systems: Spain. Washington, D.C.: U.S. Department of Justice: Bureau of Justice Statistics. http://www.ojp.usdoj.gov/bjs/pub/ascii//wfbcjspn.txt (accessed October 24, 2003).

European Legal Databases on Drugs. 2003. "The role of the quantity of the prosecution of drug offenses." www.eldd.emcdda.org/databases/eldd_comparative_analyses.cfm (accessed October 3, 2003).

"Memoria de la Fiscalia General del Estadoll (Report of the State General Attorney). Madrid, 1992. Ministry of Interior. Madrid.

Reeg, A. 1992. "Drugs and the Law in Post-Franco Spain," in *Drugs, Law and the State*, ed. by Harold H. Trayer and Mark S. Gaylord. New Brunswick, N.J.: Transaction Press.

Rodriquez, M. E., and M. D. Anglin. 1987. The Epidemology of Illicit Drug Use in Spain. United Nations Office on Drugs and Crime: Bulletin. www.unodc.org/unodc/en/bulletin/bulletin_1987-01-01_2_page 008.html (accessed January 14, 1999).

United Nations Office on Drugs and Crime. 2003. *Global Illicit Drug Trends 2003.* www.unodc.org/unodc/en/global_illicit_drug_trends.html (accessed October 24, 2003).

14

The Netherlands

Overview

THE NETHERLANDS, A HIGHLY DEVELOPED and affluent country of 16,318,199 (CIA 2004) people, borders the North Sea on the north and west, Germany on the east, and Belgium on the south. It is located strategically at the mouth of three major rivers, the Rhine, the Maas, and the Meuse and serves as an important gateway for cocaine, heroin, and hashish entering Europe. It is also a European producer of illicit amphetamines and other synthetic drugs. The majority of citizens are Dutch (96 percent), but have mixed religious affiliations— Roman Catholic 34 percent, Protestant 25 percent, Muslim 3 percent, other 2 percent, unaffiliated 36 percent.

The Kingdom of the Netherlands, as defined by the Constitution, includes the Netherlands, Aruba, and the Netherlands Antilles. The Netherlands is a constitutional and hereditary monarchy.

The Netherlands has a unitary governmental structure. Operation of the federal police, the Public Prosecutor's Office, and the correctional system all fall under the authority and control of the Ministry of Justice; the municipal police answer to the Ministry of Internal Affairs (Aronowitz n.d.). The application of laws and legal procedures is consistent across the country. The principal laws which guide the criminal justice system in the Netherlands are the Constitution, the Criminal or Penal Code, the Code of Criminal Procedure, and Special Acts. Furthermore, criminal law in the Netherlands is influenced by European Community law and European treaties. These treaties must be approved by Parliament, and duly published and incorporated into domestic law. When treaties are adopted by the Dutch Parliament they can be applied directly by Dutch courts (Hoyng and Schlingmann 1992).

Drug Offenses and the Law

The Penal Code of 1881 came into effect in 1886. It emphasized imprisonment as the principal disposition for serious, intentional criminal offenses. The Penal Code has been considerably amended since then to provide alternatives to incarceration as sentencing options. It includes amendments to change the system of sanctions by broadening the scope for imposing fines (1983). In 1984, the community service order was introduced as an alternative to imprisonment. Other reforms included introduction of suspended sentences (1986), and automatic release from prison after having served two thirds of a prison sentence longer than one year (1986). Even though the code's emphasis is on incarceration, sentences remain short and overall the Netherlands penal system was, and still is, characterized as a relatively lenient system (Tak 1993).

Among other central legislation affecting criminal justice are the Narcotic Drugs Act/Opium Act of 1928 (revised in 1976), the Traffic Act of 1935 (revised in 1951), the Economic Offences Act of 1950 (revised in 1976), and the Prison Act of 1951 (revised in 1974). The basis of criminal procedure is found in the Code of Judicial Procedure, which was enacted in 1921, and came into force in 1926 (Pease and Hukkila 1990).

The Opium Act was revised in 1976 and is the general dictate for drug offenses in the Netherlands. Drug trafficking is prohibited by law and includes the following offenses: importation, exportation, transportation, and the sale and production of drugs. Drugs are classified as either hard (heroin, cocaine, amphetamines, amphetamine oil, amphetamine tablets, methadone tablets, and LSD) or soft (hashish, hashish oil, and marijuana).

The criminal law of the Netherlands, like that of Germany, Denmark, and Austria, does not refer to use of drugs. However, possession of small quantities of hard drugs is a criminal offense and can be sanctioned by penal code. The sale and use of small amounts of soft drugs, usually under 30 grams, is tolerated in coffee houses throughout the Netherlands.

Drug traffickers of hard drugs who are not trafficking across borders are subject to up to eight years and/or a fine; those trafficking internationally can receive a maximum of twelve years. Maximum penalties for trafficking in soft drugs is two years and/or a fine, but increases to five years if a trafficker is part of an organized criminal group. Trafficking soft drugs internationally raises the maximum sentence to four years. Repeat offenders are subject to increased penalties.

Petty offences are classified as transgressions (e.g., traffic violations) and the police have the power to utilize a kind of civil agreement between the state agent (the police officer) and the offender. If the offender agrees to pay the financial penalty set by the police officer in accordance with a fixed tariff, this payment ends the case. The results of police investigation in other criminal matters are passed on to the prosecutor. More serious crimes are known as felonies, but sometimes referred to as crimes (as opposed to transgressions). Incarceration is reserved for the serious offenses, and drug offenses are considered serious.

Extent and Patterns of Use

Abraham, Kaal, and Cohen (2002) report findings from a national survey on drug use in the Netherlands. The survey, conducted by CEDRO, questioned 18,000 respondents about their use of drugs. The findings, shown in Table 14-1, indicate the prevalence of lifetime use of cannabis in the Netherlands increased from 15.6 percent in 1997 to 17 percent by 2001 (Abraham et al. 2001). Over the same time period, the use of cocaine increased from 2.1 to 2.9 percent. While the lifetime use of heroin increased from 0.3 in 1997 to 0.4 in 2001, the lifetime prevalence of opiate use decreased from 11.7 percent to 8.2 percent (see Table 14-1).

Table 14-2 shows the national prevalence of drug use in 1997 and 2001. Respondents reported whether they used various drugs within their lifetime, within the past year, and within the past month. Except for opiates, the rate of

TABLE 14-1
Drug Use among Respondents Ages 12 and Over, the Netherlands, 1997 and 2001

	Ever used		Used in the past year		Used in the past month	
	1997	2001	1997	2001	1997	2001
Cannabis	15.6	17.0	4.5	5.0	2.5	3.0
Cocaine	2.1	2.9	0.6	0.9	0.2	0.4
Heroin	0.3	0.4	0.1	0.1	0.0	0.1

Source: National Household Survey 1997 SAMHSA, Office of Applied Studies, Washington D.C.; M. Abraham, P. Cohen, M. De Winter: *Licit and Illicit Drug Use in the Netherlands, 1997* CEDRO/Mets&Schilt; *National Household Survey on Drug Abuse, 2001* SAMHSA, Office of Applied Studies, Washington D.C.; M. Abraham, H. Kaal, P. Cohen: *Licit and Illicit Drug Use in the Netherlands, 2001* CEDRO/Mets&Schilt.

lifetime use of all drugs increased from 1997 to 2001. The prevalence of use within the last year also increased for all drugs except opiates (the rate for heroin remained the same) and the rate of use within the last month increased for all drugs except opiates.

Nearly 75 percent of the country's hard-drug users, which ranges from 25,000 to 28,000, have come into contact with demand- and harm-reduction programs. From 1998 to 1999, according to the Dutch Addiction Care Information Foundation, the number of cocaine addicts who sought treatment increased by 23 percent, totaling 5,689 in 1999 (U.S. Department of State 2004). It is estimated that there are 320,000 users of cannabis.

Law Enforcement

Prevention efforts in the Netherlands bridge law enforcement and "health-education specialists" (International Child and Youth Care Network 2001). Drug policies are the responsibility of the Health Ministry and law enforcement efforts are carried out by the Ministry of Justice (U.S. Department of State 2004). There has been a significant decrease in the number of coffeeshops, seen by the decline from 1,200 coffeeshops in 1995 to 846 in 1999 (U.S. Department of State 2004). However, this has raised several concerns regarding other venues through which drugs might be sold, such as through street markets.

TABLE 14-2
National Drug Use Prevalence in the Netherlands,
1997 and 2001 (Weighted Percentages)

Drug	1997 Lifetime	2001 Lifetime	1997 Last Year	2001 Last Year	1997 Last Month	2001 Last Month
Cannabis	15.6	17.0	4.5	5.0	2.5	3.0
Cocaine	2.1	2.9	0.6	0.9	0.2	0.4
Ecstasy	1.9	2.9	0.7	1.2	0.3	0.5
Opiates all	11.7	8.2	4.2	2.6	1.0	1.0
Heroin	0.3	0.4	0.1	0.1	0.0	0.1
Other drugs*	4.1	4.9	1.2	1.8	0.5	0.8
No drugs**	5.2	5.3	10.6	11.1	17.8	18.2
Total sample 1997	21,959					
Total sample 2001	17,655					

*Other drugs are cocaine, amphetamines, ecstasy, hallucinogens, heroin.
**No drugs indicates none of the above drugs.
Source: CEDRO, Centrum voor drugsonderzoek. 2003. National Drug Use Prevalence in the Netherlands, 1997 and 2001 (weighted percentages), http://www.cedro-uva.org/stats/national.97.html.

Drug dealers may face jail time, which varies based on how long the person has been involved in dealing. Hemp growers face jail time and fines. Data in 1991 show that there were 4,261 drug offenses of which 3,580 were hard-drug offenses and 681 were soft-drug offenses at a rate of 24 per 100,000 population for hard-drug offenses and a rate of 5 per 100,000 population for soft-drug offenses (attempts included) (Department for Statistical Information and Policy Analysis, 1993). These were those offenses that violated the Opium Act. In 1991 there were 33,940 total admissions to prison, of which 32,391 (95.4 percent) were male and 1,549 (4.6 percent) were female. (Tak 1993: 52). The estimated yearly percentages for prison inmates for drug crimes by gender on September 30, 1991 was 20 percent for males and 40 percent for females. There is a higher percentage of women in prison for drug crimes than for property crimes (33 percent).

Drug Policy

In 1997, the Netherlands added measures to allow mayors of municipalities to close down premises when drug use or trafficking causes a public nuisance, and increased the scope of research into innovative drug programming by setting up evaluation teams to assess the medical prescription of heroin.

Drug abusers are generally treated within the rehabilitative/medical framework, and are not faced with stiff criminal justice sanctions. Prosecutors can order treatment as an alternative to court proceedings. The focal point of drug policy in the Netherlands is public health (Drug Policy Alliance 2003). The main components of the country's drug policy are listed by the Drug Policy Alliance as:

- the central aim is the prevention or alleviation of social and individual risks caused by drug use;
- there must be a rational relation between those risks and policy measures;
- a differentiation of policy measures must also take into account the risks of legal recreational and medical drugs;
- repressive measures against drug trafficking (other than trafficking of cannabis) are a priority; and
- the inadequacy of criminal law with respect to other aspects (i.e., apart from trafficking) of the drug problem is recognized.

The agencies involved in carrying out drug policy include "25 regional police forces and their Special Criminal Information Services; the National Police

Services Force; the National Criminal Intelligence Division (CRI) of the National Police Services Force, which coordinates efforts to counter drug trafficking; and customs authorities and the Customs Information Center" (U.S. Department of State 2004). Today, many policy directives are focused on soft drugs such as cannabis. National campaigns warning of the dangers of drug use and mandatory drug and alcohol education within schools are examples of preventive efforts.

References

Abraham, Manja D., Hendrien L. Kaal, and Peter D. A. Cohen. 2002. *Licit and Illicit Drug Use in the Netherlands 2001.* Amsterdam: CEDRO/Mets en Schilt. 169-226. www.cedro-uva.org/lib/abraham.npo01.06.html (accessed January 2, 2004).

Aronowitz, Alexis A. n.d. World Factbook of Criminal Justice Systems: The Netherlands. U.S. Department of Justice, Bureau of Justice Statistics. www.ojp.usdoj.gov/bjs/pub/ascii/wfbcjnet.txt. (accessed October 23, 2003).

CEDRO, Centrum voor drugsonderzoek. "Drug Use in the Population of 12 Years and Over in the USA and the Netherlands, 1997 and 2001." www.cedro-uva.org/stats/national.nlusa.html (accessed January 2, 2004).

CEDRO, Centrum voor drugsonderzoek. 2003. "National Drug Use Prevalence in the Netherlands, 1997 and 2001 (weighted percentages)." www.cedro-uva.org/stats/national.97.html (accessed January 2, 2004).

Central Intelligence Agency. 2004. *The World Factbook: The Netherlands.* Washington, D.C.: Central Intelligence Agency. www.cia.gov/cia/publications/factbook/geos/nl.html (accessed December 20, 2004).

Department for Statistical Information and Policy Analysis. 1993. Registered Crime in the Netherlands 1965–1991, SIBa, Ministry of Justice/CDWO, the Hague, the Netherlands.

Drug Policy Alliance. 2003. *Drug Policy around the World, The Netherlands.* www.lindesmith.org/global/drugpolicyby/westerneurop/thenetherlan/ (accessed January 2, 2004).

Hoyng, Willem, and Francine Schlingmann. 1992. "The Netherlands," *EC Legal Systems: An Introductory Guide.* Maurice Sheridan, and James Cameron (eds.), (London: Butterworth and Co., Ltd.), 1–42.

International Child and Youth Care Network. 2001. *Today 8 August 2001.* www.cyc-net.org/today/today010808.html (accessed January 2, 2004).

Leuw, Ed. 1991. "Drugs and Drug Policy in the Netherlands," *Dutch Penal Law and Policy: Notes on Criminological Research from the Research and Documentation Centre.* Ministry of Justice: The Hague, The Netherlands, November.

Opiumwet, VII 201–204 in Nederlandse Wetboeken - Suppl. 240 (November 1992); (The Opium Act of 1976; in the Dutch Penal Code - Supplement 240, November 1992; VII201204).

Pease, Ken, and Hukkila, Kristiina (eds.) 1990. "The Netherlands," *Criminal Justice Systems in Europe and North America*. Helsinki: Helsinki Institute for Crime Prevention and Control, Publication Series No. 17, 87–192.

U.S. Department of State. 2004. *Europe and Central Asia: Netherlands*. www.state.gov/g/inl/rls/nrcrpt/2000/892.htm (accessed January 2, 2004).

Tak, Peter J. P. 1993. *Criminal Justice Systems in Europe: The Netherlands, HEUNI* (European Institute for Crime Prevention and Control, affiliated with the United Nations), Deventer: Kluwer Law and Taxation Publishers.

Part V

EASTERN EUROPE

THIS SECTION OF THE BOOK describes the drug problem in Russia, Poland, Bulgaria, and the Slovak Republic. Between 1998 and 2002, problem drug use increased in Eastern Europe, although there is some indication that drug use is remaining stable in the Czeck Republic, Hungary, Slovakia and Slovenia.

In 2000 or 2001, the Russian Federation, Poland, Bulgaria, and the Slovak Republic reported increases in heroin abuse (UNODC 2003:120). While cocaine use is widespread in Western Europe, it is the fourth through sixth most common drug in Eastern Europe (131). It is even less common in the Russian Federation.

The UNODC (2003) reports that in 1991 in the Russian Federation there were 21.2 registered drug addicts per 100,000 inhabitants. The figure rose to 219.9 by 2001. There are approximately 2.5 to 3 million individuals who use drugs regularly or occasionally. The Russian Federation also has one of the highest injecting drug use (IDU)-related HIV rates in the world. The number is estimated at 319 per million in 2001.

Cannabis and opium-based products are the most common narcotics used in Poland.

Heroin is the drug of choice in Bulgaria. There are an estimated 20,000 to 30,000 heroin-dependent addicts in a country of 8.4 million.

Public opinion polls conducted in the 1990s in Slovakia reported that 63 percent of the respondents believe drug-dependent persons should be considered sick and should be treated, not punished.

15

Russia

Overview

RUSSIA CONSISTS OF TWENTY-ONE REPUBLICS, one autonomous region, ten autonomous areas, six territories, forty-nine regions, and two federal cities, Moscow and St. Petersburg. This amounts to eighty-nine members of the Russian Federation. This vertical structure is maintained by eighty-nine appointed presidential envoys.

Understanding the former Soviet Union's geography and culture is central to understanding the roots of the drug problem within Russia and the former Soviet republics. Known today as the Commonwealth of Independent States (CIS) the states have over 100 different ethnic groups located in primarily three geographic regions. Western and northern regions hold people of Slavic and European descent, Central Asian peoples live mainly in the south, and people of Mongolian and Chinese descent, the smallest group, live in the eastern region. Ethnic Russians make up over 25 million people spread throughout non-Russian republics of the former Soviet Union. This group's culture is linked closely to alcohol use, whereas those of Islamic heritage in the south, mainly shun alcohol use. The Mongolians and Chinese of the south are indifferent to alcohol but tolerate the cultivation and use of opium and hashish (Zvyagelsky 1990). The southern region, specifically Tajikistan, Turkmenistan, and Uzbekistan, produces high-quality opium and hashish, and easily transports the drugs to Moscow, St. Petersburg, and other big cities. The economic returns are enormous; a hectare of Uzbek opium brings in roughly twenty times the earnings of a hectare of cotton or a hectare of vegetables (Lee and MacDonald 1993).

In addition to the drugs produced in the Central Asian republics, the former Soviet-bloc countries are neighbors to the "Golden Crescent," a tract of land stretching across sections of Pakistan, Iran, and Afghanistan. The Golden Crescent is notorious for its cultivation of poppies and its efficient heroin refineries.

Before the dissolution of the Soviet Union, communist leaders believed that illegal drug abuse and trafficking was indigenous to capitalist societies, and that communist countries would not have to deal with the consequences of these problems. Because of this belief, the police, public health officials, and government authorities had little understanding and training to deal with drug abusers and the drug trade. Furthermore, there are very few studies available regarding drug use trends and patterns, and many officials still believe that anti-drug use education campaigns are counterproductive, in that ads will only serve to make youth curious about drugs.

Although alcohol remains Russia's main substance abuse problem, over the years, the illicit drug trade has begun to flourish and substance abuse is on the rise. During the 1990s, as borders became easier to penetrate with the fragmentation of the police infrastructure, drug traffickers were bringing in heroin from Turkey and Afghanistan, cocaine from the western countries and marijuana from Central Asia. The Central Asian republics produce large amounts of cannabis and opium and it has been estimated that over 80 percent of the illegal drugs consumed within the borders of the former Soviet Union have been grown and processed locally (U.S. General Accounting Office 1997). There is little stigma against heroin as the flood of Western movies bring in the lure of drugs among the educated youth. Increasing contact with the West not only has opened up opportunity for youth to experiment with drugs, but it has also accelerated the flow of information in the manufacture and supply of illicit drugs to Soviet criminal networks (Lee 1992).

Drug syndicates are growing more powerful as the value of the ruble has declined, and increasing demand for drugs has raised drug prices. The drug syndicate members have been successful in bribing the poorly paid law officers and military personnel and have become a huge threat as they acquire military weaponry and telecommunications equipment. Crime has flourished as economic instability and unemployment increases, creating an overall social malaise. The republics of the former Soviet Union have become major transshipment points, as drugs produced in South Central Asia and Central Asia are entering the world market. Lithuania and Latvia, because of their ports, have become particularly popular as transshipment pipelines (Davis 1994).

Drug Offenses and the Law

Russia's most important laws originate from the Criminal Code, the Criminal Procedure Code, the Criminal Punishment Execution Code, Law on the Justice System, Law on the Militia, and Law on the Status of Judges (Nikiforov n.d.). The sole source of criminal legislation is the Criminal Code. Crimes are classified into two categories: major offenses, such as rape, kidnapping, treason, espionage, crimes against the justice system, serious violent crimes, and murder; minor offenses such as offenses against property, and offenses against the public order. Drug offenses in the Criminal Code include (1) the unlawful production, transportation, storage, mailing or distribution of drugs; (2) stealing drugs; (3) inclination to consume drugs; (4) unlawful obtaining and storage of a small quantity of drugs; (5) cultivation of poppy or hemp; (6) organization of haunts for consumption of drugs. To comply with the 1961 Uniform International Convention on Drugs, Russia's Constant Committee for Drug Control of the Health Care Ministry of Russia established the list of over 400 illegal drugs including opium, morphine, hemp, heroin, and cocaine.

In Russia, drug use was decriminalized in 1991, but drug addiction continues to be regarded as a crime. Strict rules of evidence in many postcommunist countries require that offenders engaged in trafficking be caught when the act is taking place. Some countries do not have conspiracy statutes, making it almost impossible to punish known drug criminals. In addition, as of 1995, money laundering was not a crime in the CIS.

With the fall of the Soviet Union, the new republics have established separate police forces. The restructuring has exacerbated drug interdiction problems in the region due to crossborder hostilities.

Prior to 1998, Russian authorities were fairly liberal-minded with regard to the use of drugs (Smirnov 2001). Consumers of drugs were not criminally responsible. However, federal law became more severe after 1998, in which "every user automatically finds him(her)self liable to the Criminal Code." For example, possession of 0.1 gram or 1 kilogram of heroin are both punishable by seven to fifteen years imprisonment (see Part 4 of Article 228 of the Criminal Code). Russia's drug enforcement agency is the Directorate on Combating the Illicit Drug Trade (UBNON).

Extent and Patterns of Use

Historically, the Central Asian republics of the former Soviet Union used cannabis, opium, and psychotropic substances, but this use was of little concern to the ethnic Russian leaders. It wasn't until the Soviet occupancy of Afghanistan in 1979, which led to the mixing of cultures throughout the

Soviet Union, that drug use became more widespread. Alcohol had become more expensive as availability decreased. Hashish, heroin, and LSD became popular among soldiers as a means to relieve boredom and stress. Soviet soldiers returned home and continued using drugs. One study surveyed 3,000 reservists and found that 53 percent of the 1,000 respondents said they had used drugs, and over 25 percent had started while they were in the army (Shchadilova 1989).

Moscow's Narcological Hospital No. 17, the largest hospital for drug users in Russia sees roughly 20,000 patients a year, and 80 percent are heroin users (Landsberg 1999). Figures from the Central Statistical Administration, though not very recent, estimate that there were 5.5 million addicts in the countries of the former Soviet Union (M-E Files 1992) that comprised 280 million people. According to one study in the late 1980s, the drugs of choice were hashish (53.3. percent), koknar—a cheap drug made from ground poppy straw (29.4 percent), cheefir tea (13.5 percent), codeine tablets (13.5 percent), pomedol/demerol (13 percent), ephedrine (11.3 percent), and morphine (11.3 percent) (Albats, 1990). The same study found that 63 percent of those questioned became addicted before the age of nineteen and that 96 percent were residents of a city. Over 43 percent of the addicts bought their drugs from dealers, but roughly 33 percent manufactured their own. In Russia, the first widespread injecting drug was called "vint," which was produced in Leningrad between 1985 and 1986 (Smirnov 2001). By 1994, however, heroin was the drug of choice.

Drug popularity varies by region. In 2001, the Russian Federation was a major source of cannabis resin (UNODC 2003: 30). Although marijuana and hashish are generally the drugs of choice, this is more so in Russia, Kazakhstan, and Kyrgyzstan. Homemade derivatives of the poppy, such as koknar, are popular in Russia, Tajikistan, Turkmenistan, Ukraine, and Uzbekistan. Methamphetamines (ephedrine-based) are increasingly used in Slovakia, the Czech Republic, and the Baltic States (Lee and MacDonald 1993). Heroin is relatively uncommon, though injection drug use is thought to be on the increase in Russia and other parts of eastern Europe (Ruggiero and South 1995).

The UNODC (2003) reports that in 1991, there were 21.2 registered drug addicts per 100,000 inhabitants (121). This figure rose to 44.0 per 100,000 inhabitants in 1995, 109.9 in 1998, and 219.9 by 2001. In 1996, 38,843 children and teenagers were abusing drugs (121). By 2000, this figure had risen to 50,079. Paoli (2002) estimates that there were 155,971 registered drug users in state drug-treatment centers in 1995 (22). By 2000, this number had increased to 451,603 (22). According to the Russian Ministry of the Interior, there are approximately 2.5 to 3 million individuals who use drugs regularly or occasionally, an equivalent to 2.1 percent of Russia's total population (22). The number of users per 100,000 inhabitants who are seeking treatment has steadily increased from 3.9 in 1991 to 49.8 in 2000 (22) (this figure was reported by the Institute on Drug Addiction of the Russian Ministry of Health).

Of concern is the increase in HIV rates related to injection drug use. In 1996, there were only two reports of IDU related HIV cases (Smirnov 2001 from Drugtext Information Services). This number grew rapidly, reaching 15,000 out of a total of 25,842 people infected with HIV by 1999 (Smirnov 2001). Approximately 63 percent of HIV infections in 2000 could be attributed to the use of injection drugs (UNODC 2003: 122). According to the UNODC, "the Russian Federation also has one of the highest injecting drug use (IDU) related HIV rates in the world" (122). While 7 per million inhabitants reported being infected with HIV as a result of injection drug use in 1996, this figure rose to 319 per million in 2001 (122).

Law Enforcement

The Ministry of Internal Affairs compiles annual statistics on crimes based on police reports. In 1993, 2,799,614 crimes were reported and 53,200 of them were drug crimes. In 1995, there were 79,819 reported drug offenses, a figure that increased to 184,832 in 1997 and to 216,364 by 1999 (Paoli 1999: 32). However, overall, there is an absence of accurate statistics regarding rates of drug use. Most Soviet sociological and demographic data have always been filtered through the Communist Party and rendered scientifically invalid (Davis 1994). Through the mid 1990s, the Soviets had one method for collecting statistics—the Registry. The system was maintained by the Ministry of Internal Affairs. The Registry includes individuals who came in contact with the police through their political views, criminal behavior, or psychological problems.

Drug Policy

With the surge in drug use and drug trafficking during the last decade, Russia has begun to address the issues by bringing together experts from other countries and from within CIS itself. The Directorate on Combating the Illicit Drug Trade (UBNON) is the main drug law enforcement agency (Smirnov 2001). May 1999 saw the gathering of chief drug specialists of the Russian Federation's public health organizations to discuss the issues of drug abuse and exchange new results from studies in prevention, treatment, and rehabilitation. Discussions also included proposals for changing and improving legislation throughout Russia and CIS states (ITAR-TASS 1999a).

Also in May 1999, Prime Minister Sergei Stepashin signed a government decision to create an extra-budgetary fund to counter substance abuse and illegal drug trafficking. The fund will help law enforcement and other government agencies fight drug trafficking and also fund programs to combat addiction (ITAR-TASS 1999b).

Recent attempts to legalize drugs have been met with opposition, as well as initiatives to combat drugs by waging a war. Lev Levinson, head of New Drug Policy, a nongovernmental organization, attempted to soften legislation on drugs and proposed an amendment to the Administrative Code. While his amendment did not pass, it only needed 25 additional votes to pass (it received 200 votes). The Director of the Center for Research on Extralegal Economic Systems in Moscow was another proponent of reducing the severity of drug laws. His position advocates the legalization of all drugs. (Smirnov 2001.)

References

Albats, Y. 1990. "Narcotics, Narcomania, Narcobusiness." *Moscow News* 24:15.

Davis, Robert B. 1994. "Drug and Alcohol Use in the Former Soviet Union: Selected Factors and Future Considerations," *The International Journal of the Addictions* 29(3): 303–323.

ITAR-TASS. 1999a. "Drug Addiction Russia's Main Enemy Say Specialists." www.mapinc.org/drugnews/v99.n556.aO2.html (accessed on May 25, 1999).

ITAR-TASS. 1999b. "Government Sets Up Federal Extra-Budgetary Drug Control Fund," www.mapinc.org/ drugnews/v99.n556.a02.html (accessed on May 25, 1999).

Landsberg, Mitchell. 1999. "Drugs Snare Young," *The Orange County Register* [June 9,1999]. www.mapinc.org/drugnews/v99.n6l3.aO2.html (accessed on June 10, 1999).

Lee, R. 1992. "Dynamics of the Soviet Illicit Drug Market." *Crime, Law and Social Change* 17(3):177–234.

Lee, Rensselaer W., and Scott B. MacDonald. 1993. "Drugs in the East," *Foreign Policy* 90: 89–107.

Nikiforov, Ilya V. n.d. *World Factbook of Criminal Justice Systems.* Washington, D.C.: U.S. Department of Justice, Bureau of Justice Statistics. www.ojp.usdoj .gov/bjs/pub/ascii/wfbcjrus.txt. (accessed October 3, 2003).

Paoli, Letizia. 2002. "The Development of an Illegal Market." *British Journal of Criminology* 36: 21–39.

Ruggiero, Vincenzo, and Nigel South. 1995. *Eurodrugs: Drug Use, Markets and Trafficking in Europe.* London: UCL Press Limited.

Shchadilova, K. 1989. "Drug Addiction from the Viewpoint of a Sociologist, Physician, Lawyer, and Journalist." *Sotsiologicheskiye Issledovaniya* 2: 3–51. As reported in Davis, 1994.

Smirnov, Alexander. 2001. "Drugs and HIV Infection in The Russian Federation." Prepared for "Harm Reduction Initiative–RF," MSF-H, Moscow, March–April 2001. www.drugtext.org/count/Russia_drugtext_ENG.htm (accessed on October 3, 2003).

United Nations Office on Drugs and Crime. 2003. *Global Illicit Drug Trends 2003,* www.unodc.org/unodc/en/global_illicit_drug_trends.html (accessed October 24, 2003).

U.S. General Accounting Office. 1997. U.S. Heroin Control Efforts in Southwest Asia and the Former Soviet Union. Briefing Report to the Chairman, Caucus on International Narcotics Control, U.S. Senate. Washington, D.C.: U.S. General Accounting Office.

Zvyagelsky, R. 1990. "Needle in the Heart." *Soviet Soldier* 2: 70–73.

16

Poland

Overview

POLAND IS LOCATED IN CENTRAL EUROPE, east of Germany, and west of the Russian Republic. The population is 38,622,660 (July 2003 est.). The ethnic groups in Poland are Polish (97.6 percent), German (1.3 percent), Ukrainian (0.6 percent), and Belarusian (0.5 percent) (1990 est.). The religions are Roman Catholic (95 percent), Eastern Orthodox, Protestant, and other (5 percent). The national language is Polish.

In 1918, Poland won its independence from a 1775 agreement between Russia, Prussia, and Austria that "partitioned" Poland (Adamski n.d.). During World War II, it was taken over by Germany and the Soviet Union. In 1999, Poland became a member of NATO and to joined the European Union in 2004.

Since 1989, Poland has been transitioning from a Communist system toward a democracy. Its government is now a parliamentary democracy, which divides power between the legislature, executive, and judicial branches. The Parliament, containing two houses—the Sejm and Senate—forms national laws, and its members are elected by citizens of Poland who are age eighteen years or older. There are forty-nine administrative regions, or voivodships, in Poland. The central government appoints an individual to govern each region (Adamski n.d.).

The Public Prosecution Office is led by the Minister of Justice, who also "exercises the powers of Attorney General" (Adamski n.d.). The criminal justice system is comprised of four levels of courts: regional, district, appeals, and the Supreme Court. Prosecutable offenses originate from public accusations, from victims, and from private accusations. Sentences are determined by "Professional judges and lay assessors [who] together deliberate and vote on the penalty to be imposed. . . . The law requires the judge and other members of the panel to rely on three factors during sentencing: 1) evidence and its evaluation, 2) the principles of science, and 3) personal experience (Adamski n.d.).

Penal legislation is a composite of the Penal Code, the Code of Criminal Procedure, and the Code for the Execution of Penalties (Adamski n.d.). There are three groups by which offenders are classified: felonies, misdemeanors, and transgressions. Felonies include violent crimes, while misdemeanors include crimes such as unintentional homicide, incest, and fraud. Transgressions are violations of administrative regulations and other minor offenses.

Sentencing is based on the discretion of the court, although the Penal Code contains suggestions as to what sentence should be imposed. The three recommendations rely on three different end goals: just deserts, general deterrence, and individual prevention. Felony offenders can receive anywhere from three years in prison to the death penalty. Misdemeanors are sanctioned by fines and incarceration.

Poland is not a major drug producing or drug transit country. However, Poland's open borders and location as a crossroads country between Asia and Western Europe have opened it up to the exploitation of cartels and mafias. Narcotics activity in Poland is dominated by organized crime groups that work with international cartels to produce and transport narcotics. While corruption in law enforcement brought about by the drug trade is not highly publicized, anecdotal evidence suggests that corruption is a problem particularly amongst the low-level officers and border guards.

Drug Offenses and the Law

The most characteristic feature of drug abuse in Poland in the last few decades was a widespread use of opiates prepared by individuals in their homes. The opiates come from "poppy straws" which are obtained from the poppies that are legitimately cultivated for their seeds. In 1985, the Law on Prevention of Drug Abuse expanded penalties for illicit production and trafficking of drugs. But, the law did not criminalize personal use and possession. Those engaged in trading narcotics or psychotropic drugs could be sentenced up to ten years in prison, while more serious crimes, such as exporting drugs, could lead to a fifteen-year prison term. Under Article 26, Section 1 of the Act, prison sentences or fines could be handed down as punishment for cultivating poppy or cannabis. Manufacturing drugs could lead to three years in prison. According to Adamski (n.d.), "the Law of 1985 does not envisage criminal sanctions for the use and possession of drugs, but emphasizes a prophylactic, socio-medical orientation to address the situation."

This legal arrangement changed in 1997. The Law of 1997 Counteracting Drug Addiction made narcotics possession punishable by law. Chapter 6 of the law details an extensive system for calculating jail time under various circumstances (e.g., producing drugs, trafficking drugs, distributing drugs, urging others to use drugs, etc.). Article 48 explains the punishments for possession, ranging from a maximum of five years for possession of a "considerable quantity" to no penalty for possession of "diminutive quantities for their own use." In 2000, the law was amended to add more restrictive provisions on possession of small quantities and to strengthen the role of demand reduction.

Poland's desire to join the EU has prompted her to sign and ratify all three UN drug control conventions, which work hand-in-hand with the EU drug strategy. Furthermore, Poland signed the 1990 Council of Europe Convention on Laundering, Search, Seizure and Confiscation of the Proceeds of Crime.

Extent and Patterns of Use

Cannabis and opium-based products are the most common narcotics used in Poland. Although Poland is a hub for high-grade amphetamine production, cocaine use does not appear to be problematic. In 1989, there were 15,382 registered drug users (Drugtext Information Services 1995). In 1991, outpatient units treated 6,000 users and hospitals and rehabilitation centers treated 3,000 users. In 1995, it was estimated that there were 300,000 injection drug users in Poland. However, in 2001, Poland reported an increase in the consumption of cocaine (UNODC 2003: 134). Poland's Ministry of Health and Social Welfare estimates that approximately 47,000 people are addicted to drugs in Poland. Nongovernmental sources report figures that are much higher. Authorities at the National Police report an increasing trend of drug-related crimes committed by juveniles, and official estimates note that some 30 percent of minors have had some contact with drugs.

Drug-related HIV infections were first reported in 1988 (Drug Information Services 1995). It is estimated that anywhere from 75 to 85 percent of users are HIV positive, suggesting that "in Poland drug users comprise the main risk group for HIVAIDS)" (Drugtext Information Services 1995). Needle exchange programs are present in Poland, and in 1995 there were sixty-seven outpatient detoxification treatment clinics.

Law Enforcement

In 1992, 222 offenders were sentenced for manufacturing drugs, whereas only 115 were sentenced in 1990 for manufacturing drugs (Adamski n.d.). Six hundred eighty-five offenders were sentenced for cultivating poppy in 1992, whereas only 115 were sentenced in 1990 for the same offense (Adamski n.d.).

While recent years have seen a decrease in the production and consumption of low-grade heroin, illicit cultivation of poppy straw and cannabis remains a problem. Cultivation of low-morphine poppies is legal as long as growers obtain proper license. Polish police conduct annual sweeps to eradicate illegal cultivation across the country.

Drug Policy

Poland has made some substantial advances in the battle against narcotics. Currently, Poland does not have an inter-ministerial coordination body for counteracting the elements of the narcotics market. The Central Narcotics Bureau of the Polish National Police investigate narcotics cases. A Council on Counteracting Drug Abuse, which includes representatives from the Central Narcotics Bureau, the Ministry of Health, and various non-governmental organizations, was implemented in 2001.

At the end of 1999, the Polish government adopted a national plan for counteracting drug addiction. The program listed eight objectives. The objectives are designed to increase demand-reduction efforts, while taking measures to reduce narcotics trafficking. Demand-reduction involves preventative education for youth populations, rehabilitation and reintegration of drug addicts into society, and reducing the health consequences of drug abuse. The plan also looks to a national coordinating body that can orchestrate its efforts with the international community.

References

Adamski, Andrzej. No date. World Factbook of Criminal Justice Systems: Poland. U.S. Department of Justice, Bureau of Justice Statistics. www.ojp.usdoj.gov/bjs/pub/ascii/wfbcjpol.txt (accessed on October 25, 2003).

Central Intelligence Agency. 2003. Worldfact Book of Criminal Justice Systems: Poland. www.odci.gov/cia/publications/factbook/geos/pl.html (accessed October 24, 2003).

Drugtext Information Services. 1995. www.drugtext.org.

United Nations Office on Drugs and Crime. 2003. *Global Illicit Drug Trends 2003.* www.unodc.org/unodc/en/global_illicit_drug_trends.html (accessed October 24, 2003).

17

Bulgaria

Overview

BULGARIA IS LOCATED BETWEEN Romania and Turkey and has a population of 7.5 million. While 83.9 percent of the population was Bulgarian in 2001, other ethnic groups include Turk, Roma, Macedonian, Armenian, Tatar, and Circassian. The majority of Bulgarians are Eastern Orthodox (86 percent) and the rest are Muslim (12.7 percent). Bulgaria first established independence in 1908. It wasn't until September 9, 1944 that Bulgaria fell under Communist rule. The Dimitrov Constitution, which was modeled after the Constitution of the U.S.S.R., was later adopted on December 4, 1947. Eastern Europe underwent many changes with the collapse of communism during the 1980s. In 1989, Bulgaria's Todor Zhivkov was removed from power. In 1990, constitutional clauses that established Communist Party power were removed by the National Assembly. Bulgaria's new Constitution was adopted on July 12, 1991 (CIA 2004).

Bulgaria's legal system was influenced by the Soviets and is based on a system of civil law. Bulgaria also falls under the jurisdiction of the International Court of Justice (CIA 2004). Today's criminal justice system stemmed from the 1896 Penal Code, which was based on the Russian Draft Penal Code and the Hungarian Penal Code. After World War II, Bulgaria underwent many social and political changes and adopted a socialist form of legislation that defined new criminal offenses.

In 1968, a new penal code was introduced; it was based on the principles of legal institutions of classical Western European penal law. Since 1968, it has been amended to make it more compatible with international law and to promote a more flexible crime policy (Bojadjieva n.d.).

In the mid-1990s a new Code of Criminal Procedure was created that was consistent with the new Constitution of 1991 and the organization of the Judiciary Act (Book of Crime in Bulgaria 1993; Penal Code 1896, 1951, 1956, 1968).

Bulgaria defines crime as an act that is dangerous to society and is punishable by the law. The Penal Code distinguish three types of crime: severe crimes, punishable by more than five years of imprisonment or by capital punishment; particularly severe crimes, those in which the criminal act or the perpetrator has demonstrated an exclusively high degree of social danger; and petty crimes, crimes with insignificant harmful consequences. The National Institute of Statistics, which compiles information on criminal case activity in the courts, has two main classification schemes for crime: crimes of the general type (have a high level of social danger) and crimes of the private type, relatively less serious, such as those involving mild injury, injury caused to a close relative, insult, or libel. According to sections of the Special Part of the Penal Code, crimes are also classified as crimes against the Republic (for instance, high treason, betrayal, spying, diversion, and subversion), crimes against persons (for instance, murder and injuries), sexual offenses, crimes against marriage, family and youth, property crimes (theft, robbery, embezzlement), economic crimes, crimes against the functioning of state agencies and public bodies (malfeasance in office, corruption), false documenting, hooliganism, and crimes of general danger which includes drug-related offenses. Police statistics recognize two types of crime, street crimes versus the more white collar, economic crimes like embezzlement, malfeasance in office, corruption, and false documentation.

Turning now to drug use and abuse, heroin addiction is Bulgaria's major problem. Out of a population of 8.4 million there are an estimated 20,000 to 30,000 heroin-dependent addicts. Cocaine is generally too expensive for the general population, but marijuana use has become a growing problem.

Bulgaria is situated along the Balkan route through which drugs are regularly transported from Turkey to Bulgaria to Serbia. Heroin from southwest Asia and cannabis from southeast Asia flow through Bulgaria to Western Europe.

Drug Offenses and the Law

Bulgaria's Penal Code defines drug-related offenses to include the preparing, receiving (in any form), possessing, or trafficking of drugs; sowing and cultivating plants with the aim of producing drug substances without permission, and abetting a person to use drugs.

The Penal Code specifies a maximum of fifteen years of imprisonment for illicit trafficking of drugs across borders. The code also permits the seizure of assets of convicted offenders. Under Paragraph 3 of articles 354a, "punishment shall not be imposed on a person dependent on narcotic drugs or analogues thereof, provided the quantity such person acquires, stores, keeps or carries, is such that reveals the intention of personal use" (EMCDDA 2003). The code (see Article 321) also provides for punishment for those engaging in organized crime. Leaders of organized crime involved with narcotics may receive five to fifteen years imprisonment and participants serve three to ten years incarceration.

Extent and Patterns of Use

No statistical information regarding drug use and abuse trends was available, prior to 1989. In 1989 The National Information Center was established within the National Service for Combating Organized Crime (NSCOC) to collect, prepare, and exchange drug indicator information. It is estimated that 1,276 drug users were registered in 1989, most of whom abused hashish or medicines (Drugtext Information Services 1995).

Experts claim that the drug abuse problem in Bulgaria, although small, is growing. By the end of the 1980s there were networks of drug dealers and Bulgarian criminal organizations began to multiply. By the early 1990s, reports of cannabis and ecstasy use increased, especially among Bulgarian youth.

Demand for cocaine has increased, but it is mainly used by the wealthy because the price remains high. In 2001, Bulgaria reported an increase in the consumption of cocaine (UNODC 2003: 134).

In 1996, 449 persons requested treatment from programs that are a part of the National Center for Addictions. Of these persons, the mean age at first drug use was 20.3. Ninety-two percent were heroin users, and 90 percent of the clients reported they used their primary drug everyday.

A school survey of 1,111 thirteen to eighteen year olds was completed in 1997 in the city of Sofia. The results are shown in Table 17-2 (Yankova et al. 1998).

TABLE 17-1 1999 Drugs Seized in Bulgaria	
Heroin	281 kg
Opium	6.4
Cocaine	24.5
Marijuana	232

TABLE 17-2
Results of School Survey, Sofia, Bulgaria, 1997

Drugs	11–18 Year Olds, Lifetime Prevalence		
	Males	*Females*	*Total*
Any illegal drugs	11.6	15.7	13.9
Cannabis	9.2	11.3	10.3
Opiates (total)	1.9	1.5	1.8
Heroin	0.6	0.5	0.6
Cocaine/Crack	0.2	0.7	0.5
Amphetamines	1.5	0.8	1.1
Hallucinogens	0.4	2.5	1.6

Source: Yankova et al. 1998

Law Enforcement

Very few citizens have been arrested and prosecuted for drug crimes. In 1996, 161 persons were defendants for offenses against the drug laws. Forty-one people were convicted and sentenced; of these eighteen were sentenced to prison, eighteen received probation, and five only received a fine. Of those sentenced to prison, five persons were sentenced to a period between three and ten years and the remainder were sentenced for a period under three years. Table 17.3 shows the most recent statistics for arrests for drug use and trafficking.

The data are assembled by the Central Statistical Agency from other law enforcement organizations including courts, the office of public prosecutor, comradely courts, and committees against antisocial conduct of juvenile offenders and minors. The data are analyzed annually by the Criminological Research Council at the Chief Prosecutor's Office and published in the yearbook "Crimes and Convicted Persons."

TABLE 17-3
Arrests for Drug Use and Trafficking, Bulgaria, 1995–1997

		1995	*1996*	*1997*
Cannabis	Use	11	28	45
	Traffic	52	30	36
	Total	63	58	81
Heroin	Use	10	50	72
	Traffic	21	33	30
	Total	31	83	102
Cocaine	Use	8	6	3
	Traffic	3	9	5
	Total	11	15	8

Source: Yankova et al. 1998

Drug Policy

Recent drug policy in Bulgaria is based on the National Drug Demand Reduction Strategy (1996–1999) and a National Program for Prevention. The policies were aimed at bringing Bulgaria into close compliance with the 1988 UN Convention and the Global Program of Action adopted by the 17th Special Session of the UN General Assembly (New York 1990). In 1998, a bill was introduced that allowed for a special budget dedicated to the country's anti-drug strategy.

Historically, demand reduction programs have not been a high priority for Bulgaria. Drug treatment/prevention programs are centered primarily in the large cities of Sofia, Varna and Burgas. The National Drug Prevention Plan, which has been approved by the Ministries of Health and Education, focuses primarily on the schools. But the National Drug Demand Reduction Strategy has broader more comprehensive goals. According to the U.S. Department of State's recent report on international drug control, Bulgaria has been assisted in drug treatment training and demand reduction programs by the United States, Italy, and the UNDCP.

Bulgaria is part of the PHARE Multi-Country Programme for the Fight Against Drugs whose overall aim is to support the partner countries in the development of a comprehensive policy approach toward drugs, and to promote cooperation at the sub regional level and with the EU and its member states (Yankova et al. 1998).

References

Bojadjieva, Julija. no date. *World Factbook of Criminal Justice Systems.* U.S. Department of Justice, Bureau of Justice Statistics. www.ojp.usdoj.gov/bjs/pub/ascii/wfbcjbul.txt (accessed October 3, 2003).

Book of Crime in Bulgaria. 1993. Sofia: University Press.

Central Intelligence Agency. 2004. T*he World Factbook: Bulgaria.* Washington, D.C.: Central Intelligence Agency. www.cia.gov/cia/publications/factbook/geos/bu.html (accessed May 10, 2004).

Drugtext Information Services, Country Pages. 1995. *Bulgaria.* http://www.drugtext.org (accessed October 3, 2003).

European Monitoring Centre for Drugs and Drug Addiction (EMCDDA). 2003. European Legal Database on Drugs. Country Profile: Bulgaria, www.eldd.emcdda.eu.int/databases/eldd_country_profiles.cfm?country=BG (accessed October 24, 2003).

Police Department in the Republic of Bulgaria. (1993). 1992 Annual Bulletin of Crimes. Sofia, Bulgaria: Police Department.

United Nations Office on Drugs and Crime. 2003. *Global Illicit Drug Trends 2003*, http://www.unodc.org/unodc/en/global_illicit_drug_trends.html (accessed October 24, 2003).

U.S. Department of State. 1996. International Narcotics Control Strategy Report, March 1997, United States Department of State, Bureau for International Narcotics and Law Enforcement Affairs.

Yankova, Tatiana, Vassilev Gueorgui, Momtchil Vassilev, Ivanka Galova, and Rossitsa Ivanova. 1998. *Bulgarian National Report: Phare Project on Drug Information Systems, Final Phase*. http://www.fad.phare.org/dis/misc/natrep.html (accessed July 23, 1999).

18

Slovak Republic

Overview

THE SLOVAK REPUBLIC, WITH A POPULATION of 5.4 million people, is predominantly Roman Catholic. Slovak is the official language in the Slovak Republic, but Hungarian is also spoken. The country is predominantly Slovakian, but other ethnic groups include Hungarian, Roma, Czeck, Moravian, Silesian, Ruthenian, Ukrainian, German, and Polish.

Slovakia drafted a new Constitution in the early 1990s based on the principles of democracy. With the onset of new principles, hundreds of new laws were drafted, many of which affected the criminal justice system and legislation pertaining to illicit substances.

Like other post-socialist countries, the Slovak Republic only began to recognize drug problems after 1991. Bratislava, the capital of Slovakia, has highly developed chemical and pharmaceutical industries, and is located near the Austrian and Hungarian borders, making the country a prime location for producing and distributing drugs. Heroin from Turkey stops in Slovakia often headed to Austria, Germany, Spain, Great Britain, and the Scandanavian countries. These factors coupled with the influence of things Western, may have contributed to the rise in substance abuse. Longitudinal surveys indicate that more youth are experimenting with drugs and more individuals overall are using harder drugs (Nociar 1998). Prior to 1995 the problems had been mainly localized to Bratislava, but drug use is now spreading across the country—in 1994 only 16 percent of heroin addicts were from outside Bratislava, but this percentage increased to 40 percent in 1996.

Drug Offenses and the Law

There are two categories of "delinquencies" in the Slovak legal system: delicts and penal actions. The former are defined as illegal actions of persons who are of a lesser danger to society. Delicts include various standards such as the Delict law (Act No. 372/1990 of Code), Customs Law (Act No. 618/1992 of Code), Forest law (Act No. 100/1977 of Code), and the Foreign Bills Law (Act No. 528/1990 of code). Penal actions are actions which are dangerous to society. They include very serious crimes, such as terrorism, military treason, murder, and genocide.

The term "drug" is not used in the Penal Code, but instead, the code refers to psychotropic or illicit substances as "habit-forming substances." Habit-forming substances include alcohol, "stupefying" substances, psychotropic drugs, and other substances which harm the mind, the social behavior, or the distinguishing and self-controlling abilities of humans. Crimes designated as drug delicts include unlawful production and possession of stupefying and psychotropic substances and poisons. (Penal Code, Section 87,188). Drug use itself is not a crime. But it is unlawful for persons to produce, import, or export these substances. The Act Against Organized Crime (October 1994) made it unlawful to possess any amount of drugs. Penalties increase if defendants are part of an organized group, when monetary gain is high, if serious injury or death is involved, and if the offense is committed with persons younger than eighteen years of age with high monetary gains (more than 500.OOOSK). Incarceration can range from one to fifteen years. Individuals can be arrested for seducing other person(s) to use habit-forming substances other than alcohol, or to promote the spread of such usage. If convicted, the maximum sentence is one year. But if this crime is committed with youth—persons under the age of eighteen—a maximum of three years in prison can be imposed.

A loophole in the law allows individuals to cultivate marijuana for botanical, horticultural, or aesthetic purposes. Marijuana seeds can be sold in local markets (Lee and MacDonald 1993).

In 1999, new legislation was passed controlling precursor chemicals, and recodification of the Criminal Code was under preparation in 2000. In 1997, the government enacted the Law on the Anti-Drug Fund which allows for the use of financial resources for antidrug programs.

The Slovak Republic is party to the 1961 Single Convention on Narcotic Drugs, as amended by the 1972 Protocal; to the 1971 Convention on Psychotropic Substances; and to the 1988 Convention against Illicit Traffic in Narcotic Drugs and Psychotropic Substances (Nociar 1998).

Extent and Patterns of Use

Slovakia is part of the Phare Program for the Fight against Drugs, a network of organizations that work together as a program to gather and disseminate drug-related data.

Prior to the 1990s there were some signs of drug problems in the Slovak part of former Czechoslovakia, but it is only in recent years that these signs have grown. Hospitals saw the first cases of heroin abuse in 1992 (56 addicts treated) and by 1994, the growth in cases was quite large—up to 1654 (Nociar 1998).

Public opinion surveys were introduced in 1994 by the Institute for Public Opinion Research, part of the Statistical Office of the Slovak Republic. Surveys have also been developed and administered by two nongovernment organizations. The Tobacco-Drugs-Alcohol (TDA) Surveys were administered in Bratislava and three regions of Slovakia on a sample of over 11,000 pupils in 1994 and 1995 (see Nociar 1998). A similar survey known as ESPAD, was administered in 1996. Though a general trend may be established by combining both survey results, they generally are not statistically valid. In 1994, 12.2 percent of the sample said they had smoked marijuana at least once in their lifetime; the percentage was 22.8 in 1995 (TDA study) and 26.3 in 1996 (ESPAD survey). Table 18-1 shows the thirty-day, twelve-month, and lifetime prevalence for drug use for a general Slovakian sample, and a youth sample.

TABLE 18-1
Use of Drugs—Slovakia

SAMPLE: ALL SLOVAKIA	30 Days	12 Months	Lifetime
Cannabis/hashish	1.20	1.66	2.56
Solvents/inhalants	0.15	10.15	2.63
Cocaine/crack	0.23	0.23	0.30
Amphetamines/ecstasy	0	0.38	0.23
LSD/ hallucinogens	0.15	0.30	0.68
Heroin	0.30	0.30	0.30
Medical drugs	0.53	0.75	1.80

SAMPLE: YOUTH OF SLOVAKIA	30 Days	12 Months	Lifetime
Cannabis/hashish	4. 5	2.78	4.98
Solvents/inhalants	0.60	0.69	3.94
Cocaine/crack	0.12	0.23	0.35
Amphetamines/ecstasy	0.12	0.35	0.46
LSD/ hallucinogens	0.12	0.35	0.58
Heroin	0.35	0.35	0.81
Medical drugs	1.16	1.39	2.55

Source: Statistical Office of the Slovak Republic Institute for Research Opinion, 1996.

According to data from the Institute for Health Information and Statistics, the methods for drug use are as follows (1997 data): injecting—63.3 percent; smoking—6.9 percent; sniffing—10.4 percent, and eating/drinking—8.8 percent.

Summary data on persons treated are extracted from the annual reports of The Institute of Health Information and Statistics of the Slovak Republic. Data are centralized via paper forms filled out and sent monthly by all health-care institutions. The dominant drug for the last years has become heroin—the reason the selected numbers deal mostly with heroin dependence.

A large problem in Bratislava and elsewhere in the Slovak Republic is that the mean age for drug use is very low—slightly over twenty years for those treated for drug addiction in the period from 1994 to 1997. In a comparison of mean age of persons treated for drug with five other Western and Eastern European cities, Bratislava had the lowest mean age (21.7) followed by Ljubljana (24.5), Gdansk (25.9), Athens (27.5), Rome (31.2), and Amsterdam (31.8) (Nociar 1998b). With the exception of youth, there were no other categories or subgroups of drug users (e.g., minorities, the poor). This may be because a study of hard-to-reach populations has not yet been completed (but is under way).

Trends in drug usage over recent years include a growth in lifetime use of marijuana among sixteen year olds in Bratislava. Amphetamine use is also on the increase, along with ecstasy. In addition, Slovak society is shifting away from solvents and hypnotics, toward heroin. Public opinion data revealed that the percentage of the respondents in the Slovak Republic who view drug dependency as a danger to society is increasing (see Nociar 1998a). They feel that the most substantial danger is connected with the growth of criminality and the spread of HIV/AIDS. The medical view predominates among attitudes with 63 percent of Slovak's polled believing that drug-dependent persons should be considered sick, and should be treated, not punished and 37 percent are in favor of free exchange of needles to addicts. The percentage in favor is higher for youth: 48 percent of the Slovakia youth sample and 50 percent of Bratislava youth sample.

Statistics on the number of drug-related deaths exist, but are not regarded as scientifically valid. For some numbers from the Ministry of Interior's National Drug Service, see Table 18-3.

Law Enforcement

The number of persons prosecuted and convicted for violations of respective paragraphs of the Penal Code related to drugs is shown in Table 18-4.

TABLE 18-2

Absolute Numbers of Treated Drug Addicts—Slovakia

Year	Total	Heroin & Opiates	Volatile Substances	Hypno. & Sedatives	Stimulants (Incl. Cocaine)	Cannabis	Hallucinogens	Other
1992	2671	56	632	1255	111	16	112	489
1993	2567	245	416	998	243	8	200	173
1994	1189	892	139	89	29	26	5	9
1995	1239	1026	89	51	25	25	2	21
1996	1594	1289	140	63	31	51	5	15

Years 1992 and 1993 were collected by different record sheet and results are not strictly comparable to subsequent years. Year 1996—numbers may not be complete. Source: Slovakia Drug Information System, www.index.sk/diis/treat e.htm.

TABLE 18-3
Number of Drug-Related
Deaths, 1993–1997

Year	Number
1993	6
1994	12
1995	14
1996	23
1997	21

Source: Slovakia Drug Information System, www.index.sk/dis/treate.htm.

Drug Policy

Prior to 1994, Slovakia did not have a comprehensive drug policy. The basis for Slovakia's drug policy is the National Programme for the Fight Against Drugs. In 1995, the government accepted a new proposal written by the Ministry of Internal Affairs that would be in compliance with the European Drug Plan confirmed by the second pan-European Conference of Ministers in 1994. The program sets forth the strategy to combat drug use and drug trafficking, including detailed plans for the treatment of drug dependent persons. The Board of Ministers for Drug Addiction and Drug Control was created upon UN recommendations. The main role of the Board of Ministers is to oversee the implementation of the National Programme. According to the program, emphasis is put on balancing repression, prevention, and treatment.

The Ministry of Health, Ministry of Labor, and Ministry of Education are the three leading agencies responsible for drug demand reduction and the Ministry of the Interior and the Customs Directorate are mainly responsible for drug supply reduction.

Drug-prevention activities are now carried out through all levels of society, including schools and special education facilities. The media has helped

TABLE 18-4
Number of Persons Prosecuted for
Drug Law Offenses, Slovakia, 1990–1997

Year	Persons Prosecuted	Persons Convicted
1990	21	n.a
1993	27	22
1995	532	98
1996	670	263
1997	873	445

Source: Justice Information Section of the Ministry of Justice.

facilitate information exchange to the public, and among experts in the fields of prevention, treatment, and repression. Harm-reduction programs, such as methadone maintenance, and needle exchange, are being implemented in some treatment facilities.

References

Hencovska, Maria. n.d. *World Factbook of Criminal Justice Systems: Slovak Republic.* U.S. Department of Justice, Bureau of Justice Statistics. www.ojp.usdoj .gov/bjs/pub/ascii/wfbcjslo.txt (accessed October 25, 2003).

Lee, R.W. and S.B. MacDonald. 1993. "Drugs in the East," *Foreign Policy* 90: 89–07.

Nociar, Alojz. 1998a. *National Report on the Drug Situation in the Slovak Republic.* Board of Ministers for Drug Dependencies and Drug Control General Secretariat, Bratislava. Prepared as part of the Phare Project on the Drug Information System. www.fad.phare.org/dis/misc/natrep.html. accessed July 7, 1999).

Nociar, A. 1998b. Joint Pompidou Group/UNDCP Project—Extension of the Multi-city Network to Central and Eastern Europe. City Report on Bratislava (1996–1997 data). Council of Europe, Strasbourg.

Slovakia Drug Information System. www.index.sk/dis/treat e.htm.

Part VI

THE MIDDLE EAST

THIS SECTION OF THE BOOK provides information on Iran and Israel. Opium addiction has been a problem in Iran for hundreds of years. The UNODC (2003) reports that 45 percent of global opiate seizures took place in Iran. It estimates that there are 1.3 million heavy drug users in Iran. The government claims it spends $400 million annually against drugs. In 1999 Iran reported that nearly 65,000 drug traffickers had been arrested and that about 80,000 people are currently imprisoned for drug-related offenses.

Israel's drug problem began after the Six-Day War of 1967. Cannabis grown in Lebanon and Syria became more accessible as East Jerusalem and the West Bank opened to Israelis. Israel's Anti-Drug Authority estimates that there are about a quarter of a million drug abusers in the country of which 20,000 are hard drug users, most likely addicted to heroin. Fifty-five percent of Israel's Anti-Drug Authority's budget is used for treatment and rehabilitation service for drug abusers. Twenty percent is used for education and prevention programs.

19

Iran

Overview

I RAN IS LOCATED IN THE MIDDLE EAST between Iraq and Pakistan. It borders the Gulf of Oman, the Persion Gulf, and the Caspian Sea. The other bordering countries are: Afghanistan, Armenia, Azerbaijan, Turkey, and Turkmenistan. Iran has a population of 66,622,704 (July 2002 est.). The majority of ethnicities are Persian (51 percent), Azeri (24 percent), Gilaki and Mazandarani (8 percent), Kurd (7 percent), Arab (3 percent), Lur (2 percent), Baloch (2 percent), Turkmen (2 percent), while other groups make up the remaining 1 percent. Iran is the only country in the Middle East in which the official religion is Shiite Islam (89 percent). Of the remaining 11 percent, 10 are Sunni Muslim and 1 percent are Zoroastrian, Jewish, Christian, and Baha'i. The majority languages are Persian and Persian dialects (58 percent). Of the other languages Turkic and Turkic dialects make up 26 percent, Kurdish (9 percent), Luri (2 percent), Balochi (1 percent), Arabic (1 percent), and Turkish (1 percent) (CIA 2004).

Known as Persia until 1935, Iran became an Islamic Republic in 1979 after the ruling Shah was forced into exile. Since that time, Iran has struggled to reconcile its conservative religious tradition with the influences of the West. Initially, conservative clerical forces stamped out westernizing liberal elements. In 1981, this conservatism displayed hostility toward the West when militant students seized the U.S. embassy in Tehran. From 1980–1988, Iran also fought an indecisive and bloody war with its neighbor Iraq over disputed territory.

The Constitution has codified Islamic principles of government and law. Iran's president is subordinate to Ayatollah Ali Hoseini-Khamenei, the leader of the Islamic Revolution since 1989. The legislative system is composed of a unicameral consultative assembly. Conservative and liberal student groups carry some weight amongst the younger population of the country. Iran's economy is a blend of central planning, village agriculture, and small-scale private enterprise. The state owns the oil industry and other large enterprises. Despite the steady income derived from Iran's oil rich industry, leaders have discussed diversification of the oil industry and other market forms.

Iran is a major transshipment point for drugs grown in Pakistan and Afghanistan and sold in markets in the Gulf, Europe, and Central Asia.

Opium addiction has been a problem for Iran for a few hundred years. The cultivation of poppies was banned in the early 1950s, but by 1969, the government permitted limited and supervised cultivation. During that same year, the government began a program of opium maintenance for individuals sixty years or older and for those who were not good candidates for detoxification. By 1975 there were 185,000 addicts registered through the maintenance program, though officials estimate that this is roughly one-third of the actual addicts in Iran.

Addicts are viewed as having a medical problem; treatment, throughout history, has been provided by local physicians. In 1975, the Rasmar Medical Congress made drug abuse and the consequences of drug abuse the centerpiece of the meetings and thereby spurred efforts for treatment and rehabilitation of drug addicts. Opium maintenance was curtailed, and outpatient treatment became the desired method of rehabilitation.

During 1999 Iran cracked down on drug traffickers, killing over 30 people in drug busts along the border regions (Agence France Press 1999).

Drug Offenses and the Law

The Revolutionary Courts have jurisdiction over drug offenses. Narcotics offenses carry severe punishments. The death sentence is a possibility for possession of more than 30 grams of heroin or 5 kg of opium. The lower tier of punishments include imprisonment, fines, or lashes. While offenders between the ages of sixteen and eighteen are usually afforded some leniency, Iran has executed some 10,000 narcotics traffickers in the last decade.

Article 1 under Iran's Anti Narcotics Drug Law of 1988 (amended in 1989) specifies that the following acts are considered crimes (United Nations Office on Drugs and Crime 2003):

1. Cultivating poppies, absolutely, and cannabis for the purpose of production of narcotics.
2. Importing, exporting, and producing any kind of narcotics.
3. Keeping, carrying, purchasing, distributing, and selling narcotic drugs.
4. Setting up or running places for the use of drugs.

5. Using drugs in any form or manner except for cases provided for by law.
6. Causing to escape or giving protection to drug offenders and perpetrators who are under prosecution or have been arrested.
7. Destroying or concealing evidence of offenders' crimes.

Article 2 states that individuals who are caught cultivating poppies or cannabis in order to produce illegal narcotics will have their crops destroyed. In addition, if the individual is a first time offender, the punishment is a fine of 10 million rials in cash. Second-time offenders must pay between 5 to 50 million rials in cash, plus receive thirty to seventy lashes. Third-time offenders are sanctioned with a fine of 10 to 100 million rials in cash, one to seventy lashes and two- to five-years imprisonment. Fourth-time offenders are sentenced to death. Storing, concealing, carrying, smuggling, dealing, distributing, or producing poppies, cannabis, Indian hempjuice, opium, opium juice, or opium residue are subject to fines and lashes, as specified in Articles 3, 4, and 5.

Extent and Patterns of Use

Opium use has long been an issue for Iran. Traditionally, it has been grown and used by individuals. However, recent indications suggest that poppy cultivation is negligible, which prompted the removal of Iran from the U.S. Major Drug Producer's list in 1998. However, there are discrepancies in statistical tracking. The UNODC (2003) reports that the largest opiate seizure since 1988 took place in Iran. In 2000, 45 percent of global opiate seizures took place in Iran, but in 2001, this decreased to 27 percent. Iran has estimated that there are one million drug addicts and an additional 600,000 users. But a physician on Iran's national committee against AIDS has estimated the number of addicts at 3.3 million.

The UNODC estimates 1.3 million heavy drug users. 93 percent of these are male in their mid-thirties, and 1.4 percent are HIV positive. Under the NOURUZ plan, Iran will spend $68 million in their first year for demand reduction and community awareness. Twelve rehabilitation centers and thirty-nine out-patient programs are run by the Prevention Department of Iran's Social Welfare. These programs treat about 30,000 people per year, and some have waiting lists.

Law Enforcement

Law enforcement efforts include the Islamic Revolutionary Guard Corps, and the Ministries of Health, Intelligence and Security, and Islamic Guidance and Education. Their efforts are coordinated by the Anti-Narcotics Headquarters. Traditionally, Iran focused on battling illegal alcohol consumption in accordance with Islamic law. However, in 1995 the Iranian government began to recognize the magnitude of the domestic narcotic problem.

Iranian authorities claim to spend $400 million annually against drugs. They pursue an aggressive border control policy that has spent some $800 million in a system of dams, roads, channels, sentry points, and observation towers. Thirty thousand law enforcement and support personnel are deployed annually to man the border patrol effort. Authorities claim that they engage in regular skirmishes with heavily armed drug smugglers. The press reports that in 1999, authorities seized 235 tons of illicit drugs in 975 operations. They further report that 183 policemen and 740 drug traffickers have been killed in border skirmishes. Over the last two decades Iran reports more than 2700 deaths in drug-related interdiction efforts. Despite Iran's seemingly fierce efforts at border patrol, opiates continue to transit through Iran in large amounts. This is due mainly to lack of regional coordination with neighbors such as Afghanistan.

In February 1999, Iran reported to the UNODC that nearly 65,000 drug traffickers had been arrested in 1997, and about 80,000 people are currently imprisoned for drug-related offenses. However, some human rights groups have alleged that the Iranian government has been known to falsely charge political opponents with drug-related offenses as a means to quash their political efforts.

Drug Policy

Since 1995, the Iranian government has openly addressed and acknowledged their growing domestic drug problem. In June 1999, the UNODC opened an office in Tehran under a four-year agreement named "NOROUZ." The agreement also calls for $12 million in aid from the United States supported by $120 million annually from Iran. In January 2000, Iran hosted the first International Conference of Drug Liaison Officers. The meeting paved the way for better regional cooperation with European nations.

References

Agence France Press. 1999." Iranian Troops Kill 25 Drug Smugglers Along Afghan Border" (7/26/99) as part of WJIN News, www.wjin.net/btml/news/2338.htrn (accessed July 27, 1999).

Central Intelligence Agency. 2004. *World Factbook: Iran.* Washington, D.C.: Central Intelligence Agency. www.cid.gov/aa/publications/factbook/geos/ir.html (accessed October 2004).

Moharreri. 1978. *General View of Drug Abuse in Iran and a One-Year Report of Outpatient Treatment of Opiate Addiction in the City of Shiraz.* NIDA Monograph. 6981.

United Nations Office on Drugs and Crime (UNODC). 2003. *Global Illicit Drug Trends 2003.* www.unodc.org/unodc/en/global_illicit_drug_trends.html (accessed October 24, 2003).

20

Israel

Overview

ISRAEL, A COUNTRY WITH A POPULATION OF 6.1 million (Central Intelligence Agency 2004), about one-fifth of whom are Arabs, is located on the southwestern tip of Asia, along the southwestern coast of the Mediterranean Sea. The ethnicities are Jewish (80.1 percent) and non-Jewish (19.9 percent) (mostly Arab) (1996 est.). The major religions are Judaism (80.1 percent), Islam (14.6 percent, mostly Sunni Muslim), Christian (2.1 percent), the remaining 3.2 percent are made up of other religions (1996 est.). Hebrew is the official language. However, Arabic is used officially for the Arab minority and English is the most commonly used foreign language (CIA 2004).

Modern Israel was established in 1947 when the United Nations voted for partition of Palestine into the Kingdom of Jordan and the State of Israel. Israel is a democratic society and characterized by ethnic pluralism.

Although Israel lacks a formal constitution, over the years, the country has enacted a series of Basic Laws. The most far reaching are the Basic Law on Human Dignity and Liberty and the Basic Law on Freedom of Occupation, enacted in 1992. Israeli criminal and penal law derives from major statutes passed by the parliament, known as the Knesset, which is the supreme legislative body of the State of Israel. The Criminal Code was developed in 1965 and the Penal Law was written in 1977. The latter replaced the Criminal Code Ordinance of 1936, a comprehensive code based on English common law.

Each year, the Israeli National Police collects and publishes the *Israel National Police, Annual Report*. Crime statistics can also be found in the Statistical Abstract of Israel. Crimes are classified according to eleven major offenses. The major offenses are also divided into subcategories. The eleven major offenses are: offenses against human lives, human bodily harm, offenses against morals, sex offenses, offenses against public order, offenses against property, drug offenses, fraud offenses, economic offenses, administrative offenses, and licensing offenses.

There has been an increase in the number of murders, which police believe is related to the increased warring between rival drug gangs. But Israel's murder rate remains one of the lowest in the industrialized world (Bensinger 1998). The death penalty can be imposed for two types of offenses: offenses against humanity and against the Jewish People committed by the Nazis and their abettors; and for treason in wartime. In actuality, the death penalty only has been used in rare instances.

A minor in Israel is defined as a boy or girl under the age of eighteen.

Israel's incarceration rate is approximately 100 persons per 100,000 population, higher than most of Europe, but less than the United States. According to the Israel Prison Service (IPS) Annual Report of 1996, 50 percent of incarcerated criminals abuse drugs (IPS 1997). Treatment in prison is voluntary. Inmates who choose to participate are classified into three categories: drug free, occasional or heavy users, and drug traffickers. After classification, inmates are housed accordingly. Drug-free wards are set aside for the drug-free inmates, and the inmates do not come into contact with users or traffickers. Users are housed in the regular prisons and drug traffickers are segregated from all other inmates.

Drug Offenses and the Law

The Dangerous Drugs Ordinance regards the following drugs as illegal: marijuana, hashish, opium, and cocaine and their manmade derivatives, and psychotropic drugs contained on the first two lists of the UN Psychotropic Substances Convention, 1971. Illicit activities include the manufacture, cultivation, production, preparation, extraction, possession, use, export, import, trade, supply, transaction, acting as go-between, conveying in transit, diversion, moving a drug in transit, and tampering with a drug in transit, for any of these substances, if all or any of these acts are done without a permit or a license as established in the Ordinance. The Ordinance defines three general categories of offenses: (1) possession of drugs for own consumption and misuse of drugs, (2) drug trafficking and (3) enticement of minors to misuse of drugs or to traffic in drugs (Weisman n.d.). Israel views the latter to be the most serious of the offenses.

Extent and Patterns of Use

It is generally believed that Israel's drug problem began after the Six-Day War
of 1967. Prior to the Six-Day War, drug use was basically confined to small
marginal populations, but after the war drug use spread to university students
and youth in high school. Cannabis grown in Lebanon and Syria became
more accessible as East Jerusalem and the West Bank were opened to Israelis
(Shoham et al. 1976). Heroin entered the scene in late 1975. Cocaine, heroin,
and hashish are smuggled into the country from the Middle and Far Eastern
countries, as well as from South America. Much of the drug supply is intended
for European and American markets, but some of the drugs are used locally.

It is difficult to find data regarding the prevalence of illicit drug use in the
general population of Israel (Ben-Yehuda 1987). The majority of resources
found focused on drug use among youth. But, Israel's Anti-Drug Authority estimates that there are 250,000 drug abusers in the country of which 20,000 are
hard-drug users, most likely addicted to heroin.

Reports document little injection drug use, and indicate the preferred
method for heroin use is smoking or snorting. Hashish, marijuana, and cocaine are also used, but crack is still mostly unknown.

The studies that focus on drug use among youth come to the conclusion that
between the period from 1971 to 1981 drug use remained stable with roughly 3
to 5 percent of youth having used hashish (Peled 1971; Peled and Schimmerling
1972; Barnea 1978; Kandel, Adler, and Sudit 1981; Javitz and Shuval 1982).

Law Enforcement

Violators of the Ordinance are subjected to punishments as follows: possession
for own consumption or misuse—three-years imprisonment; trafficking—
twenty years imprisonment; enticement of minors—twenty-five-years imprisonment. In addition to these prison terms, the courts can fine drug traffickers—
up to the amount of approximately $908,000.

In 1989, the Law Amending the Dangerous Drugs Ordinance (No. 3), 5749-
1989, was adopted to provide for the forfeiture of some or all property connected directly or indirectly with a drug trafficking offense. Forfeiture can
only occur after the defendant has been convicted and declared by the court a

TABLE 20-1
Consumption of Hard Drugs in Israel, 1991–1996

1991	1992	1993	1994	1995	1996
7528	n.a.	6482	6594	7476	8821

Source: Statistical Abstract of Israel.

drug trafficker. Trafficking also includes possession, but not necessarily for personal use.

The Anti-Drug Authority Law of 1988 created the Anti-Drug Authority (ADA). Similar to the U.S. Office of National Drug Control Policy, the ADA reports directly to Israel's Prime Minister.

Drug Policy

The Israeli government has made it clear that illicit drug use poses a grave danger to individuals and to Israeli society as a whole, and has taken action to educate the public to the dangers of drug use. Campaigns against drug use have generally been successful, but researchers point out that Israel's national emphasis on creating and maintaining a central value system has helped deter drug abuse (Ben-Yehuda 1987; Rubenstein 1975). Although values emphasizing collectivity may be decreasing over the years, Israeli citizens still identify with the collective.

Currently, the Anti-Drug Authority (ADA) is the central policy agency on drug use and abuse. ADA's main goal is to formulate drug policy and coordinate prevention, treatment and other anti-drug activities of government agencies. Fifty-five percent of ADA's resources go toward treatment and rehabilitative services for drug abusers, and one-fifth of the budget is directed toward education and prevention programs, with the remaining monies earmarked for research, purchase of equipment for the police, and other activities.

References

Barnea, Z. 1978. A Multidimensional Model of Young People's Readiness to Use Drugs. M.A. Thesis, Institute of Criminology, Tel Aviv University. (in Hebrew).

Ben-Yehuda, Nachman. 1987. "Drug Abuse Social Policy in the United States and Israel: A Comparative Sociological Perspective." *The International Journal of the Addictions, 22(1):* 1745.

Bensinger, Gad. 1998. Justice in Israel: The Criminal Justice System. Chicago: Office of International Criminal Justice,

Central Intelligence Agency. 2004. *The World Factbook: Israel.* Washington, D.C.: Central Intelligence Agency. www.cia.gov/cia/publications/factbook/geos/is.html (accessed May 10, 2004).

Dangerous Drugs Ordinance (New Version), 5733-1973, L.S.I., New Version, vol. 3, 527.

Israeli National Police. 1997. Israeli National Police Annual Report. www.police.gov.il/english/AboutUs/Structure/01_mazap_rep1997.asp (accessed December 2, 1997).

Israel Prison Service (IPS). 1997. Annual Report for 1996. (In Hebrew).

Javitz, R., and J. T. Shuval. 1982. "Vulnerability to Drugs Among Israeli Adolescents." *Israel Journal of Psychiatry*, 19(2):97–119.

Kandel, D. B., I. Adler, and M. Sudit. 1981. "The Epidemiology of Adolescent Drug use in France and Israel." *American Journal of Public Health*, 71: 256–65.

Law amending the Dangerous Drugs Ordinance (No. 3), 5749-1989, no authorized translation, Hebrew official version published in Sefer HaChukkim 5749, 80.

Peled, T. 1971. Attitudes of Youth in School to Drugs: Selective Findings from the Study on Values, Plans and Youth Behavior. Jerusalem: Institute for Applied Social Research (in Hebrew).

Peled T., and H. Schimmerling 1972. The Drug Culture Among the Youth of Israel: The Case of High School Students. Israel Studies in Criminology, 125–51.

Rubenstein, A. 1975. *Law Enforcement in a Permissive Society.* Jerusalem: Schocken Books (in Hebrew).

Shoham, S. Giora., Nehemia Geva, Dina Kliger, and Tamar Chai. 1976. "Drug Abuse Among Israeli Youth: Epidemiological Pilot Study," in Israeli Studies in Criminology Volume III S. Giora Shoham (Ed.) Jerusalem: Jerusalem Academic Press.

Weisman, Gloria M. n.d. *World Factbook of Criminal Justice Systems: Israel.* U.S. Department of Justice, Bureau of Justice Statistics. www.ojp.usdoj.gov/bjs/pub/ascii/wflocjisr.txt (accessed October 3, 2003).

Part VII

ASIA

THE UNODC (2003) REPORTS THAT one third of all cannabis abusers, or 55 million individuals, reside in Asia (136). Roughly 8 percent of those seeking treatment have been abusing cannabis (136).

Between 1998 and 2001, twenty Asian countries supplied cannabis (UNODC 2003: 29). Furthermore, in 2001, 59 percent of worldwide heroin seizures took place in Asia (53). The greatest seizures were made in the eastern and southeastern regions of Asia. The UNODC (2003) reports that 50 percent of the world's opiate abusers reside in Asia (107).

Heroin seizures in Southwest Asia decreased in 2001, largely because of the reduced production of opium in Afghanistan (UNODC 2003). However, heroin seizures in Central Asia increased by 55 percent in 2001, in part due to the increased availability of opium in the northern areas of Afghanistan.

Cocaine trafficking is not prevalent in Asia, which accounted for only 0.1 percent of global cocaine seizures in 2000 and 0.3 percent in 2001 (UNODC 2003: 67). Areas in which seizures have taken place are India, Sri Lanka, Indonesia, Hong Kong, and Thailand (67).

21

China

Overview

CHINA IS A UNITARY STATE RULED by a central government. Made up of twenty-two provinces, five autonomous regions, and three municipalities (Beijing, Shanghai, and Tianjin), China's population tops all countries with 1.2 billion inhabitants. China is bordered by the East China Sea, Korea Bay, Yellow Sea, and South China Sea, and is between North Korea and Vietnam. The other bordering countries are Afghanistan, Bhutan, Burma, India, Kazakhstan, Kyrgyzstan, Laos, Macau, Mongolia, Nepal, Pakistan, Russia, and Tajikistan.

The dominant ethnicity is Han Chinese at 91.9 percent. The remaining 8.1 percent are Zhuang, Uygur, Hui, Yi, Tibetan, Miao, Manchu, Mongol, Buyi, Korean, and other nationalities. The major religions are Daoism (Taoism) and Buddhism. Islam is represented by 1 percent to 2 percent and Christianity by 3 percent to 4 percent (2002 est.). The official languages are standard Chinese or Mandarin (Putonghua, based on the Beijing dialect), Yue (Cantonese), Wu (Shanghaiese), Minbei (Fuzhou), Minnan (Hokkien-Taiwanese), Ziang, Gan, and Hakka dialects (CIA 2004).

China's highest state power is the People's National Control (NPC). The current Constitution was adopted in 1982, and amended as recently as 1993 (Bennett 1996).

It has only been since Mao Tse-tung's death in the late 1970s that China has begun to establish a formal and stable legal and criminal justice system. The first code of criminal law and criminal procedural law was adopted in 1970. In 1997, a new criminal procedure law replaced the "presumption of guilt" with the "presumption of innocence" to keep pace with human rights protections. Before 1997 the presumption of innocence, the exclusionary rule, protection against self-incrimination, the right to a jury trial, and protection against double jeopardy were not parts of China's criminal procedure. In addition, China revised its law on Penal Procedure, and the new revised law became effective January 1, 1997 (Mulvenon, 1997).

Drug Offenses and the Law

Historically, opium was introduced into China in the eighth century by Arab traders (Fields and Tararin 1970; Spencer and Navaratnam 1981), but it was not a problem until the seventeenth century, when it was first imported from India by the British. Opium use rose rapidly throughout the eighteenth and nineteenth century. The opium trade flourished in Europe, Africa, and Asia. Opium produced in the Mediterranean basin had a higher quality than that produced in China and other parts of Asia and, hence, opium from the Mediterranean soon became highly desired by the Chinese. After Manchu invaders overthrew the Ming dynasty in China, in 1729 the Manchu emperor prohibited for the first time opium commerce with Europeans. China believed that trade of tea, spices, and silk for opium depleted imperial reserves of valued resources. By 1793, China prohibited the cultivation of opium in China, and by 1799, prohibited the importation of opium. As smuggling flourished, the Chinese emperor ordered the strangling of opium smugglers and owners of smoking dens.

In contemporary times, the selling or importing of opium became a criminal offense in 1976, and violators of the law over the next four years were sentenced to death (Spencer and Navaratnam 1981). In late 1990s, the Standing Committee of the National People's Congress passed an antidrug law entitled "The Decisions on Prohibition of Drugs." The Decisions mandate fifteen years of imprisonment or more for: those who smuggle or sell or transport or produce 1,000 grams or more of opium, or 50 grams or more of heroin, or a large amount of other types of drugs; the core members of drug organizations that sell, smuggle, transport, or produce drugs; and those using weapons during the operation of smuggling, selling, transporting, or producing drugs; and those involved in serious cases that involve forces to resist arrest or search. Those convicted of these crimes but having a smaller amount of drugs (200 to 999 grams of opium or 10 to 40 grams of heroin) would be subject to seven or more years of imprisonment. Those convicted of drug crimes with even smaller amounts are subject to less than seven-years imprisonment.

In January 1995, regulations were put into effect to force drug users to receive treatment for drug use. The Regulations on Forcible Termination of

Drug Use mandate medical and psychological care, and legal, moral, and medical education. Individuals who use drugs again after treatment are sent to labor camps, called institutes of education through labor. In 1991, 8,344 drug offenses were reported (Guo et al. 2003).

Extent and Patterns of Use

In 1906, it was estimated that there were 2,700,000 regular users of opium in the Chinese Empire (roughly 0.5 percent of the population) (Escohotado 1999). By 1934 opium addiction was a serious problem (Vaughan et al. 1995) with an estimated 40 million persons smoking opium (Fields and Tararin 1970). Japanese opium smugglers controlled the drug market at the time, and morphine, heroin, and cocaine were easy to obtain since the Japanese government had created the puppet state of Manchoukuo (Manchuria). In addition to the tremendous supply and distribution of opium in Manchuria, reports estimate that large quantities of heroin and cocaine were manufactured in Japanese pharmaceutical firms for distribution in China.

In 1945, at the termination of Japanese occupation, the Chinese government cracked down on opium importation and use and as a result, had sentenced over 80,000 drug offenders by 1953, including approximately 800 who were sentenced to death and executed.

In recent years, opiate abuse has been on the rise in China. Officials acknowledge at least 900,000 registered drug addicts in 2001. This figure is significantly higher than the 70,000 registered drug addicts in 1990 (UNODC 2003: 125). However, the actual number of addicts may be many times higher. Identified addicts are compelled to undergo rehabilitation in state run facilities. The government also runs programs designed to educate the population on the link between IV drug use and AIDS/HIV. The number of HIV/AIDS patients in China has risen to 22,000 in 2001, almost double since 1998. About 71 percent of these victims were infected via IV drug use. Statistics show that 2,051 cities in China report drug abuse among the population. Of these, 205 cities have a drug abusing population of over 1000.

Although China claimed to have conquered its drug problem, problem drug use began to reemerge with force by 1980. Today, the government estimates that there are millions of heroin users in the country—heroin replacing opium as the most popular drug. Between 1994 and 1995, the number of registered addicts increased from 250,000 to 380,000. Youth are also using drugs in large numbers. In Guangdong Province, 80 percent of all drug users are under the age of twenty-five, and a national drug study in 1990 found that more than 85 percent of 14,000 users were younger than thirty-five years old (Ma and Bao 1993). In the 1990s, China seized more heroin than any other

TABLE 21-1
2002 Mid-year Law Enforcement Statistics, China

# of Solved Drug-Related Cases	# of Drug-Related Arrests	Opium Poppy Production (Hectares)	Heroin Seizure (kg)
45,378	38,765	169,000	4,035

Source: China Daily/People's Daily Website, 6/21/02; 6/26/02; 6/27/02.

country (Bennett 1996). It is estimated that 200 tons of illegal drugs are annually imported from the Golden Triangle region of Burma, Thailand, and Laos. In Guangdong Province alone, the cases of drug crimes solved by the police in 1994 were more than three times that of the years from 1981 to 1990 combined (Liu and Situ 1996).

Researchers believe the Chinese feel that selling drugs is well worth the risk because the profit to be gained is incredibly great. One kilo of heroin bought in Yunnan Province in 1993 (which borders Burma) can be sold in Guangdong Province (which borders Hong Kong) for $40,000, and in the United States that same one kilo is worth $100,000 (Liu and Situ 1996; Ma and Bao, 1993).

Law Enforcement

In 2002, six drug dealers were executed by Beijing's No. 1 and No. 2 People's Intermediate Courts. The Shzhen Intermediate Court also gave the death penalty to two Hong Kong drug traffickers.

TABLE 21-2
Statistics on Drug Arrests, Sentences, and Imprisonment, China, 1985–1994

	85–90	1991	1992	1993	1994
Drug cases cracked	30,000	8,344	14,701	26,191	38,033
Offenders involved,	—	18,479	28,292	—	—
Arrests	20,800	8,080	7,025	7,677	10,434
Offenders sentenced	16,000	5,285	6,588	—	—
Offenders sentenced to life imprisonment or death penalty	866	1,354	—	—	
Drug abusers registered	148,539	250,000			
Compulsory drug abstinence institutions	232	252			
Number of addicts under compulsory abstinence	41,227	46,000	50,000		
Number of illegal drug users punished	12,060	20,000			

Between 1983 and 1990, at least 1,284 drug smugglers and dealers were executed (Liu and Situ 1996). Throughout the 1990s, the government remained steadfast in its adherence to swift and severe punishments for drug offenders. Between 1991 and 1994, over 60 percent of convicted drug offenders were sentenced to more than five years of imprisonment, or life or death sentences. This ratio is much higher for drug crimes than for other common crimes. In the same time period, courts at all levels decided over 90 percent of drug cases within forty-five days.

Drug Policy

Between the 1950s and 1980, the government paid little attention to drug problems, believing that any problems were minor. To maintain its status as a "drug-free" nation, any antidrug activity was carried out quietly. But, with the resurgence of opium use and heroin use after 1980, China began to put together a strong and very public antidrug policy.

East China's Zhejiang Province has begun to take strong measures to crack down on drug use and drug related crimes. In early 1995, the city of Wenzhou established a six-month antidrug campaign which solved over 100 drug cases and arrested 300 people using drugs. Some of the drug traffickers will be sentenced to death, while many of the drug users will be sent to new drug rehabilitation centers (*China Daily*, 1998).

Drug education takes place in all high schools and public antidrug exhibitions and antidrug slogans appear in streets and public transportation stations. Citizens are encouraged to report drug offenders and drug users and can receive monetary rewards for doing so.

References

Bennett, Gary (ed.). 1996. *China Facts and Figures. Annual Handbook*, Volume 20. Gulf Breeze, Fla.: Academic International Press.

Central Intelligence Agency. 2004. *World Factbook: China*. Washington, D.C.: Central Intelligence Agency. www.cia.gov/cia/publications/factbook/geos/ch.html.

China Daily. 1998. Zhejiang Attacks Drug Problem. Criminal Justice International Online (www.acM.ui).

China Daily. People's Daily Website: 6/21/02; 6/26/02; 6/27/02.

Fields, A., and P. A. Tararin. 1970. "Opium in China," *British Journal of the Addictions* 64(3): 371–382.

Guo, Jianan, Guo Xiang, Wu Zongxian, Xu Zhangrun, Peng Xiaohui, and Li Shuangshuang. n.d. *World Factbook of Criminal Justice Systems: China*. Bureau of

Justice Statistics. www.ojp.usdoj.gov/bjs/pub/ascii/wfbcjchi.txt (accessed October 8, 2003).

Liu, Weizheng, and Yingyi Situ. 1996. "China: The Causes, Control, and Treatment of Illegal Drugs." CJ International Online. September–October, 1996, Volume 12, #5, pp 1–13. http://www.acsp.ulc.edu/oici/pubs/cji/120509.htm (accessed September 1, 1998).

Ma, Kechang, and Suixian Bao. 1993. "Zhongguo Dupin Fanzui De Xianzhuang Yuanyi Yu Duice." (The Present Drug Crimes in China: Causes and Consequences) in Chinese. In *Chengzhi Dupin Fanzui Lilun Yu Shijian* (Theories and Practices in Punishing Drug Crimes) ed. by High Court of Yunnan Province. Beijing: Press of Chinese Political and Legal University.

Mulvenon, James (ed.). 1997. Volume 21. Gulf Breeze, Fla.: Academic International Press.

Spencer, C. P., and Visweswaran Navatham. 1981. *Drug Abuse in East Asia.* Kuala Lumpur: Oxford University Press.

United Nations Office on Drugs and Crime. 2003. *Global Illicit Drug Trends 2003.* www.unodc.org/unodc/en/global_illicit_drug_trends.html (accessed October 24, 2003).

Vaughn, Michael, S. Frank, F.Y. Huang, and Christine Rose Ramirez. 1995. "Drug Abuse and Anti-Drug Policy in Japan." *British Journal of Criminology,* 35(4) 491–524.

22

Japan

Overview

JAPAN IS LOCATED IN EASTERN ASIA. It is an island chain between the North Pacific Ocean and the Sea of Japan. Japan has a population of 126,974,628 (July 2002 est.). The majority ethnicity is Japanese at 99 percent. The remaining 1 percent is made up of Korean (511,262), Chinese (244,241), Brazilian (182,232), Filipino (89,851), and other (237,914) (2000). The religions mostly observed are Shinto and Buddhism, at 84 percent. Other religions make up the remaining 16 percent. The official language is Japanese (CIA 2004).

Japan has a federal system of government, but one that it is largely centralized. The government is divided into executive, legislative, and judicial branches and much of their political system was influenced by nineteenth-century German and British parliamentary models.

Historically, Japan's legal system has been influenced by German criminal law and French civil law. But in the era after World War II, American law models became dominant. Japan has an informal system based on mediation. Arbitration is also very popular.

With the onset of the Meiji Era (1867–1912), Western culture was introduced and the government established new laws reflecting a gradually modernizing Japanese society. Criminal laws and prison laws were passed that hastened modernization. Japan adopted the adversarial system with their new Constitution in 1996. Japan's criminal code is found in the 1948 Code of Criminal Procedure and the 1949 Rules of Criminal Procedure under the

Constitutional Law. Japan's laws reflect American legal concepts in contexts important to the protection of human rights.

Japan has suspended the use of a jury system and the court is the exclusive trier of fact. Crimes are classified as crimes against the state, crimes against society and crimes against individuals. While some changes in the law were made after World War II, the fundamental structure of the laws has changed little.

Juveniles are youth under age twenty, but the minimum age limit for criminal responsibility is over fourteen years of age. Juvenile cases are handled in family court except when the crime is serious. The death penalty can be instituted for fourteen offenses, but in practice, only murder and aggravated robbery have resulted in death sentences.

Japan's criminal justice statistics are thorough in that each agency—police, prosecution, court, correction and after-care divisions—publishes their own statistics as a yearbook. The Ministry of Justice then summarizes their statistics and publishes a book, *White Paper on Crime.*

Drug Offenses and the Law

Japan's law regarding drugs is very specific. The Cannabis Control Law was developed in 1930, with revisions in 1947, 1948, and 1963. Each revision added stiffer penalties for law violations. Amphetamines became a "dangerous drug" with the enactment of the 1948 Drug Control Act. In response to an epidemic of stimulant use during and soon after World War II the Stimulant Drug Control Law of 1951 and the Narcotics Control Law of 1953 were passed by the Japanese Parliament. In 1954 the Opium Control Law punished the illegal use of opium. In addition, compulsory treatment was mandated by the Narcotics Control Law in 1963. The law introduced life sentences (before the maximum was ten years) for trafficking in heroin. It can be seen from Table 22-1 that arrests for narcotics violations dropped dramatically after the law was introduced.

In 1990 revisions were made to numerous laws in order to widen the scope of penalties and increase sentence lengths for law violators. In many instances, fines tripled and sentences grew for the possession, sale, and consumption of cannabis, stimulants, and other narcotics.

Japan has ratified the 1961 Single Convention on Narcotic Drugs, but has not ratified the Convention on Psychotropic Substances that was developed a decade later. Japan is a signatory to the 1988 United Nations Convention against Illicit Traffic in Narcotic Drugs and Psychotropic Substances and at the time increased penalties for drug offenses, making Japan one of the

TABLE 22-1
Number of Arrestees for Drug Control Violations, Japan, 1956–1990

Year	Narcotics (Heroin) Violations	Cannabis Violations
1956	1103	15
1957	1188	22
1958	1667	6
1959	1525	29
1960	2081	11
1961	1954	34
1962	2349	55
1963	2288	146
1964	847	185
1966	859	201
1966	692	176
1967	476	290
1968	227	338
1969	130	315
1970	110	487
1971	119	518
1972	204	518
1973	325	617
1974	276	588
1975	150	733
1976	84	735
1977	98	892
1978	61	1070
1979	49	1041
1980	113	1173
1981	59	1122
1982	64	1083
1983	66	1035
1984	108	1230
1985	115	1099
1986	85	1171
1987	82	1276
1988	105	1464
1989	205	1344
1990	186	1512

Source: Reproduced from Tamura, 1992, page 102. Original source: National Police Agency, 1991.

strictest Asian nations with regard to drug control. Japan introduced new legislation in 1991 to comply with the 1990 United Nations Convention against
Illegal Traffic in Narcotic Drugs and Psychotropic Substances.

Japan has a serious problem with amphetamines, which are mainly imported from other Asian countries. The government reacted by passing the
Stimulant Control Law in 1951. In 1954 the law was amended to strengthen
criminal penalties for offenses involving amphetamine. The law was somewhat successful in reducing the number of addicts, but by 1980, amphetamines experienced a dramatic resurgence.

Extent and Patterns of Use

Unlike many other Asian nations, opium addiction has not been a problem
for Japan. But, the use of opium-based narcotics can be traced to the fifteenth
century (Vaughan et al. 1995). Foreseeing a problem in the early 1900s, Japan
was the first Asian country to create strong controls against opiate use. Reports estimate that roughly 3,600 of the country's 70 million people were addicts in 1938 (compared to 50,000 of the 130 million in the United States).
Japan's first problems with illicit drug use came after World War II (and some
say as a result of the war) with the widespread use of methamphetamine
(Spencer and Navaratnam 1981). Methamphetamine was originally produced
for military use, and was soon sold in large quantities to fight sleeplessness
(Greberman and Wada 1994).

Cannabis entered the scene in Japan in the late-1970s as prosperity and
hence, disposable income, grew (Select Committee 1990). But, cannabis has
not been a major problem for Japan. A review of published statistics shows
that only a few individuals have been arrested for offenses related to
cannabis since 1948, when the Cannabis Control Law was enacted
(Vaughan 1995).

Japan's youth that are involved with substances tend to use solvents and
amphetamines, as opposed to marijuana often the drug of choice for Western
youth. Japan's first crisis involving methamphetamine abuse started in the
1950s (UNODC 2003: 147). Methampetamine production is very uncommon
in Japan, although there have been ephedrine seizures. The UNODC estimates
that 1.7 percent of individuals age fifteen to sixty-four are abusing methamphetamines (148). Up to one-third of the methamphetamine smuggled into
Japan is thought to be provided by North Korea. In 2001, after many years of
increased methampetamine abuse, Japan reported a stable rate of abuse
(UNODC 2003: 9).

Law Enforcement

The number of the Stimulant Drugs Control Law violators cleared by the police increased greatly during the period of the early 1970s to the early 1980s. It started to decrease in 1989, after exceeding 20,000 for nine consecutive years since 1980. However, it once again started to increase in 1995. The number in 1997 was 19,937, up 1.4 percent over the previous year (Ministry of Justice 1998). Out of 2,100,006 offenders disposed of at the public prosecutors offices in 1997 offenders violating the Stimulant Drugs Control Law made up 7.5 percent, the third largest crime category after larceny (39.7 percent) and embezzlement (10.2 percent). The number of prisoners newly admitted to penal institutions in 1997 was 22,667, with the largest category of offenses of newly admitted prisoners in 1997 being violations of the Stimulant Drugs Control Law (29.7 percent).

The number of juvenile violators of the Stimulant Drugs Control Law has been declining, after a peak of 2,769 in 1982. The 1994 total was 832 with a large increase again over the next three years reaching 1,601 in 1997. Regarding non-stimulant drugs, the number of juvenile violators of the Law for Control of Poisonous and Powerful Agents who were referred to the public prosecutors offices was high during the period of 1978 to 1991, roughly at 20,000. After 1991, there has been a large decrease (5,057 in 1997), almost one sixth of its highest record in 1982 (Ministry of Justice 1998).

Drug Policy

Japan's drug policy began in the fifteenth century as the country witnessed China's growing problem with opium addiction. Opium smoking was prohibited in the Edo Period (1600–1867), along with any nonmedical use of the drug. A trade agreement with the United States in 1858 forbade Americans from bringing opium into Japan. Violators of newly established laws against drug smuggling and trafficking were given the death penalty (National Police Agency 1992). During the next era between 1868 and 1912 (Meiji Restoration), antidrug policy remained strong and the government created new laws that severely punished the use and possession of opium. The government also established a massive public education campaign. Drug users were looked upon as outcasts and the public education campaign was perceived as very successful.

At the onset of World War II, Japan's drug policy consisted of strict enforcement and control on the one hand, and encouragement of drug sales and

TABLE 22-2
Number of Cases Known to the Police, Japan, 1980–1986

	1980	1981	1982	1983	1984	1985	1986
Offenses reported to the Police							
Total	1,375,411	1,463,228	1,528,779	1,540,717	1,588,693	1,607,697	1,581,411
Drug possession	7631	7695	7660	7405	7471	7371	7063
Other drug	27,647	30,483	31,840	31,483	31,725	30,190	27,102
Apprehended or arrested							
Total	392,113	418,162	441,963	438,705	446,617	432,250	399,888
Drug possession	6265	6430	6479	6202	6599	6452	6202
Other drug	15,191	17,007	18,286	18,583	18,942	18,168	16,468
Persons prosecuted							
Total	27,045	28,776	28,958	28,052	28,334	27,170	25,149
Other drug							
Offenders convicted							
Total	79,417	78,740	79,174	79,239	80,144	78,769	76,305
Drug possession	na	na	na	na	na	na	na

manufacture in China. Since 1897 the government of Japan had allowed for a government monopoly on the opium trade to generate revenue for the country. The Opium Law of 1932 created the General Monopoly Office that controlled the state monopolies. Smokers of opium had to register and pay a monthly tax.

As the war continued, the Japanese government began to encourage the use of stimulants for soldiers and factory workers (Yokoyama 1992). Drug addiction after World War II became a problem for many of these soldiers and workers and injured soldiers who became addicted to their prescribed painkillers. At the time of the American occupation of Japan, Japan's drug laws were based on U.S. legislation. The laws did not have harsh controls on stimulants, thereby fueling a growth in the problems associated with stimulant use. It wasn't until the mid-1950s that new restrictions were placed on the manufacture of stimulants. In response to the new laws, organized crime groups became involved with trafficking heroin. Trafficking in narcotics continued to grow as public sentiment changed and stimulants acquired a negative reputation.

Drug enforcement activities are performed by at least three main agencies: the National Policy Agency's Drug Enforcement Division, the Ministry of Health and Welfare, and specialized officers within other government branches. The Drug Countermeasure Institute coordinates policy among these agencies and the courts and corrections. Data from numerous sources indicate that Japan's drug policies were becoming increasingly strict in the period from 1950 to the mid-1980s (Bonner 1990; Tamura 1989, 1992). The courts saw a decrease in suspended sentences and suspended prosecutions, with a simultaneous increase in indictments for drug-related crimes.

With increasing worry that Japan's problems with illicit drugs were growing in the early 1990s, the government began drug education advertising in 1993.

References

Bonner, R. C. 1990. "Combating Drugs and Economic Crimes: An American Prospector's Perspective," in V.Kusuda-Smick, ed., *Crime Prevention and Control in the United States and Japan*, pp. 47–52. Dobbs Ferry, N.Y.: Transnational Juris Publications.

Central Intelligence Agency. 2004. *World Factbook: Japan*. Washington, D.C.: Central Intelligence Agency. www.cia.gov/cia/publications/factbook/geos/ja.html.

Friman, H. R. 1991. "The United States, Japan, and the International Drug Trade," *Asian Survey* 31(9): 875–890.

Greberman, Sharyn Bowman, and Wada, Kiyoshi. 1994. "Social and Legal Factors Related to Drug Abuse in the United States and Japan," *Public Health Reports, 109(6)* 731–737.

Huang, F. F. Y., and M. S. Vaughn. 1992. "A Descriptive Assessment of Japanese Organized Crime: The Boryokudan from 1945–1988." *International Criminal Justice Review* 2: 1957.

Ministry of Justice. 1998. *Summary of the White Paper on Crime 1998.* Research and Training Institute of Ministry of Justice, Japan.

Ministry of Justice. 1991. *Summary of the White Paper on Crime 1991.* Research and Training Institute of Ministry of Justice, Japan.

Moriyama T. 1988. "Citizen Associations and the Volunteer Probation Officer," UNICRI (ed.), *(In)formal Mechanisms of Crime Control.*

Moriyama, T. 1991. "The Response to Delinquency by Formal Agencies in Japan," J. Hackler (ed.), *Official Responses to Problem Juveniles,* the Onate International Institute.

National Police Agency. 1991. The Police of Japan.

National Policy Agency. 1992. *Antidrug Activities in Japan.* Tokyo: National Police Agency.

Select Committee on Narcotics Abuse and Control, U.S. House of Representatives. 1990. *Asian Heroin Production and Trafficking.* Washington, D.C.: United States Government Printing Office.

Shkita, M., and Tsuchiya, S. 1992. *Crime and Criminal Policy in Japan.* Springer-Verlag.

Spencer, C. P., and V. Navaratnam. 1981. *Drug Abuse in East Asia.* Kuala Lumpur, Malaysia: Oxford University Press.

Tamura, M. 1989. "Japan: Stimulant Epidemics Past and Present," *Bulletin on Narcotics,* 41: 8393.

Tamura, M. 1992. "The Yakuza and Amphetamine Abuse in Japan," in H. H. Traver and M. S. Gaylord, (eds.), *Drugs, Law and the State,* pp. 99–117. Hong Kong: Hong Kong University.

United Nations Office on Drugs and Crime. 2003. *Global Illicit Drug Trends 2003.* http://www.unodc.org/unodc/en/global_illicit_drug_trends.html (accessed October 24, 2003).

Vaughn, Michael S., Frank F. Y. Huang, and Christine Rose Ramirez. 1995. "Drug Abuse and AntiDrug Policy in Japan." *British Journal of Criminology,* 35(4): 491–524.

Yokoyama, M. 1992. "Japan: Changing Drug Laws: Keeping Pace with the Problem," *Criminal Justice International* 8(5): 11–18.

23

India

Overview

INDIA IS A PLURALISTIC AND DIVERSE CULTURE with 1,033.4 million people. Hindus represent 82.6 percent of the population; 11.4 percent are Muslims; 2.4 percent are Christians; and the remaining are Sikhs, Buddhists, and a mixture of other religions (Sharma 1996).

India became a sovereign democratic republic in January 1950 after attaining independence from Britain in 1947. A quasi-federal system of government, India has a president who acts as head of state. A prime minister advises the president. The country's twenty-five states are each headed by a governor appointed by the Union Government. There are also seven Union Territories which are directly administered by the Union Government through its officials.

The criminal justice system in India is based on the British system. It has four subsystems, those being the Legislature (Parliament), Enforcement (police), Adjudication (courts), and Corrections (prisons, community facilities). India's Penal Code originated in 1860 and was largely influenced by English criminal law, followed by the adoption of a Criminal Code in 1861. However, the Criminal Code was repealed and replaced by a new code in 1974. Criminal offenses are divided into two categories: cognizable crimes and noncognizable crime. The former are the more serious crimes, for which a police officer does not need a warrant to make an arrest. The latter are more trivial and a warrant is needed for arrest.

India maintains the death penalty for some crimes, including murder and specified offenses against the state which include waging war against the government.

India's legal system is a combination of adversarial and accusatorial. The penal system has been heavily influenced by amendments to the Narcotics Control and Psychotropic Substance Act in 1985, and the Prevention of Illicit Traffic in Narcotic Drugs and Psychotropic Substances Act of 1988 (UNODC, Regional Office of South Asia [ROSA] 2003).

Youth are deemed criminally responsible at age seven. But, if it can be proven that the child has not attained sufficient maturity to understand the consequences of an act, the child will be free from liability.

Located between the Golden Crescent and the Golden Triangle, "the world's two largest areas of illicit opium production" (UNODC, Regional Office for South Asia 2003: 6), India is the world's largest producer of licit opium. India adheres to strict guidelines to run its licit opium market, which provides the drug for pharmaceutical purposes worldwide. India has managed to regulate its licit opium production with great success, minimizing diversion of this crop into illegal markets. Essentially, the Indian government establishes a minimum crop yield of opium that its farmers can harvest each season. This minimum crop yield is adjusted yearly according to the worldwide market demand for opiates. Farmers can only harvest the crop in specific regions of certain states. Over the years, Indian authorities have been effective in eradicating illegal opium farming in territories outside those designated for that purpose.

Drug Offenses and the Law

Prohibition of "intoxicating substances" has been in effect since India's Constitution was adopted in 1950 (Raghavan 2003). All uses of opium, except for medicinal purposes, were restricted in 1959.

The primary legislation concerning illicit drugs is the Narcotic Drugs and Psychotropic Substances Act of 1985. Narcotic drugs include coca leaf, cannabis (hemp), opium straw, and manufactured drugs, which includes all coca derivatives, medicinal cannabis, opium derivatives, and poppy straw concentrate. Psychotropic substances are those listed in the Schedule of the act and include, among others, LSD, DET, and MDA.

The act prohibits cultivation of coca plants and the possession, sale, purchase, and use of coca leaves. It also prohibits the possession, sale, purchase, and use of psychotropic substances. The Act also gives enforcement authority to the Union Government (Central Excise, Narcotics, Customs) and the State Government (including Revenue, Drug Control, Excise, and the Police).

The National Crime Records Bureau of the Union Ministry of Home Affairs in New Delhi publishes *Crime in India* annually and this publication includes statistics on drug offenses. In 1990, there were 5,299 violations under the Act of 1985.

Extent and Patterns of Use

In India, patterns and choice of drug usage are related to caste, religion, and local customs and traditions. Cannabis use goes back to 2000–1400 B.C. when hemp was referred to as a medicinal plant created by God. The Shivites in Hinduism believed (some still believe) that hemp should be left for their deity in the temples. Some religious individuals believed that cannabis aided meditation, and the cut tops of uncultivated cannabis plants, known as bhang, are associated with Hindu rituals. Muslims also have used charas (resin from the cannabis plant) and hashish to aid meditation.

Opium use can be traced back to the ninth century when Arab traders introduced the drug. Opium was used as a natural medicine, and became an important item of trade in the sixteenth century. It was at this time that many individuals acquired an opium habit. However, by the time the first official study of opium use was conducted in 1893, it was determined that opium smoking in rural areas was rare (Royal Commission 1893). In 1975, the total number of registered opium addicts in India was 80,809 (National Committee 1977).

Cocaine use is not a problem in India, but opium and hashish use appear to be an issue. To learn more about its own drug problem, India's Ministry of Social Justice and Empowerment is conducting its first nationwide survey of narcotics addicts in conjunction with the UN. In 1985, the government initiated the "Scheme for Prohibition and Drug Abuse Prevention." This program helps fund hundreds of nongovernmental organizations which support 425 drug treatment centers across India. The UN has also provided assistance with developing community-based rehabilitation programs and workplace prevention programs. Also, the Center for Drug Abuse Prevention was created as part of the National Institute of Social Defense to increase the number of trained rehabilitation professionals.

The UNODC (2003) reports that India has one of the highest prevalence rates of opium abuse. Approximately 0.7 percent of men over the age of ten have abused opiates (107). Current trends indicate that injecting heroin, buprenorphine, and dextropropoxyphene is more prevalent (UNODC, Regional Office for South Asia 2003: 6).

Among persons age fifteen and older from 1997 to 1998, the annual prevalence of cannabis was 0.2–5.8 percent and 0.09–1.6 percent for opiates
(UNODC, Regional Office for South Asia 2003, Table 3.4, p. 10).

Since India sustains a legal market for opium production, there is always
the danger that licit opium can get diverted into illicit markets. Opium can
be sold to illegal buyers for twenty to twenty-five times the regular market
price, creating a constant temptation for opium farmers. Indian authorities
maintain strict controls over the amount of opium produced and extract
every gram from the producers. If opium farms are producing in excess of 5
percent of the allowable harvest, it is seized and destroyed. In 1999, about 18
metric tons of opium was seized from farmers who did not fully declare their
excess harvest. Licit opium cultivation took place in Madhya Pradesh, Rajasthan, and Uttar Pradesh during 2001 (UNODC, ROSA, 2003).

Still there has been diversion of opium into illicit markets over the years.
Exact numbers are difficult to calculate, but substantial illegal opium markets
are present in the states of Punjab, Orissa, West Bengal, Rajasthan, Kerala,
Tamil Nadu, and Maharashtra. The U.S. government is working with Indian
authorities to devise a system of tracking crop yields to help discover the
amount of opium diverted to illegal markets. Illegal cultivation also occurs,
though Indian authorities have responded well in discovering and destroying
these crops using satellite data provided by the United States and extensive
aerial surveys to discover hidden fields. In 1999 about 350 hectares were found
and destroyed.

Law Enforcement

India's Central Bureau of Narcotics is the office with the primary task of overseeing and enforcing the nation's drug policies. The office is small compared
to the size of the nation and amount of trafficking (about 400 officers nation-

TABLE 23-1
Licit Opium Production (in Metric Tons) and
Cultivation (Licensed Areas in Hectares), India, 1997–2002

	1997	1998	1999	2000	2001	2002
Production						
Opium	998	260	1,075	1,326	726	790
Cultivation						
Opium Poppy	29,799	30,714	33,459	35,270	26,684	22,847

Source: UNODC, Regional Office for South Asia 2003. *Country Profile: India*, Tables 3.1, 3.2, p. 10.

wide). But India's success against drugs comes from the coordinated efforts of several government agencies including the Central Bureau of Investigation, the Directorate of Revenue Intelligence, and the Customs and Central Excise Service. About 90 percent of drug seizures actually occur through state police agencies.

Given its size and location geographically, India experiences a large amount of drug smuggling through its borders. Over the years, heroin seizures have concentrated around the Indo-Pakistan border. Media reports allege narcotics-related corruption among local politicians, police, and government officials. Still, prosecutions are rare. The government has taken steps to reduce corruption by transferring officers regularly and concealing locations of opium production.

The areas where Indian authorities have difficulty with illicit opium cultivation are Jammu and Kashmir. Insurgent military groups are active in these areas and prevent authorities from conducting full sweeps of the landscape. Also, farmers in poor rural areas tend to give in to the temptation of large profits returned by illicit opium production. The government is working on supplying legitimate cash crops to these areas.

Indian authorities work closely with drug enforcement agencies internationally. In 1999, India made several successful interdictions and seizures with the help of other nations. In May 1999, Indian authorities seized 384 kg of hashish in Bombay bound for Canada with the help of Canadian authorities. In October 1999, U.K. customs made three arrests and seized 7 kg of heroin entering Britain thanks to intelligence provided by Indian authorities.

Cocaine use has not been a problem in India, but some estimate that in the early half of the twentieth century, there were 500,000 cocaine users (Chopra and Chopra 1965). In modern day India, cocaine is very rarely mentioned as a problem (Spencer and Navaratnam 1981).

A public opinion poll conducted in 1991 found that respondents thought the international drug trafficking problem was serious. Eighty-eight percent responded that the problem was very serious and only 1 percent said they did not think the problem was serious (Hann and Hastings 1991).

The UNODC, ROSA highlights major events occurring in India in 2002 (16). Regulatory and preventive systems have been implemented to prevent the flow of opium, although they have not curbed the illicit trafficking of opium. Much of the licit opium makes its way through illegal channels and is eventually used to make heroin in clandestine laboratories, although heroin seizures have been low since September 11, 2001. Furthermore, there is much concern over the prevalence of trafficking and consumption of amphetamines.

TABLE 23-2

Seizures (in Kilograms), India, 1997–2002

		1997	1998	1999	2000	2001	2002
Heroin	Seizures	1,332	655	839	1,240	889	712
	Cases	2,990	3,095	2,937	2,776	3,891	2,933
Cocaine	Seizures	24	1	1	0.35	2	2
	Cases	6	6	4	5	10	5
Opium	Seizures	3,316	2,031	1,635	2,684	2,533	150
	Cases	1,333	954	927	1,257	1,205	959
Morphine	Seizures	128	19	30	39	26	49
	Cases	75	56	103	142	146	75
Cannabis/ganja	Seizures	80,866	68,221	38,610	100,056	75,943	2,295
	Cases	7,062	6,018	5,935	6,073	6,467	2,170
Cannabis resin/hashish	Seizures	3,281	10,106	3,290	5,041	5,664	1,344
	Cases	2,223	2,193	2,314	2,078	2,117	
Methaqualone	Seizures	1,740	2,257	474	1,095	2,024	11,130
	Cases	207	114	8	31	8	7
Acetic anhydride (liters)	Seizures	8,311	6,197	2,963	1,337	8,501	3,284
	Cases	12	9	7	14	6	3
Ephedrine	Seizures	8,311	1,051	2,134	532	792	27
	Cases	12	15	51	8	1	

Source: UNODC, Regional Office of South Asia. 2003. Country Profile: India, Table 3.3, p. 10.

Drug Policy

India has worked on all sorts of legislation to bring its drug laws and policies up to speed and align them with recommendations of the U.N. Although there is little evidence of money laundering in India, legislation has been introduced to expand money laundering laws. In 1997, the government proposed a number of amendments to Parliament that are still under consideration. Among these are provisions that streamline the process of search and seizure by law enforcement, codification of civil forfeiture provisions to seize assets of drug traffickers, and reforming loopholes and clarifying existing drug laws that hinder prosecution of drug traffickers. The Indian government also reorganized its schedule of drug classifications to fit more closely with UN standards.

A project entitled "The extent and pattern of drug abuse in India" involved the Ministry of Social Justice and Empowerment, which is responsible for drug demand reduction programs, as well as the United Nations Office on Drugs and Crime, Regional Office for South Asia (ROSA). The project consisted of four main elements: a National Household Survey of Drug and Alcohol Abuse, a Drug Abuse Monitoring System, Rapid Assessment of a Survey of Drug Abuse, and Focused Thematic Studies (UNODC, ROSA 2003: 23). The Ministry of Social Justice and Empowerment is attempting to tackle the drug problem in India through education and increasing awareness, treating addicts, and "imparting drug abuse prevention rehabilitation training to volunteers having in view to build up and educate a cadre of drug abuse control operators" (UNODC, ROSA, *Country Profile: India*, 33).

References

Chopra, R. N., and I.C. Chopra. 1965. *Drug Addiction with Special Reference to India.* New Delhi: Council of Scientific and Industrial Research.

Indian Penal Code, 1860.

Jois, Rama, M. 1990. Legal and Constitutional History of India, Vol.I & 11. Bombay: N.M.Tripathy Ltd.

Hann, E., and P. K. Hastings (eds.). 1991. Index to International Public Opinion. Westport, Conn.: Greenwood Press.

National Committee. 1977. *Drug Abuse in India.* New Delhi: Ministry of Health and Family Welfare.

National Crime Records Bureau, Crime in India. 1991. New Delhi: Ministry of Home Affairs, November 1992.

Raghavan, R. K. n.d. *World Factbook of Criminal Justice Systems: India.* U.S. Department of Justice, Bureau of Justice Statistics. www.ojp.usdoj.gov/bjs/pub/ascii/wfbcjind.txt (accessed October 10, 2003).

Royal Commission on Opium. 1893. *Report*. Simla: Government of India, Central Printing Office.

Sharma, H. K. 1996. "Sociocultural Perspective of Substance Use in India," *Substance Use and Misuse 31* (11&12): 1689–1714.

Spencer, C. P., and V. Navaratnam. 1981. *Drug Abuse in East Asia*. Kuala Lumpur, Malaysia: Oxford University Press.

Thapar, Romila. 1990. *A History of India*, Volume 1. London: Penguin.

United Nations Office on Drugs and Crime (UNODC), Regional Office for South Asia (ROSA). 2003. *Country Profile: India*. www.unocd.org/unocd/index.html (accessed October 10, 2003).

United Nations Office on Drugs and Crime. 2003. *Global Illicit Drug Trends 2003*. www.unodc.org/unodc/en/global_illicit_drug_trends.html (accessed October 24, 2003).

24

Thailand

Overview

In 2004, THAILAND HAD AN ESTIMATED population of 64.9 million, with 20 percent living in urban areas. Thailand's population is 75 percent Thai, 14 percent Chinese, and 11 percent other. The overwhelming majority—95 percent—are Buddhists. Thailand is part of the Golden Triangle, a notorious drug trafficking and transit area comprising the border regions of Thailand, Lao People's Democratic Republic, and Myannmar (Burma). Although the government's alternative development initiative has helped decrease the production of opiates, Thailand remains a major transit area, with Bangkok an important technological center for money laundering.

Thailand is a constitutional monarchy. During the last decade at least two new constitutions were written, one in 1991 and one in 1997. The country's legal system is generally based on civil law system, but has also been influenced by common law.

Drug Offenses and the Law

It is against the law in Thailand to possess, produce, manufacture, import, export, or acquire illicit drugs. Punishment can be very stringent for law breakers, including lengthy terms of imprisonment or death. Recent problems with ecstasy and amphetamines have led the Thai government to classify these drugs as first-grade narcotics. The maximum punishment for trafficking first-grade narcotics has recently been increased from twenty years to the death sentence. Individuals who produce, import, export, or posses with intent to sell more than 20 grams of pure first-grade narcotics face the maximum sentence.

Extent and Patterns of Use

Survey data estimate that there are two million drug users in Thailand today. (UNODC 2003). The highest prevalence rates exist among truck drivers, three-wheeled vehicle drivers, fishermen, and bus drivers. Cocaine use is generally limited to the more privileged, which represent a very small portion of the population.

The United Nations Drug Control Programme surveys found that cannabis and heroin users tend to be between the ages of twenty and twenty-five years, and opium users tend to be older. Heroin users are increasingly using needles to inject the drug, as opposed to smoking it. With local production of heroin, students and other youth have easy access to the drug. Use of heroin is particularly widespread among blue-collar workers.

In addition, the surveys found that there are about 45,000 new illicit drug users each year. In 1992, approximately 32,000 people were admitted to treatment centers. The overwhelming majority of these drug-dependent persons were admitted for abusing heroin (83 percent), and another 8.8 percent for abusing opium. The largest age group represented in treatment were the twenty to twenty-four year olds.

Historically, drugs are used in Thai society to improve performance and overcome fatigue. However, during the last decade, the trend seems to be moving toward use of drugs simply for pleasure. Treatment data from Bangkok showed that clients were twenty-three times more likely to be unemployed than the general population in Thailand, where the unemployment rate is very low.

Recently, Thailand has reported significantly large increases in methamphetamine abuse (UNODC 2003: 147). The UNODC (2003) reports that "the number of methamphetamine abusers rose 10-fold between 1993 and 2001. Thailand also reported the highest methamphetamine prevalence rate worldwide . . . as well as the world's highest methamphetamine seizures in 2001" (147).

Thailand outlawed the production, transportation, use, and selling of all forms of opium on December 9, 1958 (Gray 1995; Visudhimark 1997). This law mandated that opium smokers register with the Excise Department and seek treatment within a six-month period, and as such, treatment centers

TABLE 24-1
Statistics, Thailand, 1991–1999

	1991	1992	1993	1994	1995	1996	1997	1998	1999
Opium (Hectares)									
Potential Harvest	3,000	2,050	2,880	2,110	1,750	2,170	1,650	1,350	835
Eradication	1,200	1,580	0	0	580	880	1,050	715	808
Cultivation	4,200	3,630	2,880	2,110	2,330	3,050	2,700	2,065	1,643
Potential Yield (Mt)	35	24	42	17	25	30	25	16	6
Cannabis									
Eradication	59	85	80	85	80	85	0	0	0
Seizures/Law Enforcement Data (Metric Tons)									
Opium	1.500	2,000.600	2.200	0.600	0.920	0.620	0.720	1.500	0.440
Heroin	1.500	0.992	2.100	1.100	0.690	0.390	0.320	0.530	0.310
Cannabis	54.00	87.00	98.00	71.00	46.00	44.00	9.00	6.00	45.25
Heroin Labs Destroyed	5	0	2	0	1	2	3	1	0
Narcotics Arrests (Thousands)	75	73	85	102	120	125	158	186	205

Source: http://www.police.go.th/Trenglish.htm.

were established in Patumthani (Visudhimark 1997). However, heroin use became more prevalent as users switched from opium abuse to heroin, and epidemics of heroin abuse were recorded in 1959 and 1967 (Visudhimark 1997). By 1993, there were an estimated 1.27 million drug abusers, of whom 17 percent were heroin dependents and 5 percent were opium dependents (Thailand Development Research Institute, reported in Visudhimark 1997).

The rise of HIV/AIDS infections in Thailand occurred during the late 1980s. Visudhimark (1997) reports that the "first acquired immunodeficiency syndrome (AIDS) case in Thailand was identified in September 1984." Needle exchange programs have been created for opium or heroin users of the Hilltribe people in the "Golden Triangle" of northern Thailand (Gray 1995). Gray estimates that 60 percent of the adult males within these northern villages are opium or heroin abusers. In 2000, the estimated national HIV prevalence rate was 2.8 percent—the highest prevalence rate in the Asia Pacific region. HIV prevalence among injection drug users tested ranges between 20 percent and 50 percent in and outside of Bangkok (WHD 2001).

Presently, the United States is actively involved in "drug and crime control assistance projects" (U.S. Department of State 2003) in Thailand. Law enforcement efforts in Thailand include the Office of the Narcotics Control Board (ONCB), the Police Narcotics Suppression Bureau, and other agencies. The Royal Thai Army Third Region (3RTA), the ONCB, and the Border Patrol Police are charged with "surveying, locating, and eradicating illicit opium poppy crop in northern Thailand" (U.S. Department of State 2003).

Drug treatment, as specified in the Narcotic Act, involves four phases: 1) pre-admission and treatment plan, 2) detoxification, 3) rehabilitation, and 4) after care (Visudhimark 1997).

Beginning around 2003, naturalized citizens and their families may lose their citizenship if they are found to be participating in the drug trade (Drug Policy Alliance 2003).

Law Enforcement

In 1992, Thailand convicted over 635,000 persons for consumption or possession of drugs. Fifty-four received a death sentence and 358 life imprisonment. During this time period over 90 percent of drug law offenses were solely for consumption and possession.

The Royal Thai Police is currently implementing a nationwide database system that will connect to all police stations and sub-stations throughout the country. The database system will include POLIS, a central database within the larger database network. POLIS will include the Crime Statistics Database which maintains the data on all the criminal cases throughout the country (Royal Thai Police website http://www.police.go.th/trenglish.htm 1999). The following statistics on reported narcotics crimes were available through the Web site. Between 1995 and 1998, the number of narcotics cases reported to the police and those arrested for narcotics violations increased over 50 percent.

Drug Policy

The national drug policies in Thailand are formed around international and regional cooperation and coordinative efforts. Thailand is a member of various international agencies designed to counter the region's large narcotics production and traffic. In 1999, Thailand passed money laundering legislation that brought it into compliance with the 1998 UN Drug Convention. Thailand is a member of the UN MOU on Sub-regional Narcotics Cooperation along with Burma, Cambodia, China, Laos, and Vietnam. Thailand is also a member of the UN Commission on Narcotic Drugs and is the designated co-ordinator for ASEAN's Senior Officials on Drugs group.

Thailand and the United States have enjoyed great cooperation in counter-narcotics efforts over recent years. Thailand is one of the top three countries in the world cooperating with U.S. extradition requests. Since 1991, Thailand has extradited forty-four fugitives to the United States, thirty-five of which were narcotics-related. In 1998, the Royal Thai Government and the United States established the International Law Enforcement Agency in Bangkok. The following year, the ILEA trained over 600 law enforcement and judicial officials from countries all over the region.

Prevention and demand-reduction programs are coordinated through Thailand's Office of the Narcotics Control Board. Programs are designed to reach several high-risk groups including students, fisherman, laborers, and long-haul truck drivers. School programs are geared toward training student leadership to conduct school-based prevention programs. The Ministry of

TABLE 24-2
Reported Drug Crimes, Thailand, 1995–1998

	1995	1996	1997	1998
Reported to Police	149,452	168,641	175,978	225,252
Arrested	156,906	178,994	188,866	243,661

Source: http://www.police.go.th/trenglish.htm.

Public Health has 421 registered drug-treatment centers in government and private hospitals. Thailand has also implemented a Narcotics Anonymous program to help prevent relapse addiction.

References

Drug Policy Alliance. 2003. "Thailand Drug War Continues: Now Denouncing Citizenships." www.drugpolicy.org/news/09_05_03thailand.cfm (accessed October 23, 2003).

Gray, J. 1995. "Operating Needle Exchange Programs In the Hills of Thailand." *AIDS Care, 7(4): 489-499.* www.drugpolicy.org/library/Trenglish.htm (accessed October 23, 2003).

Royal Thai Police. www.police.go.th/trenglish.htm (accessed May 17, 1999).

United Nations Office on Drugs and Crime. 2003. *Global Illicit Drug Trends 2003.* www.unodc.org/unodc/en/global_illicit_drug_trends.html (accessed October 24, 2003).

United States Department of State. 2003. "Counternarcotics and Law Enforcement Country Program: Thailand." Fact Sheet, Bureau for International Narcotics and Law Enforcement Affairs, March 11, 2003. www.state.gov/g/inl/rls/fs/18533.htm (accessed October 23, 2003).

Visudhimark, Annop. 1997. "Drug and AIDS in Thailand: Same Policies, Different Laws. How Can They Be Reformed to Obtain the Most Benefit?" Ministry of Public Health, Department of Medical Services. www.drugtext.org/library/articles/visudhimark.htm (accessed October 23, 2003).

World Health Organization. 2001. HIV/AIDS in Asia and the Pacific Region.

Part VIII

AFRICA

THE UNODC (2003) SURVEYED 111 COUNTRIES to determine the world's producers of cannabis. Of the 103 countries that supplied cannabis between
1998 and 2001, 30 were in Africa. Twenty percent of all cannabis abusers reside in Africa (UNODC 2003: 136). In 2001, the number of heroin seizures in
Africa increased, especially in southern countries. Still, the seizure rates are
not as high as they were in the early 1990s.

From South America, cocaine often passes through countries such as Nigeria, Ghana, South Africa, Swaziland, Tanzania, Kenya, and Uganda before they
reach their final destination in Europe (UNODC 2003: 67). The largest
seizures of cocaine in Africa during 2001 took place in South Africa and Nigeria.

In 2003, the UNODC reported that the abuse rate of opiates in Africa is
below the worldwide average (107). This trend has changed since the 1990s
when Namibia and Zimbabwe reported "strong" increases in heroin abuse and
other countries reported "some increase" (UNODC 2003: 126).

References

United Nations Office on Drugs and Crime. 2003. *Global Illicit Drug Trends 2003*,
http://www.unodc.org/unodc/en/global_illicit_drug_trends.html (accessed October 24, 2003).

25

South Africa

Overview

BEFORE AUGUST 1993, THE COUNTRY WAS a racial oligarchy in which apartheid controlled every aspect of life on the basis of racial classification. South Africa is currently a non-racial democracy of roughly 44 million people, the fifth largest in Africa (UNODC 2003: 3). The population is comprised of 75.2 percent Black, 13.6 percent white, 8.6 percent Colored, and 2.6 percent Indian. The main religion is Christianity (68 percent) and includes most whites, Coloreds, and about 60 percent of blacks and 40 percent of Indians. The remaining religions include Muslim (2 percent), Hindu (1.5 percent), and the rest traditional and animistic (28.5 percent).

With the fall of apartheid, criminal activity became very visible. The rapid transition to a democratic government produced conditions that are favorable to organized crime groups. Rapid transition is usually accompanied by reforms of the security forces and replacement of personnel with new individuals often not equipped to take on the new responsibilities. Similarly, judicial institutions now are responsible for protecting individual freedoms instead of repressing any opposition. Outdated laws and weak judicial and police institutions provide the right atmosphere for criminal activity to flourish. In addition, poor border controls coupled with sophisticated transport and banking systems have led the country to become a major center for the drug trade. South Africa has become a transhipment point for heroin, cocaine, and Mandrax—a synthetically produced sedative made from methaqualone powder and antihistamines. Its location facilitates the flow of drugs from Asia, Latin America, West Europe, and North America (UNODC 2002: 7).

Factors contributing to the increase in drug abuse include unemployment rates, social injustice resulting from apartheid, family anomie, and adjusting to the post-apartheid South Africa (UNODC 2002: 7).

Drug Offenses and the Law

Crimes are referred to as either "crimes" or "offenses" and generally people use the term "crime" to refer to the more serious forms of criminal conduct such as murder, theft, and rape, and the term "offense" to refer to less serious conduct (like misdemeanors in the U.S.) as contraventions of municipal by-laws (Snyman 1984: 4).

Drug use, possession, and dealing is prohibited by the Drugs and Drug Trafficking Act (No. 140 of 1992). Drugs are generally defined as any substance that produces a dangerous or undesirable dependency. Cannabis, known locally as dagga, is included as a dangerous drug. Before the 1992 Act, drug law consisted of the Abuse of Dependence-Producing Substances and Rehabilitation Centres Act of 1971 and its 1973 amendment. Penalties for minor dealing and possession were imprisonment for a period of not less than five years, but not exceeding fifteen years. A person convicted of drug offenses is not considered innocent until proven guilty, as is the case with other offenses. The 1973 amendment strengthened the 1971 law by making it difficult for the courts to impose suspended sentences, or reduced sentences.

South Africa is a signatory to the United Nations Single Convention on Narcotic Drugs (1961), the 1970 Protocol, and the United Nations Convention on Psychotropic Substances (1971). Although South Africa has not yet signed on to the 1988 Vienna Convention against Illicit Traffic in Narcotic Drugs and Psychotropic Substances, they have taken a few recent steps against drug trafficking and drug use by hosting in 1995 a joint conference between the Southern African Development Community and the European Union to discuss trafficking. The conference adopted a regional protocol on reducing the drug trade in the southern African region and stressed the need to focus on drug abuse. Drug laws are formulated through legislation such as the Medicines and Related Substances Control Act of 1965 and the South African Drugs and Drug Trafficking Act of 1992 (UNODC 2002: 45).

Extent and Patterns of Use

Between 1997 and 1998, cannabis was the most prevalent drug of abuse, respectively followed by mandrax, depressants, inhalants, cocaine/crack, ATS, LSD, and heroin/opiates (UNODC 2002 Table 6, p. 36). Estimated morbidity rates place cannabis at the highest level, followed, respectively, by mandrax, cocaine/crack, depressants, heroin/opiates, ATS, LSD, and inhalants. (See South African Medical Research Council, Draft Country Profile, October 1998).

Nigerian criminal groups have set up "permanent operational bases" (UNODC 2002: 9) in the southern regions of Africa to traffic drugs. As such, South Africa has "unfortunately become part of major international drug trafficking networks" (9). South Africa has joined a host of regions—namely Western Europe, North America, Latin America, and Asia—that produce and consume drugs (9).

A survey of urban high school students found that in 1985 almost 19 percent of students reported using marijuana. The next most popular drug for students was inhalants, followed by hallucinogens (du Toit 1991). Another study of eleventh graders in Cape Town in 1997 revealed that the lifetime prevalence of abusing cannabis was 32 percent among males and 13.1 percent among females, for glue/inhalants, the prevalence was 15.8 percent among males and 4.9 percent among females, for white pipe (cannabis/mandrax) the rate was 5.7 percent among males and 1.9 percent among females, for ecstasy it was 4.3 percent among males and 3.1 percent among females, and for crack cocaine it was 2.6 percent among males and 1.0 percent among females (UNODC 2002 Table 8, 39; see Flisher 1998).

Cannabis has been smoked by Africans for centuries and is currently the most abused drug in South Africa (UNODC 2002: 7). Cannabis is cultivated domestically in areas such as Eastern Cape, KwaZulu-Natal, Limpopo, and Mpumalanga (11), but is also imported from Swaziland, Malawi, and Lesotho (8).

Heroin and cocaine have become threats in the last decade as expanding networks of drug trafficking—principally from Nigeria—looking for new markets and new transshipment points, brought illicit drugs into South Africa. Heroin use, however, remains somewhat limited, largely because dipipanone, a synthetic pain killer, is available legally. Larger cities experience problems with heroin abuse, such as Gauteng province and Cape Town, although this concern is being heightened due to recent trends in injecting heroin (UNODC 2002: 7).

Cocaine, on the other hand, is a highly desirable drug, and becoming easier to obtain. Cocaine was more of a status drug in the 1970s and

1980s—its use confined to middle- and upper-class suburbanites. But, cocaine prices have dropped dramatically, as the trafficking network from Nigeria continued to expand. In addition, crack has recently entered the scene among cocaine users in the major metropolitan areas. Currently, cocaine is the most serious drug problem, but marijuana is the most widely abused drug in the country and almost every other country in the South African region.

South Africa is one of the world's leading marijuana producers (Gelbard 1998). In addition to these well-known drugs, South Africans are using Mandrax, also known to some as methaqualone, which is the main psychoactive ingredient in a sleeping tablet. The drug was banned in 1977, but continues to be a problem. Over the years a subculture has evolved that involves using the drug by grounding the tablet into a powder and mixing it with cannabis before smoking it. In 1996 a laboratory was found in a rural area that was capable of producing half a million tablets (Venter 1998). Today, it is the second most commonly abused drug in South Africa and is largely obtained from China and India (UNODC 2002: 8).

Longitudinal data on illicit drug usage is largely lacking. The epidemiological studies that have been conducted on substance abuse in South Africa have been poorly constructed, or done in an ad hoc manner. But the Mental Health and Substance Abuse Division of the Medical Research Council (MRC) has recently launched the South African Community Epidemiological Network of Drug Use (SACENDU). The objective is to develop a network of local stakeholders in the drug abuse area to share information and data about drug use trends. The program began in Cape Town with plans to expand to Durban and Johannesburg.

The prevalence of HIV and AIDS is a major concern in South Africa. It is estimated that 20 percent of the working population was HIV-positive in 1999 (UNODC 2002: 41). Between the years 2002 and 2012, it is expected that 3 million children will lose their parents to HIV/AIDS. The connection between HIV/AIDS and drug use is strong (UNODC 2002: Table 42).

Law Enforcement

Table 25-1 reports national arrests for marijuana, cocaine, and heroin from 1992 through 1996. As shown in Table 25-2, during the first half of 1997 there were 236 drug-related arrests in Cape Town (UNODC 2002: 20). Over half of the arrests involved cannabis. During the same period, 227 arrests were made in Durban and 417 in Guateng. In the latter half of 2001, the number of drug-related arrests was 255 in Cape Town, 162 in Durban, and 567 in Guateng.

TABLE 25-1
Arrests for Marijuana, Cocaine, and Heroin, South Africa, 1992–1996

	1992	1993	1994	1995	1996
Arrests for Marijuana Possession	6,511	4,331	3,169	2,047	637
Arrests for Marijuana Dealing	10,272	8,717	7,896	4,065	1,843
Arrests for Cocaine Possession	17	28	28	23	27
Arrests for Cocaine Dealing	108	236	266	271	65
Arrests for Heroin Possession	5	1	4	1	0
Arrests for Heroin Dealing	7	14	29	21	7

Source: Venter 1998.

A recent study by the South African Medical Research Council and the Pretoria-based Institute for Security Studies found that among a cohort of arrestees between August 1999 and September 2000, 46 percent tested positive in a urinalysis at the time of their arrest (UNODC 2002: 20). Of those who tested positive, the most common drug that appeared was cannabis, followed by mandrax (see Parry, Louw and Pluddemann 2001). Overall, the study revealed a significant correlation between substance abuse and crime.

The South African Police Service is working with citizens through Crime Stop, a hotline that lets concerned citizens pass on information about local drug dealing, and Captain Crime Stop, an educational program for children that discusses all aspects of crime, and has special units to educate youth about the harm caused by drugs.

Drug Policy

Within a few years after the fall of apartheid, South Africa released a National Crime Prevention Strategy, an eighty-page document that attempts to provide a broad vision for South Africa by restructuring and consolidating the departments involved with crime control and prevention. The document has a strong focus on prevention, but little is mentioned about prevention of drug use, specifically. A Drug Advisory Board was established under the Prevention and Treatment of Drugs Dependency Act of 1992 to advise the Minister of Welfare on issues of alcohol and drug abuse, but the board does not have the power or resources to develop and implement prevention and intervention

TABLE 25-2

Arrests for Dealing, South Africa, 1997–2001

Area	Period	Cannabis	Mandrax	Cocaine	Ecstasy	Heroin	LSD	Meth.	Other	Total (N)
Cape Town	1997a*	54%	27	10	4	<1	3	1	0	236
	2001b	29%	26	26	15	1	2	1	0	255
Durban	1997a	66%	9	11	9	0	0	5	<1	227
	2001b	27%	40	23	4	0	0	0	5	162
Gauteng	1997b	70%	12	14	2	<1	1	<1	0	417
	2001a	29%	16	33	11	2	8	1	0	567

*a = first half of the year, b = second half of the year

Source: UNODC, Regional Office for Southern Africa. 2002. Country Profile on Drugs and Crime. (Table 3, p. 20.

programming. Historically, the government response to the drug problem has been underfunded and piecemeal (Ryan 1997; Shaw 1998).

After several failed attempts during the 1980s and early 1990s to develop a national plan that would confront the drug problem head on, the Drug Advisory Board drafted the National Drug Master Plan which was adopted in February 1999 (UNODC 2002: 44). The Master Plan, drawing upon international practices, was designed to confront the government's "disjointed, fragmented and uncoordinated" (44) approach to the drug situation. It contains six main areas of focus, that involve reducing drug-related crime, protecting minors, supporting community health and welfare, strengthening research and its dissemination, encouraging international involvement, and improving communication between diverse groups (UNODC 2002: 44). By working with communities, governmental agencies, and private agencies, the Master Plan specified methods in which demand reduction could take place. Furthermore, the plan calls for educational material that accommodates all cultures, languages, and socioeconomic groups (UNODC 2002: 44).

In 2000, the Central Drug Authority (CDA) was created to push forth national drug control plans and to monitor their implementation (UNODC 2002: 44). Consisting of both government and nongovernment appointees and experts, and representing civilians, research councils, trade unions, universities, and businesses, the CDA reports progress to Parliament (UNODC 2002: 44).

References

du Toit, Brian M. 1991. *Cannabis, Alcohol and the South African Student: Adolescent Drug Use 1974–1985.* Ohio University Center for International Studies. Monographs in International Studies, Africa Series, Number 59, Athens, Ohio.

Gelbard, Robert S. 1998. "Drug Trafficking in Southern Africa," in Rotberg, Robert I., and Mills, Greg. (eds.) *War and Peace in Southern Africa: Crime, Drugs, Armies and Trade.* Washington, D.C.: Brookings Institution Press.

Rotberg, Robert I., and Greg Mills. (Eds.)1998. War and Peace in Southern Africa: Crime, Drugs, Armies and Trade. Washington, D.C.: Brookings Institution Press.

Ryan, Tim. 1997. "Drugs Violence and Governability in the Future South Africa," Occasional Paper No. 22 for the Institute for Security Studies, Crime and Policing Project, May, 1997. www.iss.co.za/Pubs/Papers/22/paper22.html (accessed June 29, 1999).

Shaw, Mark. 1998. "South Africa: Crime and Policing in Post-Apartheid South Africa," in Rotberg, Robert I., and Mills, Greg. (eds.) *War and Peace in Southern Africa: Crime, Drugs, Armies and Trade.* Washington, D.C.: Brookings Institution Press.

United Nations Office of Drugs and Crime, Regional Office for Southern Africa. 2002. *Country Profile on Drugs and Crime: South Africa.* (www.unodc.org/pdf/southafrica/country_profile_southafrica_1.pdf) (www.unodc.org/pdf/south

africa/country_profile_southafrica_2.pdf) (www.unodc.org/pdf/southafrica/
country_profile_southafrica_.3pdf) (www.unodc.org/pdf/southafrica/country_
profile_southafrica_4.pdf) (accessed October 9, 2003).
Venter C. J. D. 1998. "Drug Abuse and Drug Smuggling in South Africa," in Robert
Rothberg and Greg Mills (eds.), War and Peace in Southern Africa, Washingon D.C.:
Brookings Institution Press.

26

Nigeria

Overview

NIGERIA IS LOCATED IN WESTERN AFRICA. It borders the Gulf of Guinea and is between Cameroon, Niger, Chad, and Benin. Nigeria has a population of 129,934,911 with more than 250 ethnic groups. The majority groups of Hausa and Fulani make up 29 percent, following by Yoruba (21 percent), Igbo (Ibo) (18 percent), Ijaw (10 percent), Kanuri (4 percent), Ibibio (3.5 percent), and Tiv (2.5 percent). The majority of the people in Nigeria are Muslim (50 percent), Christian (40 percent), and indigenous (10 percent). English is the official language, although Hausa, Yoruba, Igbo (IBO), and Fulani are also spoken (CIA 2004).

The British gained control over Nigeria in 1900 and its laws—including the Criminal and Penal Code—were based largely on those in England. Differences between Islamic law and English criminal law were problematic, since many of the inhabitants of northern Nigeria were Muslims. A new Penal Code, developed in 1959, was based on the Sudanese Penal Code, because Sudan's Muslim laws were similar to the local code of the Muslims in Northern Nigeria (Ebbe 1996).

After Nigeria gained its independence in 1960, the Criminal Code and Penal Code were amended many times to more closely reflect the values and customs of the Nigerian people. Although these laws reflect much of the Nigerian culture, Nigeria generally operates a tripartite system of criminal justice where the Criminal Code (including criminal procedure) is largely based on English common law and legal practice, the Penal Code is based on the local Maliki law and the Muslim system of law and justice, and customary law is based on immemorial customs and traditions. In some parts of Nigeria the native laws and customs are written, and in some, they are unwritten.

Drug Offenses and the Law

Although criminal procedure is based on English law, Nigerians do not use a jury system or allow plea bargaining. Most persons convicted of an offense are not incarcerated, but instead receive fines, community service, or time in a labor camp. Assault and battery rarely lead to a sentence of imprisonment because they are traditional methods of settling disputes. In addition, rural areas generally handle all criminal victimizations within the village in a traditional manner.

Crimes are classified by seriousness as felony or misdemeanor, and are separated into offenses against persons, offenses against property and other offenses without victims, and offenses against local ordinance. Felonies include murder, strong-arm and armed robbery, arson, auto theft, burglary, aggravated assault, rape, grand theft, child abduction, counterfeiting, conspiracy and smuggling contraband, forgery, fraud, kidnapping, and treason. Definitions for these crimes are very similar to those in the United States.

Drug offenses are also considered felonies. Drug offenses include possession or selling of cocaine, heroin, or marijuana. All amphetamines and barbiturates are legal drugs which can be purchased in pharmacies.

The age of criminal responsibility is seventeen; youth twelve to sixteen are treated as juveniles and youth seven to eleven are treated as children. Crimes by youth under seventeen are handled by juvenile courts, which is made up of a county magistrate and a layman and laywoman.

Nigeria did not enter the drug-trade world until the mid-1980s when the Nigerian economy collapsed. Smugglers were recruited cheaply and many of those who lost their wealth were attracted to drug running, soon placing Nigeria on the map as having some of the most organized drug trafficking crime networks in the world (Gelbard 1998).

Extent and Patterns of Use

During the 1960s and 1970s, the United Nations Office of Drugs and Crime reported that the most common drugs were cannabis, amphetamines, and tranquilizers (Pela 1989). During the mid-1970s, when importation of amphetamines was banned, amphetamine abuse rates dropped. However, the use of alternative stimulants increased. Heroin and cocaine use and trafficking became a concern in 1983 (Pela 1989). Thus, drug abuse was widespread during the 1980s.

Anumonye's (1980) survey of a national sample of 2,800 students from secondary schools in 1980 found that 2.9 percent of the males and 2.1 percent of females had ever tried marijuana. Also of significance was the increase in female cannabis users during the 1980s (Pela 1989). Ebbe (World Factbook) reports that there were 588 drug cases reported to the police in 1989.

Among persons age fifteen and over in 1999, the annual prevalence rate for cocaine abuse was 0.5 percent, and for amphetamines it was 1.1 percent (UNODC 2003: 337, 342). The annual prevalence of cannabis abuse among the same age cohort in 2000 was 14.4 percent (339).

Law Enforcement

Nigeria's law enforcement agencies lack the organization and material support to keep comprehensive statistics about antinarcotics efforts. Oftentimes small-time couriers and street dealers are apprehended by local police, but the larger traffickers and organizations remain untouched. Many times, law enforcement agencies simply do not follow through with their efforts. Seizures may occur with no follow-up investigation or arrests. Asset forfeiture must be preceded by convictions, but there are few attempts at prosecuting individuals. Nigeria's law enforcement agencies also fail to cooperate with each other, adding to the general disarray.

As shown in Table 26-1, in the 1980s drug-related crime escalated and the number of drug convictions increased rapidly. From 1986 to 1989, it is estimated that women accounted for 27 percent of the total 275 drug convictions (1 Up Info, Country Study & Guide 1991). A study found that "65 percent of the heroin seizures of 50 grams or more in British airports came from Nigeria, which was the transit point for 20 percent of all heroin from Southwest Asia" (1 Up Info 1991). During the late 1980s, hundreds of Nigerians were arrested for drug trafficking in a number of foreign countries.

TABLE 26-1
Rates of Crime Based on Offenses Known to the Police, Nigeria, 1986–1989

	1986	*1987*	*1988*	*1989*
Drug Offenses	316	422	593	588
Total**	151,495	150,297	154,820	148,462

** Total includes armed and strong-arm robbery, assault, auto theft, burglary, counterfeiting, drug offenses, forgery, fraud, manslaughter, murder, rape, smuggling, and theft. From the Annual Reports of Nigerian Police Force 1986–1989 and Nigerian Year Book, 1986–1989.

Drug Policy

Nigeria is the hub of African drug trafficking. Not only are drugs distributed to African nations through Nigeria, but cartels based in this country are responsible for a large part of heroin brought into the United States and for South American cocaine distributed throughout the eastern hemisphere. Nigeria's former-military governments remained indifferent to the activities of drug traffickers. The current democratically elected President Obasanjo has firmly denounced drug trafficking in public speeches, but there has been little action to back up the strong rhetoric. Many of Nigeria's government agencies lack the material support and expertise to coordinate and effectively combat the powerful cartels entrenched in the nation, while corruption continues to cripple law enforcement efforts.

Many recent developments have focused on buttressing the nation's government ministries and agencies. Legislation is under debate that would increase government salaries to a respectable living wage. This would reduce the temptation faced by many government employees to receive bribes from drug cartels. In 1995, money laundering legislation was enacted, but its enforcement has been sporadic, and it has proven an ineffective tool in combating narcotics trafficking.

The National Drug Law Enforcement Agency is primarily responsible for combating the drug traffic. Since the new government's inauguration in 1999, the legislation has created committees to oversee the operations and performance of the NDLEA. Still, no major financial or legislative initiatives have been created. President Obasanjo has proposed some sweeping reforms. The new Ministry of Police Affairs has promised a comprehensive reorganization, and Obasanjo has requested $210 million in his budget for law enforcement. Despite these promising signs, Obasanjo has been unable to unify the nation's legislature in backing these proposals.

References

Annual Reports of Nigerian Police Force 1986–1989 and Nigerian Year Book, 1986–1989.

Anumonye, Amechi. 1980. "Drug Use among Young People in Lagos, Nigeria." *Bulletin on Narcotics* 32.

Central Intelligence Agency. 2004. *World Factbook: Nigeria.* Washington, D.C.: Central Intelligence Agency. www.cia.gov/cia/publications/factbook/geos/ni.html.

Ebbe, Obi N.I. n.d. *World Factbook of Criminal Justice Systems: Nigeria.* Bureau of Justice Statistics. www.ojp.usdoj.gov/bjs/pub/ascii/wfbcjnig.txt (accessed October 8, 2003).

Ebbe, Obi N.I. 1996. "The Judiciary and Criminal Procedure in Nigeria" *in Comparative and International Criminal Justice Systems: Policing Judiciary, and Corrections.* Newton, Mass.: ButterworthHeinemann.

Gelbard, Robert S. 1998. "Drug Trafficking in Southern Africa," in Rotberg, Robert I., and Mills, Greg. (eds.) *War and Peace in Southern Africa: Crime, Drugs, Armies and Trade.* Washington, D.C.: Brookings Institution Press.

1 Up Info, Country Study & Guide, Web site. 1991. *Nigeria.* (www.1upinfo.com/ country-guide-study/nigeria/nigeria166.html).

Pela, A.O. 1989. *Recent Trends In Drug Use and Abuse in Nigeria.* http://www.unodc.org/ unodc/en/bulletin/bulletin_1989-01-01_1_page010.html (accessed October 9, 2003).

United Nations Office on Drugs and Crime. 2003. *Global Illicit Drug Trends 2003.* /www.unodc.org/unodc/en/global_illicit_drug_trends.html (accessed October 24, 2003).

Part IX

THE PACIFIC

The South Pacific Region of the world includes Australia, New Zealand, and over a dozen islands located off the northeast coast of Australia. This section of the book discusses the drug problem in Australia, the largest nation in the Pacific.

Cannabis is the most widely used illicit drug in Australia. A 1998 survey found that 40 percent of Australians over the age of fourteen have used the drug at least once. The UNODC (2003) reports a decrease in the availability of heroin, in the number of heroin addicts who presented themselves for treatment, and in overall abuse of heroin. Australia is more of a consumer than a producer of illicit drugs. The only illicit crop cultivated in Australia is cannabis. National surveys report that the public favors allocating money for educational programs to help reduce drug use and trafficking as opposed to law enforcement activities.

27

Australia

Overview

Australia is located in Oceania. It is a continent between the Indian Ocean and the South Pacific Ocean. Australia has a population of 19,913,144 (July 2004 est.). Ninety-two percent of the population are Caucasian, 7 percent are Asian, the remaining 1 percent are aboriginal ethnicities. The majority of people are Christian (Angelican 26.1 percent, Roman Catholic 26 percent, other Christian 24.3 percent). Other religions make up the remaining 23.6 percent of the population. English and native languages are spoken (CIA 2004).

Six independent British colonies—New South Wales, Victoria, Queensland, Western Australia, South Australia, and Tasmania—became a federation in 1901, and eventually formed the States of the Commonwealth of Australia, although since then, the Northern Territory and the Australian Capital Territory have been granted self government. (In 1911, the Northern territory was carved out of South Australia and the Australian Capital Territory came into existence.)

Similar in many ways to the United States, Australia is a federalist (Commonwealth) government composed of a national government and six state governments (Biles n.d.). The Commonwealth is responsible for the enforcement of its own laws. Notably, the most frequently prosecuted offenses in the Commonwealth are those related to the importation of drugs and the violation of social security laws. The development of criminal law lies with the states. Local governments can pass legislation for the more minor social nuisance offenses.

These laws, known as bylaws, carry a maximum penalty of a monetary fine. However, non-payment of fines can result in imprisonment.

The Australian legal system, derived from that of the United Kingdom, uses the parliament to make laws. The legal system is adversarial in nature and places a high value on the presumption of innocence. There are nine separate legal systems in operation, one for each state, the federal government, the Australian Capital Territory and the Northern Territory. Although there are some significant differences among these systems, they are essentially similar in nature.

Conduct which is prohibited by law and which may result in punishment is characterized as criminal. Australia utilizes the distinction between felonies and misdemeanors, but it is more common to classify crimes as indictable or non indictable offenses. Indictable offenses include the more serious crimes of homicide, robbery, serious sexual and non-sexual assault, fraud, burglary, and serious theft. These are heard by the superior courts and may require a jury, whereas nonindictable offenses, which comprise the vast majority of court cases, are heard in magistrates courts, where no juries are employed.

As the United States uses the distinction between Type I and Type II crimes for many statistical summaries, criminal justice statistics in Australia are based on a classification scheme which divides crimes into offenses against the person, property offenses, and "other."

The age of criminal responsibility varies among the states from seven in Tasmania to ten in Queensland, New South Wales, South Australia, and the Northern Territory. The jurisdictions also set a maximum age limit for hearings in the juvenile court. This age is usually sixteen or seventeen. The minimum age of criminal responsibility in juvenile courts is seven, while the minimum age to be tried in an adult court is sixteen. A child older than the age of criminal responsibility who has been charged with homicide can be tried in adult court.

No jurisdictions maintain capital punishment as a punishment. The last execution took place in 1967. There are approximately eighty prisons throughout Australia. In May 1993, the total number of prisoners in Australia was 14,335. The rate for imprisonment in Australia was 80.6 per 100,000 population.

Drug Offenses and the Law

In all Australian jurisdictions, the possession, use, sale, distribution, importation, manufacturing, or trafficking of a wide range of drugs is illegal. Illegal drugs include: marijuana/cannabis, heroin, ice, ecstasy, amphetamines (speed, LSD), and cocaine/crack. Each of the six states and two territories have their own laws that establish penalties for drug crimes, the majority of which were enacted in the 1980s with the exception of Tasmania's Poisons Act, enacted in 1971.

The Commonwealth derives its laws pertaining to drugs from two sources: the Customs Act of 1901 and the Crimes Act of 1990, also known as the Trafficking in Narcotics Drugs and Psychotropic Substances Act (TINDAPS). The Customs Act of 1901 established the penalties of a $50,000 fine or fine of three times the value of the goods for importing or exporting prohibited imports/exports. In addition, the act established the penalty of life imprisonment for the possession, import, or export of more than commercial quantity of narcotic goods. More than trafficable quantity, but less than commercial quantity carries a possible punishment of $100,000 and/or twenty-five-years imprisonment. But, possession, import, or export of more than a trafficable quantity of cannabis would result in a $4,000 fine and/or ten years-imprisonment.

The Crimes Act of 1990 delineated penalties for cultivation, separation of drug from plants, and manufacture or possession for purpose of manufacture.

Two jurisdictions—South Australia and the Australian Capital Territory—have partially decriminalized the possession and use of small amounts of marijuana. In other states, the maximum penalty for possession of small amounts of cannabis is two years imprisonment. Possession of large amounts of illegal drugs for commercial uses may be punished with life imprisonment. Cannabis plays the largest role in drug law offenses, accounting for 82–85 percent of the total of cannabis, cocaine, heroin, amphetamine, and LSD-related offenses during 1990 to 1994. Amphetamine and heroin offenses represented a 8–10 percent and 6–8 percent, respectively, of the total during the same period. Cocaine was 1 percent or less of the total. Offenses are divided into either consumer or provider offenses. Consumer offenses are those offenses involving personal use or possession for personal use. Provider offenses include drug trafficking, manufacturing, and importing (UNODC 2003).

Cocaine and heroin accounted for the highest share of total provider arrests in 1994, 37 percent and 28 percent respectively. But most arrests are related to consumption, and cannabis consumption arrests accounted for 61 percent of all arrests. While there are no national data recording the number of drug offenders, the South Australian police reported 36,447 arrests in 2000/2001, of which 5.8 percent were drug offenses (Graycar, McGregor, Makkai, and Payne 2002: 2). Graycar et al. estimate that 6 percent of serious offenses that are recorded involve arrests for drug-related crimes (3).

Extent and Patterns of Use

In 1995, thirty-nine percent of Australia's population aged fourteen or older had tried at least one illicit drug in their lifetime, including nonmedical use of prescription drugs. With respect to annual prevalence, 17 percent had used one or more drugs in the last twelve months (Commonwealth Department of Health and Family Services 1995). The most common illicit drug is cannabis, with 31 percent of surveyed persons admitted having tried cannabis. More than half of all individuals aged fourteen to thirty-nine have tried cannabis. Hallucinogens and amphetamine type stimulants follow cannabis in popularity.

Although cannabis may be the country's most popular drug, alcohol was nominated by the population of treatment clients as the number one drug problem. Alcohol was followed by opiates, opiates/polydrug use, tobacco, and cannabis. This 1995 Commonwealth Department of Health and Family Services survey[1] estimated that there were 35,000 to 51,000 individuals undergoing some form of treatment at any one time of the year. A total of 39 percent of all substance abusers injected drugs in the 12 months preceding the day of the census.

With regard to gender, 71 percent of the substance abusers surveyed were male. Women were more likely to have problems with opiates, benzodiazepines, and with polydrug use—but not opiates. Men more often than women listed alcohol as a drug problem.

High-grade, low-cost heroin has caused a surge in heroin-related problems in Australia in recent years. The Australian states cite an increased number of fatal overdoses, particularly in conjunction with other drugs such as alcohol and barbiturates, and unprecedented pressures on methadone programs, forcing waiting lists in some states that are close to a year. Increased use of heroin is also stressing the treatment system inside prisons. There are reports of rising levels of property offenses, that are attributable to the addict population.

Cannabis is the most widely used illicit drug in Australia. A 1998 survey for Australian Institute of Health and Welfare (AIHW) reported that 40 percent of Australians over the age of fourteen have used the drug at least once. It also noted that 17 percent had used it in the last twelve months. The survey reported that 46 percent of all Australians have experimented with at least one illicit drug, and 22 percent had done so in the previous year.

Authorities are especially concerned with a growing rate of heroin use. In 1998, a survey issued by the AIHW revealed that 2.2 perent of Australians used heroin. In 1995, only 1.4 percent of the population had reported heroin use. The most affected group are men age twenty to twenty-nine. In this group, 6.2 percent reported using heroin in 1998, where as three years earlier only 3.6 percent had done so.

In 2001, there was a decrease in the availability of heroin, as well as a decrease in the number of heroin addicts who presented themselves for treatment (UNODC 2003: 8), and in overall abuse of heroin (107). Drug overdoses related to heroin use decreased by 66 percent in 2001 (UNODC 2003: 126). Many of the drug traffickers who generally supplied heroin to Australia had been eliminated, and as such, the rate of drug-related crimes and deaths decreased noticeably. More recently, however, the UNODC reported that North Korea has helped to re-stimulate the market in Australia by providing or trafficking heroin.

Recently, the states of New South Wales and the Australian Capital Territory passed legislation creating "safe heroin injecting rooms." The controversial law establishes locations where heroin users can get clean needles and inject their drug without fear of prosecution from the government. Such an approach is geared toward minimizing the deleterious health concerns of IV drug use on the streets. However, Australia's federal government intervened to delay the implementation of this law after receiving a precautionary letter from the UN International Narcotics Control Board. The law is currently being researched in light of Australia's obligations under the UN's 1988 Drug Convention.

Law Enforcement

Overall, Australia and the United States work closely to combat drug trafficking. Australia is more of a consumer, rather than a producer nation. Australia has been a target for South American cocaine traffickers, and Southeast Asian heroin. There is no evidence that Australia serves as a major transit country for the illegal flow of narcotics. Australia's large and free-flowing financial sector has made it an opportunistic place for money laundering. Some legislation has been implemented to prevent and report large or suspicious transactions.

The only illicit crop cultivated in Australia is cannabis. About 5,000 hectares of this crop has been discovered nationwide. Australia also produces licit opium on the island of Tasmania. Its facilities are strictly regulated, and controls against diversion into the illegal market are excellent.

Drug Policy

Overall, Australia's policy is based on harm reduction. Australia's National Drug Strategy places its main emphasis on the minimization of the harmful effects of drugs and drug use. Australia believes that focusing simply on specific drugs will not solve the problem. The country does not distinguish between legal and illegal drugs in terms of substance abuse, but treats all substance abuse within the same organizational structure.

When the country is polled regarding drug policy priorities, surveys show that the country would allocate most money for education, followed by treatment and then law enforcement, regardless of the drug in question. Over time, the survey data showed an increasing preference toward education (Makkai and McAllister 1998).

Federal budgetary cuts have put a strain on law enforcement activities and have made it difficult to deter the upsurge in the importation and trafficking of heroin. Budget cuts resulted in significant reductions in funding allocations to the National Crime Authority, the Australian Federal Police, and the Customs Service.

On the education side of drug policy, the Commonwealth announced a new antidrug campaign in November 1997 known as the National Illicit Drug Strategy "Tough on Drugs." Almost 90 million Australian dollars were targeted to drug trafficking (43.8 million), education (14 million), and rehabilitation and research (29.8 million).

This strategy continues to form a significant part of the national drug strategy today. In the 2003–04 federal budget the government provided funding of $316 million (Australian dollars) over four years for a range of new and continueing measures to combat illicit drug use in Australia. Australia's strategy comprises both demand and supply measures.

Note

1. The survey identified almost all drug and alcohol treatment agencies in Australia which are specialized in the care, treatment, or rehabilitation of persons requiring assistance because of problems caused or exacerbated by the use of substances, including alcohol. The survey was carried out during a 24-hour period. During the 24-hour period, individual clients within these agencies were surveyed. The response rate was 92 percent.

References

Australian Encyclopedia. 5th ed. Terrey Hills, NSW: Australian Geographic for the Australian Geographic Society, 1988. 9v. Includes articles on crime and criminology (Mukherjee), criminal law (Bennett), police, and prisons and penal systems (Biles).

Australian Institute of Criminology. Synthesis of information contained in the annual reports of Australian police forces for the year 1991–1992.

Australian Prisoners: Results of the National Prison Census, June 30, 1982. Annual release. (Canberra: Australian Institute of Criminology), 1983.

Biles, David. n.d. *World Factbook of Criminal Justice Systems*: Australia. Washington, D.C.: Bureau of Justice Statistics. www.ojp.usdoj.gov/bjs/pub/ascii/wfbcjaus.txt (accessed October 8, 2003).

Biles, David. ed. 1988. *Current Australian Trends in Corrections: Selected Papers From the Australian Bicentennial International Congress on Corrective Services*, Sydney, January 1988. (Sydney: Federation Press in association with the Australian Institute of Criminology).

Central Intelligence Agency. 2004. *World Factbook: Australia*. Washington, D.C.: Central Intelligence Agency. www.cia.gov/cia/publications/factbook/geos/as.html.

Chappell, Duncan, and Paul Wilson (eds.). 1986. *The Australian Criminal Justice System: The Mid-1980s*. 3rd ed. Sydney: Butterworths.

Chappell, Duncan, and Paul Wilson, (eds). 1989. *Australian Policing: Contemporary Issues*. Sydney: Butterworths.

Commonwealth Department of Health and Family Services. 1995. National Drug Strategy Household Survey, Survey Report. Canberra: Australian Government Publishing Service, Commonwealth of Australia. www7.health.gov.au/pubhlth/publicat/document/nds.pdf (accessed January 25, 1999).

Crawford, James. 1988. *Australian Courts of Law*. 2nd ed. Melbourne: Oxford University Press.

Graycar, Adam, Kiah McGregor, Toni Makkai, and Jason Payne. "Drugs and Law Enforcement: Actions and Options." Presented at the South Australian Drugs Summit 26 June 2002. Australian Institute of Criminology.

Makkai, T., and I. McAllister. 1998. Public Opinion toward Drug Policies in Australia, 1985–1995. Canberra: Department of Health and Family Services.

Mukherjee, Satyanshu K. et. al. 1989. *Source Book of Australian Criminal and Social Statistics 1804–1988*. Bicentennial edition. Canberra: Australian Institute of Criminology.

Mukherjee, Satyanshu K., Debbie Neuhaus, and John Walker. 1990. *Crime and Justice in Australia*. Canberra: Australian Institute of Criminology.

Mukherjee, Satyanshu K., and Dianne Dagger. 1985. *The Size of the Crime Problem in Australia*. 2nd Criminology), 1990. Bruce Swanton, and Gary Hannigan, (eds.). *Police Source Book* 2, assisted by Trish Psaila. Canberra: Australian Institute of Criminology.

United Nations Office on Drugs and Crime. 2003. *Global Illicit Drug Trends 2003*. www.unodc.org/unodc/en/global_illicit_drug_trends.html (accessed October 24, 2003).

United Nations International Drug Control Programme. 1997. *World Drug Report*. Oxford, England: Oxford University Press.

Walker, John. 1993. *Crime in Australia: As Measured by the Australian Component of the International Crime Victims Survey 1992*. Assisted by Dianne Dagger. Canberra: Australian Institute of Criminology).

Walker, John. 1992. "Estimates of the Costs of Crime in Australia." *Trends and Issues in Crime and Criminal Justice*, no.39. Canberra: Australian Institute of Criminology.

PART X

28

Concluding Remarks

W E CONCLUDE WITH THE SAME OBSERVATION that we made in the introduction. The demand for drugs throughout the world is great. Illicit drug consumption ranges from 3.3 to 4.1 percent of the world population. The United Nations Office on Drugs and Crime estimates that there are 200 million consumers of drugs around the world; 163 million consume cannabis, 34 million consume amphetamines, 8 million consume ecstasy, 14 million consume cocaine, 15 million consume opiates, and 10 million consume heroin.

In almost every country included in this volume drug use has been on the increase. The type of drug most favored varies among different societies, with cannabis or marijuana favored in most of the countries.

Concerning the questions posed in the introduction, the nations of the world, certainly those included in this volume, have begun to converge on drug policies. Going back to 1909 and the Shanghai Conference when the United States invited representatives from Austria, Hungary, China, Great Britain, France, Germany, Italy, Japan, the Netherlands, Persia, Portugal, Siam, and Russia to work together to reduce the growth and use of opium and other narcotics. Among the major resolutions it adopted, although they were nonbinding, was that opium should be limited to legitimate medicinal purposes and that each country should enact legislation aimed at suppressing opium smoking.

The Shanghai Conference was followed by the Hague Convention in 1912, which was attended by all of the same countries except Austria and Hungary. The Hague Convention made international narcotic control a matter of international law with binding recommendations. In 1921 the League of Nations

formed an Advisory Committee on the Traffic of Opium and Other Dangerous Drugs to handle all agreements regarding dangerous drugs. This 1921
meeting was followed by a conference in Geneva that began in November
1924 and concluded in February 1925. The objectives of the conference were
to reach an agreement to limit the amount of morphine, heroin, and cocaine
that could be manufactured and to limit the amount of raw forms of these
drugs—the poppy and the coca leaf. But the conference did not reach agreement on these matters because some of the countries attending refused to
agree to make opium smoking illegal. Two other conference were held before
the outbreak of World War II that also resulted in inconclusive agreements on
the manufacture of illicit drugs and on police sanctions on drug trafficking.

Following the end of World War II, the United Nations established the
Commission on Narcotic Drugs. The commission was composed of fifteen
countries that led in the manufacturing of opium or were countries in which
illicit drugs were a serious problem. The commission was responsible for
overseeing the implementation and progress of all international agreements
related to dangerous drugs and to developing a new agreement.

In 1948 the Paris Protocol was signed that brought synthetic drugs deemed
harmful by the World Health Organization under international control. In
1953, the Opium Protocol made it illegal for any country except Bulgaria,
Greece, India, Iran, Turkey, Russia, and Yugoslavia to produce opium for export. Farmers had to be licensed to cultivate the poppy for opium.

In 1961 the Single Convention on Narcotic Drugs replaced all earlier agreements. In 1988, forty-three UN member countries adopted the Convention
against Illicit Traffic in Narcotic Drugs, the main provisions of which controlled the shipment of precursor chemicals, reaffirmed the nations' commitment to reduce or eradicate the raw materials used to manufacture drugs, provided authorization to sieze drug-related assets, and granted permission to
extradite and prosecute persons charged with drug violation. There appears to
be consensus that these international controls have helped to stem the supply
of narcotics.

All of the countries included in this volume have joined the international
dialogue on illicit drugs and are parties to the international antidrug treaties
and conventions.

Of the twenty countries described in this study, the United States, Japan,
China, Iran, and, most recently, Spain and Russia have adopted the most punitive and repressive policies vis-à-vis drug use, sale, and trafficking. Canada, the
Western European countries of Great Britain, France, and Italy, and the Eastern European countries of Bulgaria and Slovakia place greater emphasis on
prevention, treatment, and rehabilitation, as do Israel and Australia.

The policies of South Africa and Nigeria are sufficiently disorganized that there is no systematic focus on repressive versus education or treatment programs. The Colombian government perceives itself as engaged in warfare within its own borders against local guerilla forces and paramilitary groups such as the Revolutionary Armed Forces of Colombia.

Index

Page references followed by t indicate tables. Those followed by n indicate endnotes.

About the Authors

Heather Ahn-Redding is a doctoral student in the field of Justice, Law and Society at American University's School of Public Affairs. She received her undergraduate degree in Psychology at the University of Michigan and her Master's degree in Forensic Psychology at John Jay College of Criminal Justice. She is currently an adjunct professor at the University of North Carolina in Greensboro.

Caterina G. Roman is a Senior Research Associate in the Justice Policy Center at the Urban Institute. Her research interests include the role of community organizations and institutions in crime prevention and neighborhood well being; the development, maintenance, and effectiveness of community justice partnerships; drug treatment policies and programs; and the spatial and temporal relationship between neighborhood characteristics and violence. She is involved in evaluating programs that support the community reintegration of returning prisoners. Her work on prisoner reentry has been published in the journals *Criminology and Public Policy* and *Justice Research and Policy*. In addition, she authored a book examining urban schools as generators of crime published by Lexington Books in 2004. She received a Ph.D. in sociology and justice, law, and society from the American University.

Rita J. Simon is a sociologist who earned her doctorate at the University of Chicago in 1957. Before coming to American University in 1983 to serve as Dean of the School of Justice, she was a member of the faculty at the University of Illinois, at the Hebrew University in Jerusalem, and the University of

Chicago. She is currently a "University Professor" in the School of Public Affairs and the Washington College of Law at American University. Professor Simon has authored 33 books and edited 19 including: *Immigration the World Over* with James P. Lynch, Rowman and Littlefield, 2003 and *In the Golden Land: A Century of Russian and Soviet Jewish Immigration,* Praeger, 1997. She is currently editor of *Gender Issues*. From 1978 to 1981 she served as editor of *The American Sociological Review* and from 1983 to 1986 as editor of *Justice Quarterly*. In 1966, she received a Guggenheim Fellowship.